SWEET LOU, MANAGER

In the late hours of Monday evening I began thinking more and more about what had changed in my life over that weekend. I felt a sense of responsibility now for the Yankee tradition, an intense desire to restore the team to the top. I recognized that I was the manager of the most famous team in all baseball, the team of Ruth, Gehrig, DiMaggio, and Mantle; Guidry, Jackson, Winfield, and Mattingly; the team all America rooted for or against but nobody ignored. Restoring the Yankees to the top. That was my job. That was serious business. There would be no turning back now. . . .

D1178389

SWEET LOU

Lou Piniella
&
Maury Allen

BANTAM BOOKS
TORONTO • NEW YORK • LONDON • SYDNEY • AUCKLAND

SWEET LOU

A Bantam Book / published by arrangement with
G. P. Putnam's Sons.

PRINTING HISTORY
G. P. Putnam's Sons edition published April 1986
Bantam edition / May 1987

ISBN 0-553-26459-1

Published simultaneously in the United States and Canada

Bantam Books are published by Bantam Books, Inc. Its trademark, consisting of the words "Bantam Books" and the por-
trayal of a rooster, is registered in U.S. Patent and Trademark
Office and in other countries. Marca Registrada. Bantam
Books, Inc., 666 Fifth Avenue, New York, New York 10103.

PRINTED IN THE UNITED STATES OF AMERICA

KR   0 9 8 7 6 5 4 3 2 1

For Anita, Louis Jr., Kristi, and Derek for their love, understanding, support, and most of all, family sacrifices, caused by the demands of my career; and for my parents, Louis and Margaret Piniella, for their endless support and unshakable faith in me; and for Anita's parents, Frank and Lucille Garcia, for their kindness and warmth, and for all my teammates on the New York Yankees.

L.P.

For Janet, Jennifer, and Ted, the greatest team I have ever known.

M.A.

Acknowledgments

Before the fact, only one man made this book possible, Lou Piniella. The idea was probably born that sunny fall afternoon in Boston when Lou saved a season with a fortuitous grab of a line drive hit. He is a man of courage, character, and decency who played, coached, and will manage with unbridled enthusiasm. I am proud to call him a friend.

After the fact, my agent Julian Bach never wavered in his enthusiasm and endorsement of this project. He is the Lou Piniella of agents, never giving less than his best, always willing to fight harder when things seem darkest.

No book is ever the work of a single creator. It is the sum total of all the hands that contribute their talents and professionalism to a common goal. I am in debt to all the skilled people at Putnam's who brought this book to life, with special warm thanks to senior editor Neil S. Nyren, who contributed so much with so little tension.

Maury Allen

SWEET LOU

Welcome Aboard, Skipper

October 24, 1985: I sat in the living room of my Allendale, New Jersey, home, sipping beer, puffing on a cigarette, and watching the World Series on television.

It was game five, and the St. Louis Cardinals were up three games to one over the Kansas City Royals, but I had a strong rooting interest in the Royals. I'd been rookie of the year for them in 1969, the first year of the expansion team's existence; in fact, I'd been the first Royal ever to get a hit—you could look it up, as Casey said. Then, after I'd been traded to the Yankees, they became our principal rivals for the American League Championship in the late 1970s and, to top it all, they were being managed by my old friend, coach, and manager Dick Howser.

Dick had won 103 games for the Yankees in 1980, but hadn't made it into the World Series—we'd been beaten in the playoffs by (who else?) Kansas City. The next year, Dick was gone—you don't lose if you want to keep working for George Steinbrenner—and now here he was managing the Royals in the World Series. The irony was too great.

About twenty minutes to nine, the phone rang.

"Anita, would you get that?" I asked my wife. "Tell them I'm watching the game. Whoever it is, I'll call back."

"Lou," she said from the kitchen, "it's Woody Woodward. He'd like to talk to you now."

Woodward was the assistant to Yankee general manager Clyde King, one of my bosses. Not the Boss, of course, but still not somebody you told to wait. I took the call.

"Are you watching the game?" Woodward asked.

"Yes. I think the Royals are really playing well now. They can win this thing."

"I think so, too. Clyde and I were in St. Louis for two games there. They aren't the same club without Coleman."

"Were you talking about deals?"

"We met with a lot of clubs. We might have something going. We were really busy. We're still working on that manager thing. We may come to a decision soon. We might make a change."

"What about Bobby Murcer? Is he going to stay in the front office?"

"Can't say yet. We have to get this manager thing settled first."

I knew what they meant by "this manager thing," of course. For weeks, the press had been flooded with rumors that Billy Martin was about to be fired from the Yankees for the fourth time. We'd finished only two games in back of the Toronto Blue Jays for the divisional championship, but the last few weeks of the season had been—to put it mildly—rough ones for Billy, marked by a string of bizarre games, *two* bar brawls, and a demand for a raise that had been greeted with withering sarcasm by George— as I said, you don't lose if you want to keep working for the Boss.

George had formally abdicated the responsibility for the managerial decision to Woody and Clyde, but it seemed a foregone conclusion. The only question was who was going to succeed Billy. I knew full well that I was one of the prime candidates, but I couldn't let myself dwell on it or try to read too much into the phone conversation I was now having with Woodward. Assistant general managers often call coaches. Sometimes they even call them to talk about the World Series. No big deal.

We talked for about fifteen minutes about this and that, then hung up. I watched the Royals win to close the

2

gap to three games to two, turned on Johnny Carson for a while and then went to bed.

The next morning I awoke early, shaved—something I try to avoid as much as possible in the off-season—then drove off to keep an appointment with my banker. I wanted him to arrange financing for some expansions I had planned for my restaurant, Sweet Lou's, and after two hours of talk, we made a deal and shook hands. When I got home Anita met me at the door. I had just had a phone call.

"It was from Clyde King," she said. "He asked you to call as soon as you got in."

Now I knew something was up. Clyde might call, Woody might call, but Woody *and* Clyde would almost never call two days in a row. I phoned Clyde at the Yankee Stadium offices.

"Lou, we'd like you to come in for a meeting. There are some things about the managerial situation we'd like to discuss. How soon can you be here?"

I looked at my watch. It was a little past one o'clock. I had some business calls to make and I wanted a sandwich in case it was a long meeting.

"Would four o'clock be all right?"

"Fine," said Clyde. "See you at four."

I tried not to get too excited on the forty-five-minute drive to the Stadium. I don't believe in thinking too much about what might happen, in case it doesn't happen, but I knew there was a chance. I just turned on the radio and tried to keep the managerial job out of my mind.

Clyde and Woody were waiting for me in George's huge office. Woody sat on one chair in front of George's desk and Clyde sat in another. *Nobody* sat behind the Boss' desk but George. I shook hands and Clyde asked me to sit down.

"Billy's not coming back," Clyde began. "We'd like to find out if you are interested in managing this ballclub. If you are, we'd like to interview you on your feelings about it, and if the interview goes well we are prepared to offer

3

you the Yankee managerial job. We haven't spoken to anybody else about this."

"Of course I'm interested," I said.

My voice was a little choked. I was nervous, but I didn't want to show it. Clyde began asking me questions about my ideas on discipline and how I would enforce it. George's name was never mentioned. It was clear Clyde understood George's attitudes and knew George was a stickler for discipline.

There were more questions about whether I felt Dave Righetti should be a starter or a reliever—I told Clyde I thought he should stay in the bullpen—about what I thought of young Dan Pasqua and Mike Pagliarulo, about what free agents we might go after, how we might get more out of some of our veteran players, and whether we should platoon our DH.

I had never been interviewed for a job before. As a player, I had always made it on my ability, and my jobs as player-coach in 1983 and full-time coach after I quit playing in 1984 had been appointments. This was a strange feeling.

As we went into the second hour of the interview, I thought back to the day that spring when George had told reporters I would manage the club someday. When he'd fired Yogi Berra and brought in Billy Martin he'd repeated publicly that I would manage. He'd even said Billy would be grooming me. Even Billy had said that. Somehow I'd thought that if it did happen it would happen differently. I'd thought I would get a phone call from George. "You got it," he would say, "and the hell with it." I remembered the day I had failed to show up for a *Sporting News* photo of the team. When Barry Halper, one of our minority owners, had asked him about my absence in the photo, George had said, "Don't worry about Lou. I'll take care of *him*. I'll make him the manager."

We talked for another hour. About six o'clock, Clyde said, "Would you be averse to having someone with managerial experience sitting on the bench next to you?"

"No," I said, "not at all."

Clyde smiled and looked at Woody. Then he looked

back at me and said, "We'd like you to manage the New York Yankees with a one-year contract for one hundred fifty thousand dollars."

This was it. I took my courage in my hands, looked at Clyde, and said, "I think I'd like a two-year contract at two hundred thousand dollars a year."

I was making nearly that much a year as a coach. I thought that figure sounded reasonable.

"I'll have to check on that," Clyde said.

We talked a bit more about the authority I would have as manager, the total input I wanted in the entire operation, the freedom in selecting coaches.

It was almost six-thirty. Clyde was finished.

"Make sure you're available over the weekend," Clyde said.

I left the Yankee Stadium offices without a final agreement. George's name had still not been mentioned. He was home in Tampa. I don't know what Clyde did after I left, but I drove up to Yonkers Raceway where I met Anita and a friend and we pointedly did not talk about the managerial situation. It was a pleasant night. A horse named Scid Dancer I owned won by eleven lengths.

After we got home, I gave Anita the whole story, told her I thought there would be some concessions on the salary and the length of contract, but that I doubted there would be any hitches. I slept soundly. I had had a hectic day.

On Saturday morning I puttered around the house, raked some leaves, fooled with the dishwasher, and made some business calls. The phone rang a few times, but I kept the talks short. Clyde didn't call. It was two-thirty. I had promised Anita and the kids I would take them hiking in the Ramapo Mountains, and I hate to break that kind of promise, so my sixteen-year-old, Louis Jr., stayed at home and the rest of us—Anita, Derek, Kristi, and myself—went off in the car.

We walked down those beautiful trails. The kids laughed and jumped through the leaves, Anita and I following slowly behind. For the first time I thought there might be a snag. Clyde hadn't called. Maybe they had changed their minds. Maybe they had contacted George after the interview and something had gone wrong. I was a little down as I drove home, a little quiet in the car.

As we walked in the door, Louis said, "Mr. King called. He called twice. He said he would call later." This was frustrating.

As I watched the sixth game of the World Series that Saturday night, the phone rang often—but it was never Clyde. It was almost always a reporter. "Is it true?" they asked. Now how in hell had they found out? "I can't comment on that," I told all of them. Kansas City won to tie the Series. Still no Clyde. About one o'clock, I went to bed, exhausted.

When I woke up in the morning, there it was in all the Sunday papers. *"LOU! LOU! LOU!"* one shouted. *"Piniella to get Yankee job."* I was glad they knew that. *I* didn't.

About ten o'clock, the phone rang again.

"Lou," Clyde began, "we'd like you to come in here early this afternoon. We'd like to get this thing settled."

When I got into the car that Sunday, I knew I would be coming home as the Yankee manager. A one-year contract wouldn't hold me back. I had played or coached for more than seventeen seasons and most of that time on one-year contracts. Besides, I knew if I did the job, I would be asked back. If I didn't, I'd be gone. The length of contract was no factor. George Steinbrenner had paid quite a few managers for not managing.

This time I met with Clyde alone in his own office in the Stadium. He sat behind his desk.

"Lou, we'd just feel more comfortable with a one-year contract, since you haven't managed before," he said. "We'll give you the two hundred thousand dollars."

My heart leaped. I tried to keep my voice even. "OK, that's fine. We have a deal."

Clyde King got up from behind his desk, walked to the front, smiled at me, and said, "Welcome aboard, skipper."

There was a lump in my throat, and I felt shaky.

Taking a deep breath, I thanked him. I had always called Billy skipper. Now Clyde had called me skipper. It was difficult to measure my emotion.

Before I knew it, I was in the office of Yankee president Gene McHale, with public relations director Joe Safety by my side. The press had been alerted in Kansas City and they were set for a conference call at five o'clock. George wanted it announced immediately. Did this have anything to do with taking the spotlight off the final game of the World Series? Nah. George is much too understated a guy ever to do anything like that.

As Joe told me the call was going through, I tried to calm my jitters. I had always gotten along well with the press, but I knew I'd be asked about Billy and I didn't feel comfortable discussing it, and I knew I'd be bombarded with questions about all my predecessors and how in hell I thought I could survive when they hadn't. Finally, I told them, "Look, I know it's a tough job—but, my God, it wasn't easy to *play* here, either." That got a laugh. "I've played here. I've coached here. I've sat in on meetings. I've *been* here. I won't be surprised."

I hoped so, anyway.

When I got home, one of the first calls was from George. It was the first time I had spoken to him since well before the regular season had ended.

"Congratulations," he said, "and remember the lessons you learned in Cleveland." In late July and early August, I'd managed five games for Billy when he'd been in the hospital, and it'd been difficult. Nobody had known who was in charge, discipline had gone all to hell, and I'd been on the verge of resigning. Oh, I wouldn't forget the lessons I'd learned there, all right. Then he said, "This surprised me. I thought you would be the manager in 1987." Right, George, if you say so—though I'd never known George to be surprised about any personnel moves on the Yankees. "Be a good leader and good luck."

Soon my parents were calling from Tampa, and Anita's parents, and some friends. Two of my old teammates I would now be managing, Willie Randolph and Ron Guidry, phoned to congratulate me and promise to help all they could. That made me feel good.

With all these calls I was feeling very sentimental and warm and fortunate; and then I started thinking about Billy. I felt sad for him. I had played and coached under him and still thought highly of his ability, but I had to recognize that the decision to change managers had not been mine to make. I remembered the last Saturday night of the season in Toronto, after Doyle Alexander had beaten us and we had been eliminated from the pennant race, and the dinner we had had together, the coaches and Billy. We had a wonderful evening and, just before we left, Billy came up to me and said quietly, "You will manage this club next year."

"No, Billy, you'll be back."

"You'll manage this club next year and you can call me anytime you want and I'll give you any advice you need."

We'd shaken hands warmly and I'd thanked Billy for those kind words, even while I'd been haunted by the sadness in his eyes.

After that emotional Sunday, I woke up early Monday morning and none of it seemed real. I thought maybe I had dreamed it all, but no, the newspapers were there and they all said Lou Piniella was the new Yankee manager. More than that: I was on the front page! "MARTIN FIRED—YES, LOU IS HIRED" ran the screamer on the *Daily News*. "BYE-BYE BILLY, HELLO LOU" headlined *Newsday*, and in smaller type "A Royal Crush Wins It for KC." If George *had* wanted to take away attention from the World Series, he'd sure accomplished his goal. But good for Dick, I thought, he's finally got his World Series. And then it struck: Next year that could be me. I could be a World Series manager. It was in my hands.

In the late hours of Monday evening I began thinking more and more about what had changed in my life over that weekend. I felt a sense of responsibility now for the Yankee tradition, an intense desire to restore the team to the top. I recognized that I was the manager of the most famous team in all baseball, the team of Ruth, Gehrig,

DiMaggio, and Mantle; Guidry, Jackson, Winfield, and Mattingly; the team all America rooted for or against but nobody ignored. A different side of my personality began to surface in those late hours, a side of me I knew had always been there but had seemed hidden behind a façade of fun. Restoring the Yankees to the top. That was my job. That was serious business.

On Tuesday, with George, Clyde, Woody, and Gene Michael, our third-base coach and former GM and manager, I attended my first Yankee staff meeting as the team's manager. We discussed personnel and made plans for the 1986 season, went over our needs and discussed our strengths, talked about trades and possible free-agent signings and our preparations for the next Yankee year.

"Remember, you're in charge," George told me when the meeting was over. "You make the rules but be sure you enforce them."

There would be no turning back now. It was my job to win, to get the Yankees back in first place, to deal with the players, the press, the coaches, the front office, and the renowned principal owner, the Boss. I had no doubt we could work together. George wanted to win, I wanted to win, and I felt in my gut we could do it as a united organization.

No matter how I had gotten to be manager, no matter how the decision had finally been made, it had been made. It was a new Yankee beginning.

Lou Piniella, number 14 on the Yankees, MGR. I was the team's fourteenth manager in the fourteenth season since George Steinbrenner had become its principal owner. I had certainly come a long way from that day late in June of 1984 when I'd decided to end my playing career, from that day in August when I'd stood in Yankee Stadium on Lou Piniella Day and heard fans issue that one, last, cascading, "Looouuu!" How long had it really been since that August? Of course—fourteen months.

Bow-Out
in Boston

The decision churned inside my head for years. I probably retired more times in my head than any man in the history of the game. I had had a remarkable career, a life filled with base hits, fly balls, "red-ass" temper tantrums, dented watercoolers, and incredible unforeseen adventures with people named George Steinbrenner, Reggie Jackson, Billy Martin, Thurman Munson, Bobby Murcer, Catfish Hunter, and Earl Weaver—but now it was coming to an end.

I always felt major league baseball was a gift to be cherished, and I had seen many players with better careers than mine tarnish themselves by hanging on too long at the end. I didn't want that to happen to me. The fans wanted me to continue, as did Yogi Berra and George Steinbrenner—but I knew my reflexes were going and my legs were no longer spry. Every day brought a great deal of pain and soreness. It was harder to go to the ballpark, harder to see my name in the lineup card, harder to concentrate, knowing I couldn't produce as I had.

The most serious problem, the ache that really forced me out, was a partially torn rotator cuff, with which I played the last three seasons of my career. I got it trying to hit the San Diego Chicken.

Johnny Bench asked me to give a batting clinic in February of 1982 for a television show he was working on,

The Baseball Bunch. I flew out to Tucson, put on a uniform, and went out to hit 150 or 200 baseballs. I wasn't in very good shape. I was never the kind of guy who believed in exercising all winter. The last time I saw a baseball each year was the last day of the season. The next time was when I pulled open my bag in spring training in Fort Lauderdale or Fort Myers or wherever I was training. I always believed it was important to work on specific skills—hitting the baseball as hard as you could, catching it, throwing it—I wasn't much for situps or deep knee bends.

I walked to the field and I took a couple of practice swings. I could see the wind blowing the flags around. I moved toward the plate.

"You ready, Lou?" asked Bench.

"Let's do it."

"You ready, Chicken?" Bench asked.

A few years before, in a playful mood, I had thrown my glove at the Chicken and screamed a few choice words, because I felt he was spoiling Ron Guidry's concentration, and basically I liked him. The Chicken, in full feathered regalia, made a few funny pitching motions, wound himself up like a pretzel, and fell down. The Chicken was ready.

I wanted to do this thing right. I have always been a perfectionist in my hitting. One time I almost scared the hell out of my wife. I keep a baseball bat near my bed during the season and sometimes take a few practice swings in the mirror before I go to sleep. One night I couldn't sleep, because I wasn't hitting well, tossed and turned in bed, then jumped up to try a new stance—I was always trying new stances. It was dark, I took a few swings—and the next thing I heard was a bloodcurdling scream. Anita had opened her eyes to see a guy standing over her bed swinging a baseball bat at her—I could hardly blame her for the shriek!

In Tucson that day we were trying to teach kids the idea of keeping your front side stiff as you drive the ball, and I probably overdid it. I kept my left side very stiff and

11

put a lot of strain on that shoulder. Bench noticed it toward the end of our filming.

"You okay, Lou?"

"My shoulder is a little tight."

"A lot of guys complain about that out here," he said.

Two or three weeks later I was in spring training in Fort Lauderdale when I noticed pain in my left shoulder when I tried to drive the ball. It lingered. I started getting cortisone shots regularly. I was under medication most of the time. It got so bad that if I played on Monday or Tuesday I couldn't swing a bat until my next start on a Thursday or Friday. I couldn't even take batting practice in between.

The team doctor, John Bonamo, was against giving me the shots, but I insisted on it. I was getting paid to play and I wanted to do it. I knew it was the only way I was going to be able to get out there. Without an occasional shot I had no chance. Once I loosened up and got the sweat going I had no problems, but after the game and the next day, the pain was awful. I had never been a training room player. I never got rubdowns. I never had ankle injuries. Now I was in there so often I was embarrassed.

I knew the time to exit was right there on my doorstep when the ball no longer jumped off my bat. The trainers had to work on me six or seven days to get me out there for two days, and even then I couldn't drive the ball. Line drives that used to fall for doubles were now being caught. The ball would hang and the outfielder would just get to it. I would drive a ball deep and think maybe I had a home run and then the ball would seem to sag and the outfielder would have time to eat a salami sandwich before catching it easily in front of the wall. Home run hitters feel it in their hands. Reggie Jackson knows when he hits one, that's why he can stand and watch it. Graig Nettles knows, Mike Schmidt—I was a line drive hitter, I never knew. I hit only 102 homers in my career. I would hit a ball well, run hard to first, and take a little peek over my shoulder. Once in a rare while I could let up and coast because it had cleared the fence. Now I could never let up. Nothing cleared the fence. I no longer had bat speed. I no longer drove the ball hard. It was time to go.

The Yankees had always been a proud organization, but the 1984 edition of the team did not measure up to the teams of the past. It was a patched-up team, and it was getting old. George, Yogi, and Clyde King, the general manager, discussed it in the spring, but decided to see if they could squeeze out one more season from the veteran players.

"Let's see how far we can go," George said at one meeting. "If it doesn't work, we can start changing during the season."

George knew he was in tough competition, not only with the rest of the American League for the pennant, but also with the Mets for the heart of New York. They were getting better and we were standing still and that drove him crazy—he couldn't *stand* for the Mets to get more attention than the Yankees—but he didn't want to give them an edge by going with inexperienced, unknown players just for the sake of a change. He asked me to try it for one more year. I was going to be forty-one that August and I had been playing baseball professionally since 1962.

George wanted to keep me around as a player because I provided leadership. I told him, "George, you can get a fan out of the stands or a general out of the Army to provide leadership. If he doesn't produce, nobody will listen to him anyway. A leader on a ballclub is a player who produces. It is as simple as that."

He understood I had to hit the ball, catch the ball, throw the ball to help the club win—and it got to the point where I just couldn't do that any longer. Even though I was hitting .300, it was a soft .300. If we had had a better team and I could have just pinch hit or played once a week I might have helped. Since we were going so badly, they needed more out of me, and I couldn't deliver.

At the end of May I walked up to Clyde in the corner of the clubhouse and told him I wanted to talk. We went into Yogi's office while Yogi was on the field. "I can't do it anymore. I want to bow out."

"I'll have to talk to George about this."

Two weeks later George summoned me to his office. He sat behind his large desk and I could see the autographed picture of his pal, Cary Grant, behind him and the large sign on his desk: LEAD, FOLLOW OR GET THE HELL OUT OF THE WAY. I sat in the soft leather chair shaped like a fielder's glove in front of his desk and tried to think how to begin. I'd been in this office many times before, but this time it was different. We were talking about my career as a player for the New York Yankees and with a few words it would be over.

George knew why I was there. "Lou," he said, "you have always been an integral part of this ballclub. Nobody will take that uniform away from you. You have to make the decision yourself. If you want to play, no matter what you can do, you can play out the rest of the year. If you don't, it is up to you."

"George, I've thought about this a long time. It's time."

We talked about the ballclub a long while, about the young players who could replace me and all the things we had examined in spring training. He listened carefully and I could see he was sad but agreed. George is a tough businessman. He has done a lot of things people don't like, but on that day, as I sat in his office, I could only thank him for saying how much I meant to the ballclub and how I could continue for the rest of the year as a player if I wanted. I'll appreciate that until the day I die.

The ballclub went up to Boston and somehow the information leaked out that I was retiring. My hotel phone began ringing off the hook, so a press conference was hastily called in Clyde King's suite and I officially announced my retirement. Yogi was there, as well as my good friend Bobby Murcer. June was a bad time for Yankee retirements. The previous June it had been Bobby's turn and I had been there. Now it was my turn. It was an emotional press conference and there were a lot of tears—there have to be tears when you give up the thing you love. I had prepared for this for a long time, but still my knees buckled. Playing baseball was something I had done, wanted to do, and loved to do all my life. Now it was over, with a snap of the fingers.

The conference ended, and I went back to my room, deeply depressed. Something was still missing. Then it shot into my head. "I want to retire at Yankee Stadium. I want to retire wearing the Yankee white pinstripes, not here in Boston in the road grays."

Bobby was with me. "I want to retire at home," I said.

"Man, you better get on the phone and rectify this right away," Bobby said.

"I want to retire at the Stadium. I don't want to retire in Boston."

"Here's the phone. Call Clyde or George or somebody."

I called Clyde. He said, "You'd better call George."

I called George and told him I wanted to retire in New York. I wanted one more game in the Yankee uniform.

George made the arrangements with the press and the announcement was changed to say I would retire in New York on June 16 at our Saturday afternoon game against the Orioles. Meanwhile, I still had that night against the Boston Red Sox.

It was right somehow that the last road game should be in Boston. Our rivalry was the most intense in all baseball, but I had always been treated well there. There were always New York fans, sometimes, it seemed, more of them than Boston fans, and I often heard the cries of "Lou, Lou, Lou," as I walked up to the plate at Fenway in a big game. I would look out at that short wall, the Green Monster in left field, hear the crowd yell and feel the adrenaline flow. It seemed that there was much more emotion in a game there.

As I walked to the plate for my first at bat in my last game in Boston, the sounds started to swell around me. I heard the public address announcer call my name and then announce it was my final game in Boston, and the applause began to rock through the park, louder and louder and louder, and I could feel the emotion in my body, and my lips grew dry, and the tears came to my eyes again. It seemed as if the applause went on for an hour. I was embarrassed and wanted it to be over, but it continued to swell and cover me like a blanket.

I went three for three that night. It felt like the ghosts of the past were in my blood. I made a couple of great catches and drove in a couple of runs and played like the young guy I used to be. When the game was over I felt a tremendous high. My teammates all congratulated me and I started thinking that maybe I had made the wrong decision, maybe I could still play, maybe I had rushed this thing. A game like that can bring doubts about quitting. But I knew I couldn't change my mind.

I pulled off my gray Yankee uniform with the large number 14 on it for the last time and threw it across the floor. I knew I would never wear it again as a player. I took a long, warm shower and thought of how lucky I was to be leaving there with such a wonderful game. I was a little late boarding the team bus; George had come down from the clubhouse and was sitting up front as I climbed on.

"What are you doing to me? You can still play," he said with a smile. "We're going bad and you put on a performance like that? You can still play."

I walked to the back of the bus and sat down. There wasn't much else to say—I was too choked up. I will always remember that farewell in Boston. Later I sent a telegram to the Red Sox general manager, Haywood Sullivan, thanking him and the Boston fans for their reception, and another one to the *Boston Globe*.

I was all wound up on the flight back to New York and felt as if I could play the next two days of my career that very night. Bobby and I talked about memories and games we shared, about the joy of being a big league ballplayer and a Yankee, about the laughs and the sorrows, about how much we missed Thurman and a lot of other guys who weren't with the Yankees anymore.

The plane landed in Newark and I took a cab to my home in New Jersey. It was about 1:30 in the morning when I put my key in the door. Anita was up waiting for me. Her eyes were red and I could see she had been crying. I stretched out my arms and she grabbed me and we gave each other a long, emotional hug.

"It's over this time, isn't it?"

"This time it's for sure," I said.

We stood there silently for several minutes and the tears ran down our cheeks. This time it was for sure.

We sat around the kitchen table for another hour and talked about our past and our future and about what a different turn our lives would take now. By morning some of the emotion had worn off and I sat alone at the table having a cup of coffee and reading the sports pages to see how my retirement had been reported. My son Louie, fifteen, came up to me, holding a newspaper in his hands. He had read the story. He looked at me and smiled.

"Dad, you're retiring. You mean it this time."

"Yes, I do, son."

I told my other two children, Kristi, twelve, and Derek, five, and they took it well. I was relaxed as I sat there reading the paper and sipping my coffee. We had a game that Friday night and then my final game as a player Saturday, so I had a light schedule that day—a long coffee breakfast, maybe a run over to my restaurant for an hour or so to check on things, then back to the house for a nap and on to the ballpark.

Anita got up and came into the kitchen. She saw me reading the paper and sipping my coffee. She had a smile on her face. I knew she was about to give me a zinger. She was about the best at that outside of Catfish Hunter.

"You know," Anita said, "I'm too young to be a coach's wife."

Tampa's Terrible-Tempered Teen

It was long before people talked about the term "extended family," but I guess that was the environment into which I was born. There were my parents, Louis and Margaret, and my mother's parents, Marcelinno and Beñina, who had come from Spain, and my mother's brothers, Joe and Mac, and my uncle Mac's wife, Gloria, who moved in after they got married, and then I came along at Centro Espanol Hospital in West Tampa on August 28, 1943. We all lived in a three-bedroom house at 2919 St. Conrad Street in a neighborhood made up mostly of Spanish families and some Italians. My parents, of course, spoke English, but neither of my grandparents did, and I spoke only Spanish until I went to school. The nuns taught me English, but, boy, it wasn't easy. My tongue always seemed to be in the wrong place!

Tampa was known as a port city then, and as the cigar center of America. A lot of people worked in those cigar factories, including my mother, who was a secretary for the Morgan Cigar Company, while my father sold cigars, cigarettes, candy, and household drugs store to store. They worked hard all week and came home tired, so my grandparents just about raised me. About the only time we could do anything as a family was on the weekend.

But, ah, those weekends! That was when we played baseball. My father pitched, my uncle Joe played first base, and my uncle Mac third in the inner-social league that played at old Cuscaden Park in Ybor City and MacFarland Park in West Tampa—a night game on Tuesday or Thursday and a doubleheader on Sunday. I was a bat boy for my father's team when I was real small.

Even my mother played baseball and basketball—she was a good athlete—and once in a while she would get into arguments just like my father and my uncles. One day my father was pitching a game, it was a big spot, and my father nailed what he thought was strike three. The umpire called ball four.

"How could you call that a ball?" my father yelled.

"It was outside," the umpire said.

"Down the middle, it was right down the middle," my father shouted.

"Get back on the mound or I'll throw you out of the game," the umpire said.

"Throw me out? Throw me out? I'll show you who can throw me out."

He flung his glove and kicked some dirt and stormed off the field. Then my uncle Joe started up on the poor umpire and walked off. My uncle Mac got into it and he was gone. Soon people were yelling from the stands, and before you know it the game was over and the whole place was in an uproar. People watch me play and think *I* get excited. They should have seen my family play. The fans got into those battles, there were fights on the field, guys rolling in the dirt, lots of screaming—it was the norm.

One day my father was playing in a game against a local rival. The score was tied and it was a big pitch. My father bent down for the signal. He shook his head three or four times and all of a sudden here came the catcher running out to the mound.

"Damn it, I've given you every signal I've got. What the hell do you want to throw?"

"Just get down there behind the plate and I'll throw what I want."

"Who the hell are you to tell me to get behind the plate?"

"Now just shut up and get back there or I'll let you have it."

All of a sudden my father let go with a haymaker and the catcher was down. He rolled over and wrestled my father to the ground, the two of them whacked away at each other, all the other players ran over to break it up, the fans came down from the stands, and everybody was having a heck of a time. That went on for fifteen or twenty minutes. Finally, they all became exhausted, the catcher went behind the plate, my father went to the mound, and the game continued as if nothing had ever happened.

Things began improving financially when my father bought his own business. It was a distributorship in Tampa and my mother quit her job at the cigar factory to go to work with him. She handled the books and paid the bills and was available to play on the softball team. My parents didn't play on the same team very often, but they saw each other play a lot. They would battle on the field for every call and the discussions would continue all the way home. We'd get to the house, my mother would start the dinner and the discussion over the play would start up again. I had a lot of interesting dinners. I don't remember many quiet nights in my house after those games.

In the summer of 1956 the West Tampa Pony League team swept through the opposition and wound up playing for the national championship in Ontario, California. It was my first plane ride, my first trip outside Tampa—and almost a fatal experience, as it turned out.

We had won our games out there and had a day off while the other two contending teams played each other for the right to meet us for the title. My best buddy on the team, Paul Ferlita, his parents, and I drove up to the top of Mount Baldy to get a view of the countryside. I jumped out of the car.

"Scappy"—my father's nickname was Scappy and my close pals called me Scappy, Jr.—"where are you going?" shouted Paul.

"I want to get a view from the top here, I said.

"Wait a second, let me get up there with you."

Before I could answer, I stumbled on a loose rock and was over the edge of the cliff, racing helplessly down the mountain, seeing the water several thousand feet below, my feet bouncing on the rugged ground, and then suddenly running in the air, falling over now as I lost control of myself, tossing and turning and bouncing on that hard ground, growing dizzy from a blow to my head, losing all sense of direction and balance and falling, falling, falling. A huge boulder rushed up at me and beyond it was nothing but a steady incline to the bottom of that cliff, to the water below, to a certainly fatal fall.

The boulder caught me.

"Lou, Lou, Lou," I could hear Mrs. Ferlita calling from the top of that mountain. It wasn't quite the same tone of affection I would hear later from the fans at Yankee Stadium. "Lou, Lou, Lou." I couldn't respond. I was too frightened and bruised and shocked.

Sam Ferlita saw that I was two hundred feet below the road and it was impossible to reach me. He ran to his car and drove to the nearest ranger station. After what seemed like hours but probably was no more than twenty minutes, a ranger helicopter began whirling overhead. A park ranger dropped a long ladder, came out of the plane to pick me up, and carried me back up and into the plane. I was rushed to a local hospital where they examined my head and found nothing. Bad joke. But I did have severe bruises and bumps on my head, a minor concussion, shoulder pain, bruises, and a broken ankle. The strange thing was they examined my ankle and didn't find the break. They kept me in the hospital overnight and let me out the next day.

I was supposed to pitch that final game but my ankle was so blown up I could hardly walk. Somebody else pitched and I played outfield. We lost the game and blew the Pony League title. The ankle continued to bother me for years and was one of the reasons I began to concentrate more on baseball than basketball, even though basketball was really my best sport. I loved the speed and movement of the game, the freedom of expression it gave me. The game really fit my personality, but it just hurt too damn much when I jumped up for my shot and came down hard on that ankle.

We never won the Pony League title, but three players from that team made it to the big leagues, so it must have been a pretty good club. Besides myself there was Ken Suarez, a longtime American League catcher, and Tony La Russa, who was later signed by Charlie Finley for a big bonus and never became a big league star. That's probably why he turned to managing. I remember him jokingly saying, much later, "The toughest thing for me as a young manager is the fact that a lot of these guys saw me play. It's hard for me to instruct them in anything, because they know how bad I was!"

By the time I entered Jesuit High I was a pretty accomplished basketball and baseball player. I made Catholic All America as a basketball player, averaged thirty-four points a game and led the team to the regional finals at Tampa. The wheels were already in motion for the terrible-tempered Lou Piniella of later years and Coach Paul Straub spent a lot of time getting me out of the Precinct of Discipline. That was run by Father Lashley and I would be sent there after school for carrying on in class, rolling marbles across the floor of the classroom, throwing erasers, putting chewing gum on the teacher's seat, or hiding the teacher's roll cards in a closet. I wasn't a bad kid, but I was a cutup.

Coach Straub would have to rescue me from these after-school detentions so I could practice with the basketball team.

"This is the last time I am going to help you, Lou," he said one day.

"I'm sorry, I really am. It won't happen again."

A week later it happened again.

"You see this figure I'm drawing on this paper?" Father Lashley said. "It's a jackass."

"I see it."

"You will not leave this class until you draw one hundred of these figures on the paper, cut each of them out and write on the bottom of the picture, 'My name is Lou Piniella. I am a jackass.' That's what you will write. Now get to it."

Not even Coach Straub could save me from that. I am a jackass.

The temper surfaced again in the spring of 1961. Jesuit went to the regional basketball finals in Tampa. I had a pretty good game, but we lost and returned home the next day. It was the first day of baseball practice and I went out for the team again. We had a game against Jefferson in three days.

"I want you to pitch, Lou," said baseball coach Jack O'Connell.

"I can't, Coach. I've just finished basketball and I'm not ready."

"I think you are. You throw today and you'll be ready for the game."

"My arm isn't ready. I'm not pitching."

"Damn it," said Coach O'Connell, "if you're not pitching, you're not on this baseball team."

"Screw it. Then I'm not on the damn baseball team."

That little temper tantrum probably cost me seventy-five thousand dollars.

Scouts had been talking to Coach O'Connell about me and several of them thought I could be signed after graduation in June as a pitcher for about seventy-five thousand dollars. I threw real hard, I had a lot of strike-outs and I was developing into a big kid. It seemed the Latin kids grew taller and heavier than the American kids by the senior year of high school. After that a lot of the Americans kept growing and most of the Latins stopped. I never could figure out why.

The season started and I went to the games and watched my friends play baseball.

"Lou, why don't you apologize and tell him you can pitch," Kenny Suarez said.

"I won't do it. Why the hell should he use me when I'm not ready?"

"That was a week ago. Your arm is rested now. C'mon, apologize to him so we can get a chance to win the state title."

Lou Piniella was too stubborn, too proud, and probably too dumb to apologize. I sat there all spring watching my friends play baseball and eating my heart out.

The scouts can't talk to you until you graduate and they had cooled off by then, since I had nothing to show them for my senior year. I went into the American Legion summer program, hit my usual .500, but it was clear I wasn't ticketed for the pros just yet. I signed a letter of intent to play basketball and baseball at the University of Tampa. My mother was thrilled. I felt fortunate to get a free ride.

"Lou, I'm so happy," my mother said. "I'm so glad you are going to college."

"I'm going, Mom. But I haven't promised I'm staying."

"We'll see, we'll see. There is plenty of time to discuss that."

By September of 1961 I was a college student. Several schools had been after me, but I was happy I stayed in Tampa. I still felt a little shy, a little insecure, a little immature to go to school out of town. And if I still entertained any thoughts of professional basketball, one final college incident ended all hopes of that.

I made the basketball team as a freshman guard on the varsity. I wasn't playing much, maybe five or six minutes a game, but it was still fun. I got to work out with the big guys, eat with the varsity starters, take all those trips. Late that season we were playing a big game against the University of Louisville in Freedom Hall in Louisville. They were highly ranked, maybe in the top ten, and if we could knock them off it would be quite a boost for our program. I was thrilled just being there.

"Piniella!"

I heard my name screamed at me by our basketball coach, Bob Lavoy. One of our guards had gotten into early foul trouble. I ripped off my sweat pants, pulled off my shirt, and leaned on the sidelines waiting for the next time-out. My heart was thumping. There were twenty thousand people in that huge arena and I was getting into the biggest college game of my life.

I brought up the ball—and was fouled. I stood on the line, took a deep breath, and pushed the ball up. Air ball. A little later I drove to the basket—and got pushed. Two free throws. Missed them both. Then came a third try after another foul. This one hit the rim. Three fouls, four chances, all misses. I didn't know if it was nerves, the big arena, or that I was a lousy foul shooter. Anyway, I felt miserable. The half ended and we trudged into the locker room. I sat down on the bench with my head in my hands. The door slammed shut and Coach Lavoy, a big, tough former professional basketball player, looked over toward me in that silent room.

"Lou Piniella," he said, slowly dragging out my name without much warmth. "Lou Piniella," he repeated. Then he paused so the entire team could pay attention and make sure they knew who he was talking about.

"All-American high school basketball player," he screamed, "my ass!"

You could hear the heavy breathing in the room as he bit off those words. I looked up at him, stared at the angry face and shouted at the top of my lungs.

"You can't be so smart either," I bellowed. "You recruited me!"

The Life I Chose

Somehow I lost my dedication about basketball around that time. One day, I was sitting in a neighborhood college hangout called Sam's having a couple of beers and reflecting on my future. I was all of eighteen years old then and I knew the drinking age was twenty-one, but I didn't care.

We were all having a grand old time when the door sprang open, a blue uniform showed up and somebody that had seen this act before yelled, "Cops. Let's go." I raced up the side stairs of Sam's to the roof. It was a two-story building and I got to the top and thought I could jump off and get away. I jumped off, all right. I didn't get away. I landed on my ankle, hurt it again, fell on the ground, and felt a nightstick in my ribs. I had jumped off the building into a collection of cops. They put me into a squad car with my ankle throbbing and drove me downtown to the Tampa police station. They asked my name and phone number. Then they called my house. My father answered.

"Mr. Piniella, we have your son, Louis, down here in the Tampa police station."

"What has he done?"

"Drinking at Sam's and he's under age."

"Is he all right?"

"Yeah, he's all right, but somebody will have to come down here and bail him out and sign for him. He's a minor."

"Let him stay there. Maybe he'll learn something. I'll pick him up in the morning."

After a night in the Tampa jail I had to face my folks when they came to get me out. The tongue-lashing I got was enough to convince me that a couple of beers was hardly worth the trouble. That incident took care of my hanging out for a while and took care of what was left of my basketball career. My ankle was too swollen to play basketball on and I was finished for the season.

When the baseball season came around, I was ready, had a good year, and one sunny June afternoon, I pulled up at our house to see a couple of strange cars parked in our driveway. My mother came out to the front yard.

"Do you want to play baseball professionally?"

"Are you kidding? Of course I do!"

"Well, there's a gentleman inside the house waiting for you and he is ready to offer you a professional contract."

It all seemed to happen very fast. Scouts had been watching me ever since my second or third year of high school—the coaches had told me so—but I had never talked to any of them. Under the rules in force then, before the institution of the amateur free draft, any club could contact you and make an offer. We went inside.

"Hi, I'm Spud Chandler," the man said. "I represent the Cleveland Indians."

"Hi, nice to meet you. I certainly know who you are."

Chandler had pitched eleven years for the Yankees, won 109 games, including 20 games in two separate seasons, and had one of the highest winning percentages in baseball history at .717. He had retired to Saint Petersburg, Florida, and scouted the area for the Indians.

"We are prepared to offer you a ten-thousand-five hundred-dollar signing bonus, a seventy-five-hundred-dollar progressive bonus and seventy-five hundred dollars extra against your education if you sign with us. I have discussed this with your mother and she says whatever you decide to do is fine. It's up to you."

"I'll sign."

That was it. I didn't argue about the price, I didn't ask

him to come back in a week, I didn't tell him to wait while I called the Tigers or the Cubs or the Yankees to see if anybody else was interested in me. I had no agent because agents were unheard of for high school or college players in those days, maybe even for professional players. He simply pulled out a contract, I signed my name to it, my mom signed as required because I was still a minor—and I was a professional baseball player. It all happened in a matter of minutes.

People complain about the huge salaries in baseball today, a million a year, a million and a half, two million. I made four hundred thousand dollars on the final year of my playing contract in 1984, but I can understand the money being made by Dave Winfield or Gary Carter or Mike Schmidt. They are superstars of the game. They bring people into the ballpark. They sell tickets and make a lot of money for the owners. When I signed for that $25,500 bonus, I was giving up college, my home, my family, and a lot of comforts for that small chance at professional baseball. About one in one hundred kids signed make it to the big leagues. Fewer than half of those last more than a couple of years. It is not outrageous for a few to make two million dollars. They are the rare exceptions. Most baseball players never even get as high as Triple A and maybe, even today, make no more than twenty-five thousand dollars a year. The minimum major league salary is sixty thousand dollars a year. My plumber makes more than that, and he can't hit a curve ball.

Now I was about to embark on that journey, about to settle into the life I had chosen.

It would all begin in a small, quiet southern town called Selma, Alabama, soon to become infamous as the center of one of the ugliest civil rights demonstrations of the 1960s, but in the soft summer days of 1962 the home of the Cleveland Indians Class D baseball team.

My mom put out a great dinner the next night, invited some friends over, and sent me off to professional baseball with a warm feeling. I had planned to leave the next morning in my car and drive straight on through to

Selma. My uncle Mac decided he would go along with me. At daybreak we loaded the car with a couple of suitcases and a small bag containing my gloves and spikes. My mother came to the door as I was about to leave.

"Try hard, do your best," she said. "Be a good boy."

"I will, Mom, I will."

"Make sure you call us collect as soon as you get settled there."

"Don't worry, Mom, I'll be fine."

She grabbed me and gave me a huge hug. She seemed to hold on for a long while and I could see tears at the corners of her eyes. We didn't say much more, but I felt a lump in my throat and I had trouble holding back my tears. I was eighteen years old, but I was still her baby boy.

"Let's go, Lou," said Uncle Mac, who seemed as excited as I was. He was forty years old and I'm sure had dreamed of this moment himself once.

"Bye, Mom. I'll call."

We drove through downtown Tampa, the sun just breaking through the clouds, the air warming up quickly as it does in south Florida in June, and headed north and west for the state of Alabama.

"Just remember to play hard all the time," Mac said as the miles raced on.

"I know that. I will."

"Managers in baseball want talented players, but they want guys who will play hard every day they are out there. Just give your best. Don't let down. I know you'll do fine. I know you can play. The Cleveland Indians know you can play or they wouldn't have given you the twenty-five thousand dollars."

"Boy, was I sorry to see that amount printed in the paper. They printed that and then they printed that Tony La Russa had been signed for a hundred thousand last year out of Jefferson. I don't think he is seventy-five thousand dollars better than me. Do you?"

"It doesn't matter what kind of bonus you get to sign.

It only matters how well you play at Selma and how fast you can get to the big leagues."

I started to think about that for a minute. The big leagues. What a strange thought. The big leagues were for my heroes, Al Rosen and Ted Williams and Tampa man Al Lopez. I was just going to Selma, Alabama. I was just getting a summer job as a professional baseball player. There was no thought of the big leagues. It was a dream too great.

We checked into the Cloverleaf Hotel in downtown Selma, and the next day we drove out to the ballpark together. I walked into the small clubhouse. It was about two o'clock in the afternoon and the manager, Pinky May, a former big leaguer, was in his office. His son, Milt, who was then about ten or eleven years old and would later be a big leaguer himself, was in his father's office shining his shoes.

"Hi, I'm Lou Piniella. I just arrived here from Tampa," I said.

"Welcome, Lou. We expected you. Get suited up and I'll show you around. You'll be in the lineup tonight, center field and batting sixth."

Tonight! So soon! I swallowed hard and ran to put on the uniform of the Selma Cloverleafs. Pinky May came to inspect me and pointed at my feet.

"Those spikes don't fit. You can't wear spikes here that are big like that with the ends curled up."

"These are the shoes I wore all through college."

"This is professional baseball, Lou. I'll let you wear a pair of my shoes and then you buy yourself a new pair when the sporting goods salesman comes around. Make sure they fit."

Professional baseball . . . we walked outside and I got my first look at the neat little park. The day was bright and sunny and the air heavy and humid. I was glad we were playing at night. We walked back inside the clubhouse and Pinky introduced me to a few of my early-arriving teammates. They weren't very friendly.

"These guys don't seem too happy to see me."

"I had to release one of their buddies today to make room for you on the roster. They're upset. Just play ball. It'll pass."

I had joined the club as an eighteen-year-old kid out of college with a decent bonus. I was a prospect and the Cleveland organization would do everything it could to see that I became a major league ballplayer. The kid they'd released had been in their organization for three years at Class D baseball. He had never progressed and now, with my arrival, the organization had decided to release him. He had to go home, a failure, to face his family and friends, to tell them he wasn't good enough, to return to school or get a job as a grocery clerk or start a new life somewhere. He would always dream of what he could have been as he read years later of Lou Piniella getting a big hit in Yankee Stadium or making a great catch in Fenway Park or throwing someone out in Comiskey Park. In the next few weeks ten or twelve more kids, eighteen, nineteen, or twenty years old, would join that ballclub and others, twenty, twenty-one, twenty-two would be called into Pinky May's office, told they weren't good enough, given a check to cover their expenses home, and sent away with their hopes and dreams shattered. Not one single player on the Class D Selma Cloverleafs of 1962 made it to the big leagues for even one day, except me. Think of that when you think of the outrageous salaries being paid to a few major league players today. I was paid six hundred and fifty dollars a month that summer, the largest amount any player on that team received.

That first night I walked to the plate, a little nervous, but confident I could hit professional pitchers because I had always been able to hit, in the Pony Leagues, high school, American Legion, college baseball. I was a hitter, period. While driving to Alabama, Uncle Mac had suggested I would see more curve balls in professional baseball than in college baseball.

"You've got to close your stance so you can protect that plate against those big curves," he said.

"I'm a good fastball hitter. I have to be able to handle the curve if I'm going to make it with these pros."

"Close up, close up. You'll handle it."

My stance was closed as I dug in at the plate. I hadn't been in pro baseball ten minutes before I changed my stance, and I continued to change it for the rest of my career. I practiced it at home in the mirror, late at night in hotel rooms, early in the morning at breakfast, late in the afternoon in the clubhouse. I was always looking for that perfect stance. Couldn't happen.

The first pitch was a fastball for a strike. I guessed the next one would be a curve. I was right. The pitch was coming in high across the letters, breaking away, moving toward the outside of the plate, as I sent that message from my brain to my eyes and hands in a flash: Swing that bat. Hit that baseball. Drive it hard. Run like hell. The ball floated off the end of my bat and blooped toward the right field corner. I saw it fall safely as I raced to first and turned toward second. The right fielder hustled over, picked it up, and threw to second base. I was always a good slider and I had already slid in safely, bounced up quickly, and was dusting myself off with a professional double on my first professional swing when the ball arrived.

The next time up I struck out on a curve and walked slowly back to the dugout in disgust. Maybe professional baseball wasn't going to be all that easy after all. I put my helmet down gently, picked up my glove and sat in the corner. For this failed at bat the dugout walls and the equipment bag would be safe. It wouldn't always be so.

For the next three weeks I played every day, but my average stayed under .200. I wasn't hitting the ball with authority. When I did hit it hard, it was right at people and I started pressing. I was a big kid by now, six feet two inches tall, nearly 190 pounds, and I was hitting the ball like some Little Leaguer. What had happened to my quick bat and college power? After a game in Pensacola, Florida, Pinky came up to me in the clubhouse. He had benched me for a couple of days as I struggled.

"Lou, let's have breakfast tomorrow. I'll meet you in the coffee shop at nine o'clock."

"Okay, Pinky. I'll be there."

I wasn't concerned about a release. It was too early for that and my bonus was too large for such a quick decision. I knew he wanted to help.

"Lou," he began that morning, "the reports we had on you were very good. You were a pull hitter and drove the ball hard. You're not driving the ball hard. You're pushing it. Is there anything wrong?"

"Well," I began, rather shyly, "my uncle and I were driving here from Tampa and we were discussing the amount of curve balls I would see in a professional game and we decided to change my stance."

"Change your stance? What the hell for?"

"To hit the curve ball."

"Listen. You have to prove you can hit the *fast*ball. Nobody plays in the big leagues without being able to hit the fastball first. If you want to be a hitter, get back to that original stance and pull the ball. Hit it hard. Show us you have power and strength. We'll teach you how to hit a curve ball. I guarantee it. First I want you to hit the fastball, regain your confidence, get comfortable with your swing."

I don't think I'd realized just how much changing my stance had altered my swing, but that night I went back into the lineup, opened up my stance—and hit a long homer. Oh, did that feel good. I started hitting the ball hard again and pretty soon I was batting third instead of sixth and the club was winning. The second half playoffs were coming up and I had become one of the two or three best hitters on that club. Everybody was friendly to me. Nobody seemed to remember anymore that I had been brought to the club in June and replaced an old buddy. With all the new players coming in, I was one of the old buddies now.

As my hitting improved, the days seemed to fly by. I lived in a big old rooming house in downtown Selma—everything was downtown Selma—and paid a hundred dollars a month for a bedroom, dinner, and breakfast. A sweet old lady rented out the rooms in her home—it must have been quite a mansion before the Civil War—and we were about fifteen minutes from the ballpark on the outskirts of town. Other players lived in the house as well, including two young Latins, Fernando Rey from Mexico and Adolpho Hernandez, a lefthanded pitcher from Havana, Cuba. We palled around together because neither of them could speak a word of English and it helped to have someone who could. It is difficult to understand just how hard it is for a scared Latin kid from a foreign country to play baseball here. He can't speak the language, he doesn't know the customs, he is usually much younger than the other players, and he is almost always homesick. With my Spanish, I tried to make them forget their troubles and feel comfortable. I have always gone out of my way to help young Latin players. They need more help than the kids from Iowa or California.

There were no blacks in the Alabama-Florida league, and there never would be. The following year, Governor George Wallace killed it. Baseball was integrating everywhere, and it was the only league in organized baseball with no black American players. They would take Latins into that league, but they wouldn't take blacks. When baseball proposed integrating the league for the 1963 season, Governor Wallace said they wouldn't have it. Baseball insisted. Wallace wouldn't budge. The league simply folded and the players were scattered elsewhere. The fans in these southern cities were denied professional baseball. In the coming years, Selma would become famous for civil rights riots and demonstrations. For me it was all presaged right there when Governor Wallace took professional baseball out of Alabama rather than let any black man on the field.

As my hitting came along, so too did that terrible Tampa temper. I wanted to play and I wanted to do well, and when I didn't I would heave a bat, or show emotion by punching a dugout. One night we were playing a big game, the bases were loaded, one man was out and I was up. I had a chance to blow the game open—and I took a curve ball for strike three. That was all I needed. I stormed back to the dugout and watched the next guy foul out to end the inning. I was still smoking when I started moving to center field.

A huge rain barrel that we used for drinking water stood next to our dugout. It was filled from a hose before the game, kept cool with a couple of chunks of ice from the clubhouse refrigerator, and served as our water fountain. Ky Littleton, a nice young man from Columbia, South Carolina, was our shortstop and my good friend. He picked up my glove and lobbed it to me as I walked onto the field. I grabbed the glove, took one more step and heaved it right into the water barrel. It immediately sank to the bottom.

"Hey, Lou, let's go," said Littleton. Well, what was I going to do now? I couldn't play center field without a glove.

I leaned over the barrel, reached in for my glove, lost my balance on the wet turf and fell head first into the icy water. I could feel water sucking into my lungs and Littleton tugging at my knees trying to pull me out upside down from that damn thing. As he got me part way out, the whole barrel tipped over and all the water ran all over me. I just sat there on the ground, soaked and coughing, as the fans, who had witnessed the entire fiasco, of course, roared with laughter.

"When I yelled for you to soak your head," one fat fan bellowed, "I didn't really mean it."

You'd think that would have taught me something about holding my temper. I just had to take my frustrations out on something. Once, in Kansas City, I attacked a watercooler so ferociously I knocked it over. I looked at it lying there, dented, and decided to buy it. I had it shipped to my home in Tampa, and every once in a while during the off-season I'd give it a good kick, just to stay in practice.

Despite such appearances, though, I was steadily becoming more professional. I was learning to play every day, to play under lights, to hit good fastball pitching. One day in August, Pinky May called me into the office before a game and presented me with a check for ten thousand dollars: The signing bonus had come through from the Cleveland club. That's when it hit me—I was a *pro*. I took that check and placed it in the glove compartment of my car, concerned that I would lose it or someone would steal it from me. Of course, someone could have stolen my car while I was playing and gotten the ten thousand with it, but that never occurred to me. I was the first customer at the bank the next morning. When I went back to Tampa at the end of the season, I had the ten-thousand-dollar bonus and some eleven hundred dollars I had saved from my salary.

Not long after I received the check, Pinky May told us that Hoot Evers, the Cleveland farm director, was coming down to watch us for a week. When he arrived I was in a hot streak and hit over .500 while he was in town. I would finish at .270, hit eight home runs and knock in forty-four runs. I knew I was helping myself. I called home.

"Mom, the Big Guy from Cleveland was here. I'm doing real well. Things are going great."

"Keep it up, Lou. Finish strong. We are looking forward to seeing you next month. We miss you."

"I miss you, too, Mom."

We went to the playoffs and won, and I couldn't wait to get home, to see my family and friends, to tell everyone about the excitement of being a professional player, to march into my high school coach's office and my college coach's office and tell them what I had done. I wanted to brag a little. Why not?

I was a prospect.

Little Napoleon
and Me

On November 26, 1962, I was drafted by the Washington Senators organization for eight thousand dollars, the first player chosen in the minor league draft. I thought I would be closer to the major leagues and get a salary raise. All that really happened was I learned that baseball was a dog-eat-dog business—and that the ballplayers were the guys getting chewed up.

Shortly after the first of the year in 1963, I received a contract from my new team, and a note from my new boss, George Selkirk. He was the Washington Senators' general manager and had been a Yankee outfielder, the guy who had succeeded Babe Ruth in right field at Yankee Stadium. He had also learned how to negotiate from Yankee GMs Ed Barrow and George Weiss, two guys who threw around loose change as if it was manhole covers. Selkirk's first contract to me called for the same six hundred and fifty dollars a month I had made in the Cleveland organization. If the owners today wonder why players support free agency and arbitration and all the rule changes in contract negotiations, they can ask any player who broke in before the rule changes began. Young ballplayers were hammered at every turn when it came to money. General managers like George Selkirk did more to make the players' union strong than all the Marvin Millers in the world.

I was hurt, angry, and very bitter about the whole thing. I sat down and began a letter. "Dear Mr. Selkirk, I received your contract and it must be the wrong one. It calls for six-fifty a month and that is the salary I made last year. I showed I could play professional baseball in 1962 and I expect a raise, a substantial one, for 1963." I sent that off and felt pretty good about it. I was only nineteen years old but nobody could take advantage of me. His reply came in the mail a few days later. "Dear Lou, your contract calls for six-fifty and that is what you will be paid. You are only a Class D ballplayer and you haven't proven yourself yet. I am enclosing these scouting reports, which indicate that several of our scouts believe you will never be more than a Triple A player. If you want any chance at all in this organization, sign this contract and send it back to me by return mail."

I wondered why the Washington Senators would draft me if they thought I'd only be a Triple A player. But he did send along those scouting reports and it sort of scared me. I signed my name to that contract.

Now I know better. Ballclubs would have eight or ten different scouts look at you over a season. Maybe three or four didn't like me. Maybe five or six liked me a lot. He didn't sent along those scouting reports. Scouting is a delicate art at best. There are as many failures as there are successes. If you want to get under George Steinbrenner's skin a little bit, remind him about the Yankee scout who went to Mexico to watch a fat little lefthander pitch. He called George and said he wasn't worth the fifty thousand dollars the kid was asking. George didn't sign him. The Dodgers did. Fernando Valenzuela is probably worth five or six million on the open market now. Oh, yes, George fired that scout in a hurry after Valenzuela became a star.

There was no other place for me to go. I was a Washington Senator or I could stay home.

"Listen," my mother said, when the letter arrived from Selkirk. "What's the difference if you make six-fifty, seven-fifty, or eight-fifty now? You won't make any real money until you get into the big leagues anyway."

I put the signed contract in the mail, but I never forgot the lesson. Baseball is a game and I enjoyed playing it, but it is also a business and you have to be able to support your family. Ballclubs play hardball when it comes to contract signing, on all levels; it was true then, it's true now. They are always trying to save money on salaries.

Soon I was on my way across the state of Florida to check in to the Thunderbird Hotel in Pompano Beach for spring training. The next day I was at the ballpark and introduced myself to Senators' manager Mickey Vernon.

"You're in the right ballpark, kid, but the wrong clubhouse."

There were six young players in the visitors' clubhouse. All six of us wound up in B ball in the Carolina league in Peninsula. Still, we got a chance to work out with the Senators and, in the middle of March, I was sitting on the bench, watching the spring training, trying to pick up as much as I could before they made the minor league cuts—when Mickey Vernon turned to me.

"Piniella, get a bat."

Hey, was this my chance? I felt the adrenaline pumping as I walked up to home plate to face Diego Segui, a Cuban righthander pitching for the Kansas City A's. He threw me a slider for a strike, a slider for a ball, and another strike for strike two. I cocked my bat. I was going to cream this one. A fourth slider broke outside, and I chased it with one hand on the bat, sort of failing at it the way Dave Winfield does sometimes when he loses his bat. Strike three. I returned quietly to the bench. That was my entire spring training performance and career with the Washington Senators.

When I arrived at the Pensacola training camp I checked in at the old San Carlos Hotel. I had come from my nice beach hotel at Pompano with two guys in a huge room to a large room with ten guys in small bunks plus one closet and one small bathroom. Quite a bit different.

"How was it up there, Lou?" several players asked me.

"It was great. A lot more meal money," I said.

That wasn't all that was different, of course. Conditions in the Carolina league were rough. It was a shoestring operation and we wore the same dirty uniforms for a week during spring training. Either you washed them yourself—which nobody ever did—or you played with them dirty. We rode smelly buses without bathrooms, drinking water, or leg room for eight or ten hours at a time without a rest stop. We had a schedule to meet. We had drivers, but they would switch off with a veteran player once in a while to get a snooze. It was a little hairy going around on some of those curving roads when the veteran outfielders were driving. We'd get to a park, haul our own stuff to the field, and start batting practice with a lot of well-used old bats. Major league ballplayers who have never played in the minor leagues simply can't understand the conditions. It can be hell sometimes and it takes an awful lot of desire to hang in there. Even now, when big league players are making millions of dollars, minor league conditions in the lower leagues are still not what they could be. That's where they ought to organize for improved conditions.

I had a fine year at Peninsula, however, and a few days before the end of the season, manager Archie Wilson called me into his office.

"Lou, I have some good news for you. It will be announced in the press today that you have been named the best rookie in the league and you will be joining the Washington club next week."

"That's great! Terrific! When do I report up there?"

"They'll let you know in a day or two."

But instead of going to the Washington Senators, I went to the hospital.

It was a Sunday afternoon and the following week on the road would finish our schedule. We decided to have a farewell party, because a lot of us would never be seeing one another again. That's always the way it is at the end of any baseball season. We got a few of those local Virginia beauties, a few cans of beer, and just enough junk food, and had ourselves a party after the game. Everybody was having a lot of fun, laughing and dancing to records and drinking beer. I had my eye on one cute girl and, fooling around, wanted to chase her a bit. She started backing away for fun, playing hard to get, and I followed her through the kitchen, through the living room, and out toward the front door. It was open on that nice late-summer afternoon and she ran out and closed it hard behind her. I just kept running after her and put my left hand through the glass door. Suddenly, my blood was everywhere, on the glass door, on the floor, all over my clothing, and on everybody else who tried to help. Somebody thought to get some towels out of the bathroom. They wrapped my arm and took me outside to a car. We drove as fast as we could to a Peninsula hospital.

The doctor had to put thirty-seven stitches in my left arm.

"Son, you are very lucky," the doctor said. "That cut goes a little deeper and you might have been in serious trouble."

"You don't think thirty-seven stitches in my left arm is serious for a ballplayer?"

"I mean if that had hit an artery there might not be any ballplayer here."

The Washington ballclub was notified immediately, of course, and it changed their plans for me. Instead of going to the big leagues, I was sent home.

Wilson had been filing good reports on my playing ability all season, but he had also told them they had a temperamental Latin on their hands. I think I lost some favor with him when I left him standing in the shower all soaped up with no hot water. That usually gets a guy upset.

We had been playing in Wilson, North Carolina, and with two out and two on in the top of the ninth of a one-run game, I had had a chance to win it with a hit. Instead, I had struck out to end it. The guys came into the clubhouse to shower and I stayed on the field kicking dirt, screaming at the top of my lungs, and heaving my bat against the screen. Then I finally went inside to shower.

By that time the manager, who was pretty upset himself at losing a tough game like that, was the only one left to shower. I just stormed in there and turned on the water faucet. When the water didn't come out as fast as I wanted, I pulled at the shower head and ripped it clear off the wall. Poor Archie Wilson. He was standing there all soaped up. No water.

"Goddamn it, Piniella," he screamed. "Get some water in here."

"How the hell am I going to get water? The damn faucet's broke."

"See that bucket? Pick it up and go across the field to the home clubhouse and fill it up. Then bring it back here and don't spill a damn drop."

I pulled on my pants and trudged across the field.

"Gotta get some water for the skipper," I told the clubhouse boy. "Damn faucet's broke."

Wilson made me bring him six buckets of water before he would come out of that shower and allow me to be free. I felt like Gunga Din.

Even though I played well all summer things like that seemed to happen. Like the day I made the trainer cry. It cost me seventy-five bucks of my six-hundred-and-fifty-dollar-a-month salary.

We were in another tough game and I was jammed by a pitch in a big spot and hit a soft roller to second. A quick fielding play turned it into a double play, and when I got back to the dugout I kicked the first thing I saw. It was the trainer's bag with all his medicines and equipment. There was a jar of acid in there that he used on cuts. I heard something break when I kicked the bag, but I had no idea what it was. An inning or so later the game ended. I picked up my glove. The trainer picked up his bag—and everything he had in there came falling out, the medicine jars, the tape rolling all over the field, the bandages falling in the dirt, the headache pills bouncing on the ground. He stood there, motionless, his leather bag torn at the bottom by the acid, his prize collection scattered. Then he started crying. I felt bad. I wasn't very mature.

"Damn you, Piniella," shouted Wilson. "This will cost you."

After the incident with the glass door, the Senators no longer considered me a fair-haired prospect. Concerned about my arm, they ordered me to play winter ball in Nicaragua, where I didn't do very well, dropping my standing even lower. Then, I had no sooner checked into spring training when the National Guard called me to active duty and ordered me to report to Camp Gordon, Georgia. George Selkirk, the Washington GM, wasn't very pleased.

He mentioned me in a newspaper article. "Our players are generally smart enough to take care of their military obligations in the wintertime. Piniella picks the baseball season to serve his time. I don't think he's very serious about his career." Well, that upset me. How was I to know when the National Guard would call me? The Vietnam War was heating up and they were calling lots of guys. I'm glad Selkirk didn't blame the war on me.

In July I was discharged from the service and rejoined the Washington ballclub. I worked out with them for a couple of weeks waiting for assignment to one of their farm clubs. One afternoon the clubhouse man told me Mr. Selkirk wanted to see me. The Senators were playing the Orioles that day.

A small gray-haired man was sitting in Selkirk's office.

"Lou, I want you to meet Lee MacPhail. He's the general manager of the Baltimore Orioles. You're with them now. We traded your contract."

"What? I just got here!"

"We think you have a fine chance to become a big league player," MacPhail said. "We are very happy to have you."

Three years in professional baseball and three organizations. What was going on here?

MacPhail said the Orioles wanted to send me down to the Class C Aberdeen, South Dakota, club.

"Class C? I've played two years and I hit .310 at B ball. Why Class C?"

43

"We'd just like you to play three weeks out there, get your swing back after the military, and we'll bring you up to the Orioles in September."

Well, I didn't like the first part of that, but the bit about September sounded pretty good, so I flew out there the next day. The manager of the Aberdeen club was a very nice, very fatherly man named Cal Ripken, Sr. I hit a double the first time up there and he greeted me on the bench later as if I had just delivered the winning hit in the World Series.

It was a good club. Also on the team was a handsome, skinny kid pitcher named Jim Palmer, who was winning a lot of games, and a tall skinny shortstop named Mark Belanger, who could make every play you could imagine. They even had a good bat boy. He was only about four or five years old, but he was a handsome little devil and he used to catch a ball pretty good on the sidelines. He was the manager's son, Cal Ripken, Jr., and about twenty years later he would be the MVP of the American League.

After twenty games there, during which I hit .270 and threw only a few bats, the Orioles were true to their word and I was called up to the Baltimore Orioles. I had just turned twenty-one. The manager was Hank Bauer, who immediately reminded me of the tough old sergeant I had just left in the National Guard. Gruff and noisy, leathery-faced, he intimidated me the first time he spoke to me.

"Piniella, you're here to work," he shouted. "We didn't bring you here to get a month's big league salary. We want you to learn some baseball while you're here. And remember that I'm hard on young people who break curfew on the road and goddamn it, I expect you to pay attention to what goes on here."

I guess that was Hank Bauer's way of saying hello.

Bauer had been a tremendous player with the Yankees, a fierce competitor and one of the greatest World Series clutch players in history. They used to say he welcomed young players by staring at them. That was enough to keep them in line. His favorite expression when a player on the Yankees wasn't hustling was: "Don't screw around with my money."

The Oriole players were all very kind and helpful to me and I made sure to do what Hank Bauer told me and learn some baseball. I didn't play much, but I kept my eyes open. A week after I got there I did get up to pinch hit for Robin Roberts, later to be a Hall of Famer, in a game that was not settled until the last out. I was the last out. I hit the second pitch on the ground off Fred Newman of the Los Angeles Angels.

Robin Roberts came up to me in the clubhouse after the game, and said, "Young man, I could have done that myself." He never took a loss easily. That's probably why he became a Hall of Famer.

All the next spring I worked out with the Orioles in Miami, but I knew I wasn't going to make the big club. Everyone assumed I was ticketed for the Orioles club in Elmira, New York, and I kept hearing the name of the same guy all spring.

"Boy, he's tough. He'll bite your head off. You gotta watch this guy. Everybody says he will be the next manager up there. He wants to win every game he plays. He'll do anything to win," one player said.

Another said, "If you play golf with him make sure you let him win. If you don't, you'll pay the price. Yeah, Earl will make you pay, all right."

When the assignment finally came down, I was told to report to Columbus, Georgia, the Orioles minor league headquarters. The drive took twelve hours and I did it straight through and arrived at about three o'clock in the morning. I was dead tired when I got there, went straight to the camp coordinator's office, reported in, got a blanket and a pillowcase, and went right over to the barracks to which I had been assigned. All the Orioles minor leaguers trained there and each team lived in separate barracks, lined up in cots the way it had been in the National Guard. I was too tired to care. I pulled off my shoes, pulled the blanket over my head, and immediately fell asleep.

About half an hour later, some short, pudgy guy with a crew cut shined a flashlight in my eyes and jolted me awake by rattling the bed.

"Who are you?" the little guy screamed.

"Who the hell are you?" I screamed back.

Upset that so many of the players had been breaking curfew and coming in late, the manager of the Elmira club had decided he would police his team. He made a run through the barracks every night to see if all his players were in, and when he was shocked by a player he didn't expect, it drove him wild. When I questioned his right to be waking me up after a twelve-hour car ride, he went insane. You would think I was an umpire. After I told him my name and told him I was assigned to that club, he began bellowing loud enough to wake up the entire barracks.

"The audacity of this guy," he screamed. "He comes in here and thinks he can just settle down and take over this club. If any of you guys think you can just become big leaguers by showing up and doing any damn thing you please, you are sadly mistaken. This isn't a goddamn country club. This is a training camp for ballplayers, not to say any of you are going to *be* real ballplayers. I'll be goddamned if anybody is going to tell me how to run my team."

The veins were sticking out of his neck. I could see his eyes staring through me. His voice sounded as if he had swallowed a bag of marbles. His butterball belly bounced against the metal bedposts. That was my introduction to Earl Weaver, my Elmira manager, and a man with whom I would continue to meet under interesting circumstances for the next fifteen years.

Weaver was the first manager who really intimidated me. Except for Bauer, my previous managers had all been gentle fellows, low-key and pleasant, as epitomized by Cal Ripken, Sr., who would put his arm over your shoulder, talking in a soft voice and helping you every way he could. Now I was confronted by this chubby little guy with a gruff voice. He led us in two-a-day workouts and after dinner, at night, he'd run up and down that training area.

I kept asking myself the same question all spring, "What in the hell am I getting myself into?"

Things were pretty tough from the start with Mr. Weaver. I had never been north of Virginia and the snow was still on the ground, the trees were bare, and the temperatures were below freezing when the team arrived in Elmira in upstate New York. I was a kid from Florida and that was not my idea of optimal baseball conditions.

After we arrived, I rented a house with Mark Belanger and Steve Caria, and two weeks later got the first shock of my baseball career. I was benched for not hitting. That made me hate Earl Weaver. Oh, I couldn't stand to look at him.

A couple of days later we were in a tight game and he called me to go up and pinch hit. I struck out and flung the bat. Then he told me to go into the game in left field. The game went twenty-four innings, we lost it in the twenty-fourth inning, and I ended it by striking out again.

"You're worthless," Weaver yelled.

"How would you know? You haven't seen enough of me," I yelled back.

"Get outta here. Get your clothes and get out of this clubhouse. You're suspended. You are no longer on this ballclub."

Lou Gorman was the assistant farm director of the Orioles and Harry Dalton was the farm boss. They called me and said that I was still highly thought of, that I would stay at Elmira and that I would simply have to do my best to get along with Earl.

"Obviously you have a volatile temper," said Gorman, "and so does Earl. But Earl likes you. He thinks you can play."

"I can't play for that man. He's a dictator. He just wants to bark orders."

"Look," said Gorman, "he has a strong personality, you have a strong personality, but he thinks you can still become a big leaguer. Will you try to get along with him?"

"He's got the worst temper of any man I've ever met and he's telling *me* to curb *my* temper?"

"Ahh, that's Earl. That's just his way," Gorman said.

Two days later, serving my week of suspension, I was still asleep in bed when the feisty little guy showed up at my house.

"What in the hell are you doing in bed?" he shouted.

"I'm suspended, remember? You told me not to come to the ballpark."

"Forget what I told you. I need you. Get your ass dressed and out to the park. I lost an outfielder last night."

When I got to the park I looked at the lineup card. He had me in there all right—batting eighth. That was embarrassing, hitting eighth in front of the pitcher—there was no designated hitter in those days—and I almost blew up again. But I controlled myself for a change. I wanted to play very badly. Soon I was hitting the ball well again, moved up to fifth in the lineup and eventually to fourth. I hit three home runs in one game and that had never been done before in Elmira's Dunn Field, which was a big park. The next time I faced that pitcher—I've blocked his name from my mind—he hit me on the left hand. I'd already doubled off him the first time up and he'd evidently decided enough was enough. I was out for ten days.

When I got back in the lineup I continued hitting well. I also did something else to help my career there. I stayed away from Earl Weaver. When I saw him on the field, I went the other way. I sat about as far away from him as I could during the game. I stayed out of his card games and I never played golf with him—I knew I'd never be willing to lay down for him. It worked pretty well, and the more I hit the less I seemed to be bothered by him, anyway.

He never said so in so many words, but he never thought I would be a big leaguer, no matter what Lou Gorman had said. I think he began to accept the fact that I had ability, but I believe he thought my temperament would keep me from the big leagues. He thought I was too hot-headed, too red-ass to make it—this from a guy who once climbed a light standard to hold up a game because he disagreed with an umpire's call.

By the end of the season, I must admit, I had learned a lot of baseball from him. Mostly I had learned the importance of winning. Until then I had been concerned with my individual records and performances, and my own development as a player. Weaver taught me that, on a professional level, there was nothing more important than winning, no matter who contributed. He instilled in me his own burning desire. I am indebted to him for that. By the end of my career, with maturity, I had come to respect him as one of the finest managers I had ever seen—even if we never exactly became pals. It shows you what a few gray hairs will do.

I hit only .249 at Elmira for Earl, but I had eleven homers and sixty-four runs batted in, and improved all season. The injuries and the suspension kept my average down. A few days before the season ended Weaver called me into the clubhouse.

"I'll be managing the Baltimore Triple A club in Rochester next year. I want you with me."

"Thanks. I think I can handle it."

I expected to go to spring training in 1966 with the Baltimore club and hoped I would be assigned to the Rochester club, just one phone call away from the big leagues. All winter I wondered if Earl would keep his promise. He never had a chance to.

The Road to
the Big Leagues

Late that winter the phone rang in Tampa. My mom said it was the ballclub and I was certain they were calling to give me some spring training information or maybe a raise. Even though I'd hit only .249, George Scott had won the batting title with a .292 mark, so my average hadn't been so bad after all.

"Lou," said Harry Dalton, "we've traded your contract to the Cleveland Indians."

"You what?"

"You'll be getting a call from Gabe Paul, the Cleveland GM, before long. He wants to discuss certain things with you. Good luck."

That was it. My Baltimore career was over. That's the way things happen in baseball. One day you're working for Baltimore, and the next day you're working for Cleveland—just as fast as that.

"We'll take you to spring training," Gabe Paul began, "if you agree to an experiment for us. We need a catcher. We'd like you to try it. If you agree, you can come down to spring training early, work on learning the position, and train with the big club. The meal money's better."

Gabe Paul had been a traveling secretary for the Cincinnati Reds. He always talked about meal money. It reminded him of his youth. He had been the traveling secretary when Willard Hershberger, a catcher on the

Reds, committed suicide by cutting his wrists in his Boston hotel room. The joke is that Gabe ran back to the room to collect the rest of Hershberger's meal money for the trip. I flew to Tucson and was introduced to the Cleveland manager, Birdie Tebbetts, an ex-catcher who would work with me. He tried hard. He showed me how to set myself, how to release the ball, many of the tricks of the trade. He even showed me how to wear the catcher's equipment, the "tools of ignorance"—"Anyone who would wear all that stuff in August," they used to say, "can't be too smart."

"Tomorrow," Tebbetts said in mid-March, "you'll be catching batting practice."

One of the coaches was on the mound when they sent me in for batting practice. I had worked well in the drills, catching and throwing the ball easily, handling pitched balls well, and squatting without discomfort. Even the batting practice started easily. The coach's stuff was soft and the batters ripped at it. I didn't catch many pitches and the few that I did were soft tosses. I started feeling pretty good about this thing. By then, the real pitchers were ready and loose. "Sudden" Sam McDowell was my first pitcher. And my last.

McDowell was the hardest thrower in the league, and the wildest. He bounced balls in front of the plate off my knees. He threw so hard I missed pitches and they struck me in the chest. He moved the ball so much there were endless fouls, and most of them bounced off my neck, shoulders, thighs, and wrists. I just didn't know how to avoid getting hit. Finally, Sudden Sam finished pitching and walked off the mound. I lifted my mask and walked off behind him.

"I'm through," I told Birdie Tebbetts. "I'm dead through with this."

"You sure?"

"If I have to catch to play baseball," I told Tebbetts, "you can give me a ticket and send me back to Tampa, Florida."

"You better go see Gabe."

I was one discouraged man when I walked into the GM's office.

"Gabe, I just can't catch. I don't like it. I'm an outfielder and that's the way I like it."

"Fine. You gave it a shot."

"Can I go back to the outfield now?"

"Yes, certainly. As a matter of fact we have been watching you and we didn't think you'd make it as a catcher, either."

Soon I was on my way back to the minor league camp with the Portland club. Johnny Lipon, a kind, gentle man, was the manager there. He liked me as a player, saw that I had much potential as a hitter, but worried about the Latin temper. Lipon had a habit of pulling on his ear and calling the players "Biggie," for big leaguer, when he addressed them.

"Damn," he said one day. "I like you as a player, Biggie, but you have got to get rid of the red-ass. No way you can play in the big leagues with that red-ass. You've got to calm yourself down and just play baseball."

That was my minor league turning point. I was now at the Triple A level, a step away from the big leagues, I was on a club with several players who had been there already—Stan Williams, Duke Sims, Bob Tiefenauer, George Banks—and I had to prove that I belonged. I began to get the message with another slow start at bat that the .249 at Elmira had been no mistake. It hadn't been the cold weather or the big ballpark or even Earl Weaver. It had been more fundamental than that. My career was at a standstill, or even starting to slip a little backward, for an age-old reason. I couldn't hit the breaking ball very well. The slider was running me out of baseball. I had to learn to hit it or my career was over. There was no other place for me to go.

A word about the slider: It is the pitch that has changed the game of baseball. It is thrown on the same plane as a fastball, and breaks sharply away from the hitter, maybe six, seven, eight inches. It is thrown at the same velocity as a fastball, maybe a few miles an hour slower. Since the break is not as pronounced as that of a curve ball, the pitchers get it over more frequently. The curve ball is thrown on a higher plane and slower. Even if it fools you, you can recock and still hit it. There is no recocking with the slider. You must go through with your swing because it goes too fast to give you time to reload. You can see the spin, but unless you anticipate it or the pitcher hangs it, there is not much chance of your hitting it solidly. It is a very tough pitch. The umpires will also call more strikes on sliders than they will on curve balls— the slider is always closer to the plate than the curve ball.

Besides the slider, the only other pitch that really bothers many hitters is the purpose pitch. The purpose of it is to scare the hell out of you. Most pitchers don't want to hit you in the head. If they do hit you, they feel it is your fault for not getting out of the way. They simply want you to move off the plate to make their outside pitches, especially that damn slider, more effective. I was hit in the head only once in my career. It was in 1971, I was with Kansas City, and we were playing Detroit. Billy Martin was the Detroit manager. He was playing tough baseball even then. I was hitting well against them, so Martin brought in a hard-throwing sidearm righthander named Chuck Seelbach. Seelbach hit me in the side of the head and I was out for about a week.

I've faced other head hunters as well. When they want to hit you they throw high, mostly as the trunk of your body, especially at the ribs where it is difficult to get away. Some guys do aim higher, even at the head. Jim Coates was a head hunter. He was mean. I think he enjoyed it when he hit you—if it was in the head, it was in the head. So what? Jim Perry threw at your head. He pitched outside so much he wanted you to get off the plate. Gaylord Perry had that spitter, and once in a while that thing would come splashing at you and in. Bob Bolin and Stan Williams wanted to hit you and then they wanted to fight you. They were big and they enjoyed it. Intimidation—that's the name of the game and it works.

A week after Seelbach hit me I returned to the

lineup. I had been kept in the hospital for observation and treatment for a mild concussion, and I thought I was over everything, but when I walked up to the plate my knees shook and I couldn't pull the trigger. I was more concerned with not getting hit than with hitting. Some guys never get over it—the rest of their careers they're waiting for the ball to zero in on them. Fortunately, I got over it in a few games and started hitting again, but those were a nervous few at bats. The thing was, in those days throwing at the batter was an accepted part of the game. Now, if a pitcher hits you, you drop your bat, go after him, and soon there is a brawl on the field. They always remind me of the fights my father's team used to have.

Right then, however, it was the slider I was having trouble with. Lipon saw what was happening and summoned me to his office.

"I'll come out early tomorrow if you want to work," he said.

"What time?"

This was serious business. I had a manager who cared about me and was willing to give up his free time to help me, so I sure was going to take advantage of it.

We went out early and hit a hundred, two hundred, three hundred balls every day. Then I played in the game and concentrated on doing what I had been taught. I moved off the plate. I changed my stance. I waited on the ball. I went to a heavier bat so I could get a piece of the ball and hit it hard somewhere. I became a contact hitter and the home runs be damned.

My average was under .200 when Lipon started working with me. By late July and early August I had become one of the better hitters in the league. I hit well over .300 for the last four months of the season. The next season in Portland, I did it again: .308 with eight homers and fifty-six RBIs. I had learned to hit a baseball for the first time in my life. I had learned how not to pull off a baseball, how to hit the ball hard to the right, how to hit and run, how to establish bat control. I had established myself with the style of hitting that would be my trademark in the big leagues for many years to come. Johnny Lipon did that for me.

There was one thing Johnny Lipon couldn't do for me, though. I'm sure you've guessed it . . .

One day in 1967, I was up in a big spot and struck out. I reacted as I sometimes did—flung my helmet, threw my bat, and raced full speed to the outfield to get rid of some of the frustration. I didn't stop running until I reached the outfield fence. We had a portable wall out there and I gave it one swift kick, as if the wall was responsible for my strikeout. All of a sudden the wall came tumbling down, burying me under the planks. I couldn't move—I felt flat as a pancake. A couple of my teammates finally had to shove the boards away to pull me out.

The next day, when I arrived at the park, Lipon quietly called me over to the corner of the dugout. He showed me a punching bag that had been cemented to the corner of the dugout.

"Punch this when you are mad, Lou," he said, "and leave the damn walls alone."

The Portland papers made a big deal of it. You would think I was the only red-ass player ever to play in the Pacific Coast League.

My confidence was growing after the 1967 season. I knew for sure I could play Triple A baseball. I was a hitter. The next year was going to be my year—I could feel it in my bones.

That wasn't all my bones were feeling. One night the previous winter, a few of us had been hanging out in one of the local bars in Tampa having a couple of beers. A buddy of mine had come in with a date. She was a striking-looking girl, dark-haired, with a great figure and a warm smile. My buddy, Ron Perez, introduced me to her.

"Lou," he said, "this is Anita Garcia. Anita, Lou Piniella, he's a ballplayer."

The three of us talked a bit about some people we knew, and Ron and Anita finally took off. I didn't think much about it because Ron was dating Anita and I wouldn't have dreamed of calling her. A few days later, Ron came into the same place. He was alone.

"Hey, Lou, how are you?"

"Ron, how are you doing? Where's that girl, what was her name, Anita, that you were with the other night?"

"Oh, we broke up," he said. "I'm not seeing her anymore."

I thought of those green eyes and that great smile and that wonderful figure, and I said to Ron, "Do you mind if I call her?"

"No. Not at all. We're finished. I'm not going to see her anymore."

Ron gave me Anita's phone number and the next night I called her.

"Anita, this is Lou Piniella. Remember me?"

"Yes."

"I got your number from Ron."

"I thought so."

"Would you like to go out Saturday night?"

"I'm busy."

"Oh. Okay, I'll call you again."

"If you want to."

It wasn't the most encouraging phone conversation I'd ever had with a girl. I waited a few days and then I called again.

"Anita, this is Lou Piniella."

"Yes."

"I wondered if you might be free next Friday night. I'd like to take you out."

"I'm busy, but please call me again."

"Oh, I thought you might not be busy because I asked you out for Friday night."

"Sorry, I'm busy."

The sound of the phone hanging up was like a thud in my ear. I waited a few more days. I kept thinking about calling again. I also kept thinking about being turned down. I didn't want to go through that scene again. A few days passed, I sat in the neighborhood hangout, had a couple of beers, got my courage again, and dialed her number.

"Anita, this is Lou Piniella."

"Yes."

"Well, I'd like to take you out. How about Saturday night. Are you free?"

"Well, I think I have something Saturday night. I'll have to check it. Maybe you can call later in the week and I'll see."

"Anita, I'm a professional baseball player. I'll be going to spring training in a few months and I won't be around. There is also something else about a professional baseball player. You get three strikes in this game and then you are out. I have called you twice and you were busy. This is my third call. If you turn me down again that will be three strikes and you'll be out. I sure won't be calling again."

"Well, is that right?"

"Yes. That will be it. Three strikes and you're out."

There was a pause and then I could almost feel her softening. She must have liked my determination or my ultimatum or something. She finally said, "What time, Saturday night?"

We went to a movie that Saturday night, enjoyed being together and started dating fairly regularly around Thanksgiving time. She met my family, I met hers, everybody liked everybody else, and by the time I left for spring training in late February we were engaged. I called her regularly from spring training, and finally decided I was old enough at twenty-three and settled enough as a ballplayer to get married. I flew back from spring training in Arizona and we were married on April 12, 1967. Anita had been Miss Tampa in 1962, and I was a big league prospect, so the story made the local papers. Not all that much goes on in Tampa—it was big news!

There were some rough times at first—believe me, it isn't easy being married to a ballplayer. I was moody at times in those days, somewhat insecure about my career. I would come home after a bad day and brood silently. Not too much conversation. Maybe just a small hello. Then a lot of silence. I would walk around the apartment, move to the largest mirror we had in the house, and swing that bat back and forth, back and forth, sometimes for an hour or two. I'm sure there were nights Anita thought I had gone off the deep end. She was always very positive about my career. She taught school every year in Tampa and reminded me we could always survive no matter what happened. But I wanted to make it in baseball. There was a lot of pressure, we had a lot of arguments, money was tight. No matter how much a ballplayer makes on the big league level, his marriage is always under financial strain on the minor league level. I owe a lot to Anita. She was always level-headed, strong, and confident about my future success even when I wasn't. I love her very much, especially for sticking with me in those tough early days.

Now, a year into the marriage, we were both beginning to feel a little bit more comfortable about our situation, a little more comfortable with each other—and we both were confident that 1968 was going to see my breakthrough to the Big Club.

There was only one problem. Its name was Alvin Dark. Alvin Dark didn't think I could play big league baseball, and his opinion mattered. He was the manager of the Cleveland ballclub. Dark had been a fine player with the New York Giants and the Boston Braves before finishing with a couple of other clubs and turning to managing. He had worked hard to achieve his baseball success and he thought the rights and privileges of baseball had to be earned on the field. One of the privileges was the club bull sessions.

As on any team, the players liked to horse around with one another on the bus, in the clubhouse, in the dugout. Dark was sometimes cold, uncommunicative, and he didn't like the idea that a young player like me, who had not proved himself as a big leaguer, was fooling around with the stars of the club such as Luis Tiant, Leon (Daddy Wags) Wagner, and Duke Sims. He stared at me a great deal and would pointedly turn away when he saw me joking around with the regulars. They didn't care. Most of them enjoyed horsing around with me. Dark ignored me throughout spring training. I got very few at bats and I knew my chances for making the Cleveland club were slipping. About a week before spring training ended, the clubhouse man told me Dark wanted to see me. Three or four of us were lined up outside his office. He was performing the ritual of spring, telling young, ambitious, sometimes talented players they were not good enough for the big club. I stormed out of Dark's office and stormed into Gabe Paul's office.

"What in the hell is going on here, Gabe?"

"We think you need a little more seasoning on the Triple A level."

"What the hell for? I've hit .300 there, I've proved I could play. I should be on the big club!"

"Now don't you worry, Lou," Paul said, "you're only a phone call away."

By this time I was smoking and that did it. I reached into my pants pocket and pulled out a dime.

"Here's a dime," I shouted. "Don't forget to call me collect."

Then I stormed out of Gabe's office. It seemed I was doing a lot of storming and door-slamming that spring. They kept Richie Scheinblum and Jose Vidal and sent me out. That was enough to make any young player slam a door.

With the passage of time, I realized I probably hurt my own chances of making the club that spring. I wasn't ready for baseball in March. I had spent a good part of the winter attending college classes at Tampa University, working part-time for E. F. Hutton, attending a couple of night classes, setting up a home with Anita, and visiting my friends. It hadn't left much time for working out with a bat. When I got to camp I couldn't show much power because I was no longer pulling the ball. My arm was only average to begin with, and I didn't have the running speed of Lou Brock or Mickey Rivers; it took me longer to get ready, so I had to play in a lot of games to show what I could do, to illustrate to the manager that I was a good hitter, that I could field, that I ran and threw well enough and that I knew how to help my team win. There was no way to show that in six at bats. That is why power hitters get a longer look. Line-drive hitters better come to camp ready.

When the Indians assigned me to Portland again I decided not to go. I went home to Tampa instead. Before I left, I told Gabe Paul I wouldn't play in Portland for the minor league salary of fifty-five hundred dollars a year they had offered me. I had to have the major league minimum of seventy-five hundred. I told Gabe I would not report unless I got a big league contract.

"Over my dead body," said Gabe, who watched the owners' money as if it were his own—which is why he worked in baseball for fifty years. "Go home. Nobody threatens me."

I went home and sat around moping about my career going down the drain over those two thousand dollars. I had been married a year and now I was out of a job. Baseball is certainly a precarious life. I thought I had been very smart about all this and now I wasn't so sure.

"You've put six years into baseball and now you will lose your whole career over two thousand dollars. Is that smart?" my mom said.

"I can't give in now. I'll look foolish."

"You'll make it up later. If you had told me the two thousand meant that much to you, I would have given you the two thousand dollars," she said.

Now I really felt bad. I knew she wanted me to go back and play—but I just couldn't call the Indians and apologize. I was too stubborn. I waited. I had one thing going for me. The league was expanding in 1969. They could sell me the next season to an expansion club and collect one hundred and seventy-five thousand dollars for me. They weren't about to let me walk away. Finally, a week after I got home, the phone rang. It was Gabe.

"We want you to go to Portland," he said.

"How much will you pay me?"

"Lou, you know we can't pay you a big league salary in Portland."

"How much?"

"We'll split the difference. We'll give you a thousand dollars more."

"I want two thousand."

"We can't do that. We'll give you fifteen hundred if you leave today and that's our best offer."

"I'll take it."

There was no reason Gabe couldn't pay me the two thousand dollars extra. Plenty of Triple A players were making more than the big league minimum. He was just playing hardball with a young ballplayer. He saved the Indians five hundred dollars. If you save five hundred on every player, it adds up. That's why Gabe walked away with a million-dollar cash bonus when he left baseball in 1985.

By mid-season I was hitting well over .300 for the Portland club and would finish at .317. July passed. No word from Cleveland. August passed. No word from Cleveland. Actually, I couldn't blame them for that. I tried to knock down another wall, this time chasing a fly ball, and dislocated my shoulder. I missed the entire month of August. Then September came. I was playing again, but— no word from Cleveland. I was beginning to resign myself to finishing out the season in Portland, when Red Davis, a fine, funny, patient fellow who had taken over from Johnny Lipon, called me early in the month.

"Lou, you're to join the big club in Cleveland tomorrow."

You could hear my shout a mile away.

"This time," Davis said, "you'll stay." I stayed all right, but not with the Indians.

I flew to Cleveland, reported to the ballclub, and suited up for a game that night against Minnesota. Left-hander Jim Kaat was pitching for the Twins. My name was on the lineup card. Just like that! Alvin Dark said nothing to me, but I just went out and hit with the regulars.

The first time up, Kaat threw me a fastball and I hit a shot on the ground down the line to third base. The third baseman juggled it and made a bad throw. I thought it was a hit, the official scorer called it an error—I didn't care. I had hit the ball hard, that was what was important. The next time up, I lined out deep to left field. I still didn't have a big league hit, but I had hit two balls on the nose. The hits would come. Now I was ready for my third at bat as the Twins changed to a righthanded pitcher in the fifth inning. I started up to the plate swinging a couple of bats. Out of the corner of my eye, I saw another player in a Cleveland uniform coming off the bench. I can't remember who it was, all I remember is saying to myself, "What the hell is this guy, Dark, trying to do to me? Doesn't he know that I killed righthanded pitchers all year long in Portland? Why in hell would he be sending up a right-handed hitter?"

I dropped my bat and my helmet, walked back to the bench, and sat there. I watched the hitter ground out or pop out, or some damn thing, and then I walked back into the clubhouse. I was as dejected as I had ever been in a baseball game. Here I was, a guy who had just been brought up from Triple A with a .317 average, a solid professional hitter, a player who had improved tremendously in the organization over the last few years, finally, at twenty-four years of age, ready to take on the big leagues— and now the manager was already stopping me from showing what I could do. If the Cleveland organization didn't want me, that was fine. I was certain one of the expansion clubs would. But here was Alvin Dark pulling me from the lineup because a righthanded pitcher was coming in—trying to label me a platoon player before I had even played a full big league game for the Indians. That was too upsetting.

In spring training I had thought maybe there was some mistake. But now I was sure. Alvin Dark was a tough guy to play for and that was all there was to it. I was convinced I had to get out of the Cleveland organization.

As a student of Gabe Paul's, I decided to take the big league meal money the rest of the month, travel in big league luxury and enjoy big league life. I did some throwing in pregame drills and convinced scouts my arm was sound. I even got one significant at bat when I hit a sacrifice fly in the bottom of the ninth to win a game for the Indians against California. Alvin Dark even congratulated me as I ran to the bench. Maybe he wasn't such a tough guy after all. You see how the mind changes?

On October 15, 1968, I skipped my afternoon class at Tampa University and went home to wait for a phone call. The expansion Seattle Pilots and the Kansas City Royals were picking players off the big league clubs that day. Cleveland had sent me a letter saying I had not been one of their protected players, but advising me I would be pulled off the list if I was not picked in an early round. I desperately wanted to be selected.

Tom McEwan, the sports writer for the *Tampa Tribune* and a friend, had promised to call me as soon as something came across the wires. I paced the house, as nervous as a cat. Finally the phone rang. It was Tom.

"The first round just came through, Lou. Seattle picked Chico Salmon, Kansas City went with Roger Nelson."

Salmon was a big league utility player and Nelson a capable pitcher. They would fit in with an expansion club because of their experience. I waited.

The phone rang again fifteen minutes later.

"Lou, you have just been picked by the Seattle Pilots. Congratulations."

I let out a great big sigh of relief. Another round or so and I'd have been one of Dark's minions again. Seattle was perfect. I knew the area and I knew they could use someone like me. I'd actually thought Kansas City would pick me, because Joe Gordon, the former manager who was a big league scout, had watched me play quite a bit in Portland, but I didn't care. I just wanted a chance to play.

They sent me a contract raising my salary by a thousand dollars to a grand total of ten thousand dollars for the 1969 season. It seemed dazzling to me at the time. I signed it and sent it in the mail as fast as I could.

I flew to spring training in Arizona and met my new

manager, Joe Schultz. "Young man," he said, "do you drink Budweiser?"

"Well, no, not really," I replied.

"Young man," the manager said, "you have to pound that Bud. That's what we do in the big leagues."

It was Joe's way of getting close and friendly with the players, showing them he was really a regular guy.

The Seattle club was a strange operation. Most of the players drafted were older players—Tommy Davis, Dick McAuliffe, Don Mincher, Rich Rollins, Mike Hegan, Mike Ferraro, John Kennedy. I was one of the few younger players, which I liked, because I knew I had a chance for a long career there. On, yes, there was one other notable player there, a smallish pitcher who couldn't throw very hard. His name was Jim Bouton. He was a strange guy and seemed more interested in asking personal questions of everybody than in pitching. He walked around the clubhouse all the time, talking, probing: What about this? What about that? Where did you play? How did you like that manager? It all seemed out of character with the life of the clubhouse—too nosy. Little did we know that he was running home every night and putting all the answers on tape. It was quite a shock when he came out with *Ball Four*.

Spring training began, I was hitting the ball well—and then they stopped playing me. Oh, no, I groaned, not again! I started reading in the papers how Seattle had drafted older players and felt it had to play them. And I thought being younger was an *advantage*. Showed how smart I was. In the midst of my gloom, Marvin Milkes, the general manager, called me into his office. "We're talking a trade with Kansas City. They'll be calling you soon."

That was the last straw. "What am I, a floating tent show?" I wondered. "Washington, Baltimore, Cleveland, Seattle, now Kansas City. What in hell is going on?"

"OK, I have Cedric Tallis on the phone, Lou. He wants to welcome you to the Kansas City ballclub."

I heard a cultured English accent over the phone.

That was "Sir" Cedric Tallis, the GM of the Royals, and my new boss.

"Lou, we traded for you because we need a right-handed hitting outfielder and Seattle wanted our lefthanded hitting Steven Whitaker. We have good reports on you. How soon can you get here?"

I listened to his praise and a thought jumped into my mind. I had to have more money. I hadn't played a nine-inning major league game yet, but I asked for a raise!

"You traded two players for me. That must mean you want me."

"Lou, we'll give you a twenty-five-hundred-dollar raise."

"I'll be on the next plane."

Off I went to Florida and the next day was in my first game for spring training. Joe Gordon was the manager. I *knew* he liked me in Portland.

"I want to see a lot of you," said Gordon. "You'll be leading off."

So for the first time in my career I led off and, in my first spring training game for the Royals, I hit a home run against Steve Carlton, a future Hall of Famer. Then I got a double off Carlton. I was three for four on the day and played a good center field. This was more like it.

Three days later, we flew to Kansas City, played a couple of exhibition games against the St. Louis Cardinals and started the season against Minnesota. Their opening-day pitcher was a tall lefthander called the Blade, Tommie Hall, and I was the leadoff hitter and center fielder. I opened the 1969 season with four straight hits. I was four for five on that first day and the big story in the Kansas City papers the next day—the Royals' rookie sensation. I got written up by the wire services and in a day or two I was getting headlines across the country.

I liked the manager, I liked the coaches, I liked the general manager, and I liked the owners. All the years of struggle, all the frustration, all the unhappiness and disappointment, all the doubts were now forgotten. I was a big leaguer.

Rookie of the Year

The Kansas City ballclub was young and enthusiastic and filled with players in the same situation as me—struggling to establish themselves as big league players and proud and happy that the years of struggle in the minor leagues had finally paid off. We were a close bunch—Jerry Adair, Paul Schaal, Wally Bunker, Dick Drago, Jim Rooker, Moe Drabowsky, Joe Foy, Joe Keough, Tom Burgmeier, Ed Kirkpatrick—and spent a lot of our off time together. None of us owned homes, because we didn't know how long we would be there and we couldn't really afford homes, anyway. We all lived in apartments, and Sunday after games we would get together in somebody's yard and drink some beer, tell some lies, and have a grand old time. There might be as many as twenty players and their wives together at one time and it was great fun. It never was that way with the Yankees. Players stayed by themselves in their own homes, in their own towns, and rarely, if ever, got together socially. It was one of the things I enjoyed about playing in Kansas City and missed in New York.

Our son, Louis Jr., had been born by then and Anita spent a lot of time with the other young mothers on the team when we were on the road. There was always somebody close, always somebody to lean on, which was not the case with the Yankees where most families felt alone because they lived so far apart. The Royals were truly one big, happy family. The Yankee players were close in the clubhouse, on the field, and on the road, but at home we all went our separate ways. Maybe that is the price a ballplayer must pay for playing in New York.

Things went very smoothly from the first. I was hitting the ball well. I was popular with the fans. The other players all liked me. The newspaper men wrote glowing things about me. I hardly ever threw a batting helmet or kicked a watercooler—didn't have to. I was hitting most of the time.

It was a doubleheader against Oakland that I hit my first major league home run. The pitcher was a big righthander named Jim Nash. He was about six feet five inches tall and 220 pounds, and could throw hard. He didn't have much of a breaking ball and I knew I could hit him. Sure enough, the second time up he threw me a high fastball and I creamed it. It went sailing over the left-field fence in old Municipal Stadium in Kansas City for my first big league homer. Nowadays if a guy hits his first big league homer he stops the game, gets all the players to autograph it, does a little war dance, takes a bow, and waves to the fans. I just hit it, circled the bases, shook my teammates' hands, and forgot about it. I expected to hit a few more.

In the second game the pitcher was another hard-throwing Oakland righthander, one of Charlie Finley's bonus babies, who would help lead the A's to five straight pennants and three straight World Series victories—my future buddy, Jim (Catfish) Hunter.

Hunter tried to sneak a fastball by me down and away, and I unloaded. The ball sailed well over the left-field fence, more than four hundred feet away from home plate. When Catfish joined the Yankees, I reminded him of it.

"Remember that one I hit off you?"

"Don't remember," Catfish would say.

"It was in Municipal Stadium, a fastball down and away."

"Don't remember it."

"The ground crew thought it was a thunderstorm, the ball hit that roof so hard, and they had to rush in and cover the field. They thought that storm would be over the stadium any minute."

"Jim f——g Wohlford," Catfish would say, in reference to the journeyman player Kansas City kept to play left field instead of me when they sent me to the Yankees. "Jim Wohlford."

Catfish and I used to have great times on the Yankee bus, needling each other about home runs and strikeouts and blunders. Catfish handled me pretty well in Oakland, because the ball didn't carry well in that big park and the weather was usually cool, but I got him in Kansas City, especially when it was warm and he sweated a lot and lost some of that fastball. He tried to finesse a little in Kansas City because he couldn't generate the same power, and I could handle finesse pitchers. That's how I established myself in the Pacific Coast League—by the time I left the Coast League, I was actually a better curve ball hitter than a fastball hitter.

Cat soon became a premier pitcher in the American League and it got harder and harder to hit him. Our clubs were in the same division and we got to play against each other a lot. It was actually something of a relief when we both ended up on the Yankees in 1974 and 1975. Of course, Catfish arrived as an instant celebrity because of that big bonus contract he had signed—the first free agent to get truly outrageous money, something like three million bucks for five years—and then he lost the first four starts.

"How in the hell could Mr. Steinbrenner give you that much money? Boy, he's gotta be dumb to do that," I told him one day.

"I hope I don't get arrested for stealing money," he said.

Catfish had a slow Carolina drawl and tried to sell the idea that he was just a slow-thinking, big old farmer from North Carolina who wasn't too sharp. But he couldn't fool anybody. Catfish Hunter was one of the smartest guys I ever met in baseball, on or off the field. He got that three-million-dollar deal, played brilliant baseball for five years, and then quit when he was ahead. That was one slick Carolina farmer.

Despite all the money, attention, and pressure, Catfish was completely comfortable as a Yankee and quickly accepted. Two years later, another former Oakland A, Reggie Jackson, joined the Yankees. It was like night and day. Catfish could take the kidding and Reggie couldn't. Everybody laughed with Catfish, everybody laughed at Reggie. Catfish joined the Yankees and his attitude was, "I'm gonna help this club." Reggie joined the club and his attitude was, "I'm gonna carry this club." Catfish was a good ol' boy. Reggie might want to think that his troubles were caused by the fact that players were jealous of him and nobody ever seemed jealous of Catfish, but that had nothing to do with it. Catfish Hunter knew how to get along with people. Reggie Jackson didn't want to bother. More about that later.

After that home run off Catfish, I stopped doubting that I could play in the big leagues. I hit the ball consistently and to all fields. I hit the old professional pitchers and the young pitchers. Not a single pitcher in the league that year really caused me to worry. A lot of them got me out, of course, but I was rarely overpowered at the plate or made to look foolish with an unsuspected breaking ball.

Soon I began to understand the differences between the big leagues and the minors. The pitchers threw a bit harder, their curve balls and sliders broke more sharply, and they threw more changeup pitches to get you off balance, but the important difference was, big league pitchers could hit a spot. If you were a high ball hitter, you saw hard, low stuff. If you liked the ball on the inside of the plate, they fired that good, hard outside fastball at you. A big league pitcher had an idea of what he was doing out there. It was no longer just grease up that old arm and let 'er go. Those guys were truly professional, working hard to get you out and make a living, while you worked hard to make sure they didn't make too much of a living off you.

I ended by batting .282 with eleven homers and

sixty-eight RBIs and the Baseball Writers Association named me rookie of the year. You can imagine how I felt about that! I also knew I had been lucky, though. *The Sporting News* chose Carlos May of the White Sox, who had eighteen homers and sixty-two RBIs, and batted .281, and he might have won my award, too, if he hadn't injured his thumb in a training accident while on military reserve duty.

I went home that winter and lay around for a while, then those old off-season worries began assailing me, and I decided to work out. I had been cheating myself for a long time and I was concerned about the sophomore jinx. Pitchers had started getting me out at the end of the season with good, inside fastballs. Was I a one-year flash? Were they wise to me now that they had already seen me? Would I go backward the way I had in Elmira in 1965 under good buddy Earl Weaver?

Cedric Tallis, the friendly GM, invited me to Kansas City to appear at a banquet and talk contract. I drove up to the stadium with Anita, not knowing what he might offer. I had twelve thousand five hundred dollars for the 1969 season.

"Young man, we think you had a fine rookie season," he said.

"I think I can do even better." Why tell him of my doubts.

"We think so, too."

"What are you offering me?"

"We are prepared to pay twenty-five thousand dollars for the 1970 season if you will sign this contract now."

Will I!? "Where do I sign?"

Tallis pulled the contract from his desk drawer and pushed it over to me. I picked up the pen and signed on the line. By the time I left the stadium, however, I was beginning to wonder if I had acted too fast. Maybe I should have haggled a little. Anita was waiting for me outside.

"What happened?" she asked.

"I think I cheated myself."

"Did you sign?"

"Yes. They offered me twenty-five thousand dollars and I signed it. I could have gotten more."

"When you walked in there wouldn't you have been happy if they offered you twenty-five thousand dollars?"

"Yes, I would have."

"Then be happy," Anita said.

She always has a way of getting to the point.

When I got to training camp in the spring of 1970, I found that Joe Gordon had been fired. I thought Gordon had done a good job with our expansion ballclub. He was an old Yankee star, believed in leaving the players alone most of the time, enjoyed a nip of gin every so often, and could laugh with the players. Some people in the organization, however, thought he was too easy and too close to the players. When a few of our players were caught out late, some executives were shocked. A breakdown in discipline, they charged, and brought in the chief scout, an old sergeant type named Charlie Metro.

Charlie was a tough guy. One day I was in the bathroom shaving after we had lost a tough ballgame.

"This isn't a goddamn barber shop!" he yelled. "No shaving in here."

The clubhouse man was instructed to throw all the cans of shaving cream out.

After we lost another tough game, he shouted, "Get that food out of the clubhouse. Nobody's eating in here. Think about your mistakes instead of eating."

The worst game to lose was the final game of a road trip or the last game of a home stand before a road trip. Then he would enter the clubhouse and scream, "No beer on the plane. No beer on the plane." Even more upsetting than the denial of these traditional baseball privileges were his mad exercises. He instituted a program of horrible stretching calisthenics on the field after batting practice before each game. I began to dislike the man. Big league baseball wasn't just running and hitting and throwing. It was also learning to adjust to managers.

The Royals train in Fort Myers, Florida, and in that

March heat, the Royals of 1970 ran, ran, and ran some more. Charlie Metro decided we hadn't run enough in 1969 under Joe Gordon, and that we were going to make things happen on the basepaths. He even brought in the track coach from the University of Kansas to teach us running techniques. We ran so much we hated to come to the park. This wasn't baseball, this was track. I once heard Whitey Ford's line about running pitchers. "If running was so important to pitchers," Ford said, "Man O' War would have won twenty games every year." That's how I felt about Metro's running. Metro got so wild about it that he forced us to run several miles on the grounds outside the complex. At least that only lasted a day. Four of our players got bitten in the legs by stray dogs. After that, we confined our running to the complex. The Royals didn't want to pay for any more rabies shots.

Charlie Metro played me every inning of every game in spring training, and by the end of March I was getting fatigued. I was only twenty-six years old and I had worked hard that winter, but playing in that Florida heat every day didn't leave me much when the season started.

I was in the opening-day lineup against the Oakland A's as we faced my old buddy, Catfish Hunter. He really had his stuff working that day, and I had an oh-for-four without hitting one ball hard. I was discouraged, felt tired, but figured I would soon get a couple of hits and be fine. Enter Mr. Metro.

I got to the ballpark early the next day because the baseball writers were presenting me the rookie of the year award. I was excited, of course, wanted to have a good batting practice and get some hits. When I came into the clubhouse, a boy walked over to me and said, "Charlie wants to see you in his office as soon as you get in."

"You wanted to see me, Charlie?"

"Yeah, Lou, sit down."

"If it's about the rookie award, I'll hit with the early group."

"No, it's not that. I'm gonna give you a day off. You seem tired."

"Tired? Tired? You play me in every inning of every goddamn game in spring training, you have the Kansas track coach running us until I can't lift my legs, and I go oh-for-four in one game and you say I need a rest?"

"You didn't swing the bat good."

"Look, I'm being presented the rookie award, my family is here, it's only the second game of the season. Let me play tonight and you can rest me tomorrow, if you want."

"You're not playing tonight."

"It's embarrassing not to play tonight with that award . . ."

"You're not playing," he shouted, "now get out of here."

Boy, did I dislike Charlie Metro after that. Add him to the list of managers I had to adjust to. Earl Weaver, Alvin Dark, Charlie Metro. They presented the rookie award to me and I had tears in my eyes, not because I was emotional over the honor, but because I was frustrated about not playing. I sat on the bench all that night and just got hot. He sat me down the next night, too, and I continued to fume. I was twenty-six years old. I wanted to play. If I was thirty-eight and getting an award and the manager didn't play me, I'd've been content. I'd've taken the money and sat quietly and enjoyed the game. But this was too much!

Well, things changed. All spring Metro had complained that his special uniform pants had not arrived. He wanted pants with western pockets, so he could put his hands in them from the side, and a watch pocket. Baseball pants only have pockets in the back.

"Where are my pants?" he asked the clubhouse man the first day of the season.

"They'll be in soon."

"Where are my pants?" he asked a few days later.

"Any day now."

Finally came the great day. The huge package arrived from the pants manufacturing company. Charlie opened it and they were perfect. Great big western-style pockets. Great big watch pockets. Perfect fit. He was grinning from ear to ear as the players arrived, walking around the clubhouse showing everybody his new pants, bragging about how he was really comfortable in his uniform now, and watch this club roll.

That night he was fired.

Charlie got to wear his fancy pants only one night. He was called into the office after the game by Cedric Tallis and sent packing. We had been playing about the same as we had in 1969, but Tallis thought we should have been playing better. Some players had also been grumbling to the front office about Metro's tough tactics, but general managers don't listen to any of that if a club is winning. If the club is losing, they use it as an excuse for firing the manager. As far as I'm concerned, managers are fired for one reason alone: not winning. The rest is window dressing— except, maybe, if you are the manager of the New York Yankees and George Steinbrenner is the owner. More later about George and his skippers.

Our new manager was Bob Lemon. He was wonderful to be around. He had been a tough, hard-throwing righthanded pitcher with the Cleveland Indians, and wound up in the Hall of Fame, and he'd been coaching and managing in the Coast leagues before getting his big league chance. He was friendly, easy-going, direct, and honest. He called all the players "Meat," as in meathead, and would sit on the bench with his arms crossed as if his attention were elsewhere. But he knew what was going on. He had a big, red nose like Rudolph the reindeer and never denied that he took a drink or ten on occasion. His managerial philosophy should be engraved on his plaque at Cooperstown. "I never take a game home with me," Lemon would say, "I leave it in some bar along the way."

Even with the change in skippers, though, we still finished fourth. I had beaten the sophomore jinx, batted .301, had eleven homers and eighty-eight RBIs, and convinced myself I would be hitting line drives for a lot of years. I was happy all winter, especially Christmas Day, when our daughter Kristi was born, and I waited for my 1971 contract. It arrived with a thud.

After having a second big year, I'd received a much smaller raise than I expected. The Royals offered me thirty thousand dollars, a five-thousand-dollar raise. That was pitiful after the year I had had. Then I read in *The Sporting News* that Amos Otis, a young outfielder we had obtained from the Mets, had gotten a big contract worth fifty thousand dollars. The story said the Royals were concerned about making this sensitive young man happy. Otis had batted .284 with the same eleven homers, and had only fifty-eight RBIs to my eighty-eight—and he'd gotten a raise double mine. If I had been in the clubhouse instead of in my own home, I would have torn it apart.

I finally signed a contract for thirty-three thousand dollars and reported to spring training with a chip on my shoulder.

"Lou, you don't seem yourself," Lemon said.

"My mind isn't on baseball."

"Is there anything we can do for you?"

"Yeah," I said, "get me Amos Otis' contract."

Spring training was a drag. I didn't work very hard, I was overweight, my mind was on my contract instead of the pitching, and I got off to a horrible start in the season. On May 5, 1971, things got worse. Cleveland righthander Steve Hargan hit me on the thumb with an inside fastball and I was out over a month with a broken bone. As sometimes happens in baseball—and out of baseball—a bad break turned out to be a damn good one.

My thumb bothered me most of the season. I often swung with only one hand on the bat and managed a .279 year with only three homers and fifty-one RBIs in 126 games. The Royals asked me to go to Venezuela that winter, play some baseball and get my hand strong again. I agreed. It was one of the few times I didn't question a managerial decision and it was most fortunate. I got to meet and work with Charley Lau.

Charley is gone now, a victim of cancer while in his prime, and he is missed as a friend, a confidant, and the best damn hitting instructor I have ever worked with. Johnny Lipon helped me learn how to hit to right field. If people remember me as a professional hitter, a stylist with the bat, and if I am able to make a living now in baseball because I can teach hitting, it is because of Charley Lau. I weep at the cruelty of his death.

Charley's secret as a hitting instructor was that he cared about the individual. He was willing to work hard. He could communicate. "Weight back, weight back," he would say in that soft voice of his. "Be quick, be quick," he would repeat as you hit buckets upon buckets of baseballs. Then he would walk out to the mound, reload the pitching machine, pick up loose balls and let you hit buckets upon buckets of baseballs again. He was generous with his time. If you wanted to work, he would work with you. He would never cut you short. When the games began, he would feel worse when you took an oh-fer than you did. He was a caring man.

The 1972 season began and I ripped the ball from the start. I was practicing Charley's style, getting that weight on the back foot, exploding with power at the ball and driving baseballs off the walls with regularity. I would wind up hitting thirty-three doubles to lead the league, eleven homers again—I might have gotten six or eight more in a smaller park—batted .312 and made the All-Star team for the first time. I not only made it, I was the fourth-highest vote-getter in the American League. Was I high when I flew from Kansas City to Atlanta to play against the National League that July for the first time. Only one man could spoil my All-Star time. And he did. Earl Weaver.

Weaver had taken over the Orioles in the middle of 1968 and managed them for the first time over a full season in 1969, my rookie year. We had spent a lot of time bellowing at each other in Baltimore and Kansas City, with Earl especially rough on me on those marvelous occasions when I would strike out in a big spot and the bats, helmets, resin bag, weight donut, and sometimes the bat boy would go flying. "Get hot, Piniella," he would yell, knowing I was as hot as I could get. "Get hot." The entire Baltimore bench would join in the fun.

Now I walked into the Peachtree Hotel in Atlanta, feeling giddy at the chance of playing with and against the best of the game, excited beyond belief that my parents and my wife and kids would see me play in this big event, just floating with joy. Weaver knocked the air out of my balloon.

"Hey, Lou," I hear a gravelly-voiced man holler. I knew it was Earl. Only one man in America has that sandpaper voice. He had won the pennant with the Orioles in 1971 and so was the manager of the American League team. My lips tightened.

"Hello, Earl. Congratulations."

"Leave your glove at home," Weaver said. "You're not playing the outfield."

Can you imagine a son of a gun like that? I was fourth in the fan voting. I was the everyday left fielder of the Royals. I was one of the best hitters in the league. And this little fire pump of a guy was taking me off the team before I could get on it.

"Leave your glove at home," he repeated, and walked off with a smirk.

That night I sat on the bench feeling completely deflated. Earl had done a wonderful job of taking the joy out of the game for me. Kansas City had had its entire outfield, Otis, Richie Scheinblum, and myself, named to the team and that had pumped all of us up. I was a hot hitter and would wind up second in the batting race to Rod Carew's .318, with a chance to win the title down to the last couple of days. The All-Star game would have been a high. No, no, Mr. Weaver had to zing me again.

He was true to his word. I didn't have to bring my glove, but at least he did send me up as a pinch hitter against Mets lefthander Tug McGraw. I had watched every All-Star game on television since I'd been a kid, and now I finally had my chance to play in one. I was excited going to the plate and was reminded by Otis, who had played with him in New York, that McGraw threw a screwball. That's exactly what McGraw threw me on the first pitch. I saw it well, timed it well, followed Charley Lau's teaching, and hit it hard off my back foot. It was a long fly to center field—that was caught for the out.

"Why didn't you take a couple of pitches and get more television time?" Anita asked me after the game.

"Yeah, I should have. I should have run the count as far as I could and let the broadcasters talk a little bit about me. I'll do it next time."

There was no next time. I had a bad year for Kansas City the next year and then I went to the Yankees. There were too many good players on the Yankees for me to make the All-Star team again. I still have the silver tray they gave to the players. I'll break bread on it someday with Earl Weaver.

The rest of the 1972 season was very positive. I hit well, played good defense, even stole my career high of seven bases, if you can believe that. The winter was just as pleasant. We bought a home in the Kansas City suburb of Leewood and decided to make our home there full time. I also bought a Honda dealership and was working for an investment banker in Kansas City selling municipal bonds. We had built up a nice circle of friends. Anita was very happy there and we had our first daughter, Kristi, so big brother Looie had somebody to play with.

In January, I received my 1973 contract from the Royals. The previous year I had moved up by three thousand dollars to thirty-six thousand dollars and felt comfortable with it. After all, I had been injured in 1971, I had had a bad year, and even a token raise was appreciated. Now, however, I was coming off the best year of my life. I had become a very popular player, and a colorful one at that—the sportswriters had taken to calling me Sweet Lou in the papers, partly for my happy-go-lucky smiles when things were going well and, more sarcastically, for when I heaved bats and pounded watercoolers during my tempers. I always managed to cool off after the games, though, and never took it out on the press—after all, they never got me out on a bad pitch, so I never blamed them. I tried to be cooperative; they were doing their job and I was doing mine. Soon the Sweet Lou began meaning just that. Then I would go crazy in a game and a teammate would yell with a laugh, "Sweet Lou, my ass."

After all I had done, though, my 1973 contract called for forty thousand dollars. Amos Otis had signed for a hundred thousand. Remember, this was 1973, before free agency. One hundred thousand dollars was big, big money. Babe Ruth only made eighty.

I sat down and wrote the Royals a nasty letter. I said I had had a great season, I deserved more money, I felt unappreciated and I was tired of being a nice guy over a contract. "What's more," I wrote, "if that's all the Kansas City organization thinks of me, maybe it's time to sell my contract to another club." Cedric sent me another contract calling for a small additional raise to forty-two thousand dollars. "That is as high as I can go," he wrote. "If you think you deserve more, it is out of my hands. You can negotiate directly with the owner, Mr. Ewing Kauffman."

The next day the phone rang. It was Mr. Kauffman's secretary. "Mr. Kauffman would like to see you in his home in Mission Hills, Mr. Piniella. Can you make it?" I said I would, but I was nervous about it. What I needed was an agent. He could milk some more dough out of the old man. I was just a novice, a piece of meat coming in to be chewed up by this successful, experienced businessman.

"Lou, how are you. It's so good of you to come."

"Good to see you, sir."

I had resolved before I went there that night I would ask for seventy thousand dollars, but not take a penny less that sixty thousand dollars, *not one penny less*, no matter what he told me.

"Lou, you like Jack Daniels, right? Here, let's have a drink."

We had a drink or two or three and talked about the ballclub, about how close we were to winning, how I was becoming an important leader on the club, how the organization would soon be turning out fine young players from the academy they had established in Florida. Actually, only Frank White, the second baseman, would amount to anything out of that academy and it would soon be closed. Ballplayers are born, not made. Then we had a couple more drinks and Mr. Kauffman suggested we play a little liar's poker. He knew I liked the game. We tossed around a few bills for a while, I was pretty lucky and all of a sudden I was up five hundred dollars.

About one o'clock in the morning, I went home. I had agreed to a contract for fifty-two thousand five hundred—and the five hundred from liar's poker made the contract fifty-three. On top of that, he promised me five thousand dollars more to build a pool or an addition to my house in Kansas City. All in all, I felt satisfied.

It didn't take long for me to be unhappy again. I walked into the clubhouse in Fort Myers for spring training, two weeks late because of the contract dispute, heard some more about Amos Otis' one-hundred-thousand-dollar contract, heard that our little shortstop, Fred Patek, had signed a seventy-thousand-dollar contract, and found out that several pitchers had negotiated deals well in excess of what I had gotten. I shouldn't have considered the contracts of other guys. It shouldn't have bothered me. I shouldn't have paid attention. But I did. I was human. Now I was damn unhappy again.

Then I realized our new manager was Jack McKeon. I had enjoyed playing for Lemon. Add Jack to the list. Weaver, Dark, Metro, McKeon. Maybe baseball would be better off without some managers.

The Road to
the Bronx

Jack McKeon had been the manager of the Kansas City farm club in Omaha, and in the final month of the 1972 season, Bob Lemon had been nice enough to invite him to travel with the parent club. He watched the games from the press box and would come down afterward and discuss the game in detail with various players. He was a short, overweight, talkative, friendly guy with a cigar always in his mouth, who liked to stir things up and buddy up with the press. And he was a champion second-guesser.

Second-guessing is a baseball disease. It destroys more clubs than sore arms. McKeon helped sour the front office on Lemon and grease the skids. He wanted the managerial job badly and everybody knew it. Lemon wasn't a gut fighter. He acted as if he could take the job or leave it. Nothing got him excited, not even McKeon's agitating. He would leave the game behind him each night and come in the next day, that big nose all painted red again, determined to do the best he could. If it wasn't good enough, he would try harder the next day. He was an easy man to second-guess because he never fought back. We would meet again under even more intriguing circumstances.

"You're late and you look out of shape," McKeon told me when I arrived.

"I'll be ready when the bell rings."

"You'd better be or you won't be playing."

I had just missed the batting title by six points to one of the greatest hitters in the history of the game, and already my job was threatened. McKeon was moving up fast from the outside on my list. (McKeon is now the GM of the San Diego Padres—hope you're happy there, Graig!)

My mind remained on my contract. I struggled to get in shape. I wasn't very enthusiastic about my work. McKeon soon noticed and called me into his office.

"Look, Lou, we are counting on you this year."

"I'll be ready when the bell rings. I told you that."

"We need more than that from you. We are looking for leadership. I want to see you set an example for these young players. You've been here a long time. You can show these guys the way. We can contend for the pennant if you play as a leader."

Spring training moved along and Jack continued to talk to me about this leadership role. He wanted me to help other players. He wanted me to suggest ideas. He looked to me to encourage our younger players. I wasn't ready for it. I was twenty-nine and had been in the league five years, but I was too concerned with my own performance. I played hard, I rooted for my teammates, I wanted us to win, and that was it. As far as leadership was concerned, I figured that was the manager's job.

The season began without much success. I struggled at bat in the first few weeks. I blamed it on the weather, a Florida boy playing in a cold northern climate, but of course, the previous year, after working with Charley Lau, I had hit nothing but ropes all of April. Now I blamed it on the weather. I was overweight and out of shape. My bat was slow. I struggled just to get my average up to .250. And of course there was Jack McKeon. I didn't like his manner, his tone of voice, his sarcasm—and the feeling was mutual. He didn't like me very much. I just couldn't play for the man.

The club was doing reasonably well and I played almost every day, though I got the feeling it wasn't because he thought I could do the job, but simply because nobody else could do any better. I got hits here and there, but never could achieve any consistency. I would finish the season at .250, the lowest full-season mark in my career, hit nine homers and knock in sixty-nine runs. By early September I started getting the message.

Kansas City had brought up some young players, a few of whom McKeon knew personally from when he had managed at Omaha. He was particularly fond of Jim Wohlford.

"Who got you out of Kansas City, who took your place in Kansas City?" Catfish Hunter would be yelling on the Yankee bus a few years later. "Jim Wohlford." Well, Jim Wohlford was now playing left field and I was sitting on the bench the last few weeks of the season. It was becoming clearer and clearer that I had overstayed my time in Kansas City. Nothing was up to date there for me.

It all came to a head late in September when we played a three-game series against the White Sox. They started three lefthanders, Wilbur Wood, Jim Kaat, and Terry Forster. As a righthanded hitter I expected to play all three games even if Jack wanted to look at Wohlford, also a righthanded hitter, in one of the games. Instead, I played in none of them.

The next night we were scheduled against the Texas Rangers. Their pitcher was Jim Bibby, a big, mean, hardthrowing righthander who wasn't afraid to pitch inside and didn't concern himself too much if one of those fastballs wound up in your ribs. Now I came to the ballpark expecting another night on the pines. I peeked at the lineup card and saw my name listed in the third batting spot. I walked into the manager's office.

"What's the problem here, Jack?"

"What do you mean?"

"We just finished a series with the White Sox and faced three lefthanders and I didn't play."

"Yeah, I need you tonight."

"Why tonight, against this big righthander?"

"Amos is scared to hit against him, he throws too hard for him and he tried to hit him."

83

"You got this hundred-thousand-dollar outfielder and he's scared to play against this guy, and you are going to do me the favor of letting me face him and letting me get hit. Is that it?"

"Damn it. I'm the manager and I make out the lineup card and you're playing."

"Is that right?"

"Yeah, that's right, now get your ass out of here and on the field."

"Well, damn it, I got news for you. I ain't playing. Get yourself another left fielder."

"You're playing and that's it."

I stayed in the clubhouse for the rest of batting practice and Jack didn't come near me again. Game time approached and we all went to the dugout. The umpires gave us the sign and the Kansas City Royals ran out to take their positions. The National Anthem began and the Royals stood at attention on the field—all eight of them. Jack knew I wasn't playing but he hadn't had time to tell Wohlford he was. I stood at attention in the corner of the dugout. Like Earl Weaver had said that night in Atlanta, I didn't need my glove this time either. My name had been on the official lineup card, so when McKeon sent Jim Wohlford out to left field, I was through for the day. I went in and dressed and went home.

The next night I was cooled down, McKeon was cooled down, Wohlford hadn't hit Bibby and things were settled. There were only a couple of weeks to go.

"Lou, I'll forget what happened last night," McKeon said. "Let's just play hard and finish out the season. We can finish second, have a good year, and we'll work this all out later."

There were only a handful of games left. I tried my best, played when Jack put my name on the card, watched Wohlford when he didn't, and counted the hours until the end of the year. For some reason, I did think it would all work out somehow, and I was in a pretty good frame of mind when the season ended.

Anita and I talked over my situation and she reminded

me about the five thousand dollars Ewing Kauffman had promised me as a bonus to fix up my house when the season was over. Now it was over. I didn't see the check. The next night I called him. This time I'd do it over the phone, stay away from the Jack Daniels and stay away from the liar's poker.

"Mr. Kauffman," I began, "this is Lou Piniella."

"Lou, nice to talk to you. Sorry about your off year. Those things happen. Next year you'll do better, I'm sure."

"Actually, Mr. Kauffman, that's what I want to talk about. You said you would give me that five-thousand-dollar bonus to repair my house and expand it. I don't think I should put it into my house if I won't be here next year."

"Nonsense. You just had a bad year. We like you, Muriel and I, and we want to keep you with the Royals for many years to come. We are building this club. We'll have a winner here soon and we want you to be part of it."

"Well, Mr. Kauffman, Mr. McKeon and I have not seen eye to eye this year. I think there is a mutual dislike and maybe we'd all be better off if I went someplace else."

"Now, listen, Lou, we like you here, we want you to be happy and we assure you that you will be with this club."

"Well, all right then, when can I expect my five thousand dollars?"

"The five thousand dollars? Oh, that. Well, I'll tell you what. I'll get that out to you first thing in the morning."

"Now you say I'm going to be with this ballclub. If I thought I wasn't, I'd put this five thousand in my bank account instead of in my house."

"You are very popular here in Kansas City, Lou. Everybody likes you, you'll be with us. Go ahead and look at swimming pools."

A few days later the five-thousand-dollar check arrived, and Anita and I figured we would certainly be remaining in Kansas City now. We decided we didn't need a pool, but we had a new room added on as a den, with a marvelous bar and a fireplace, and decided to celebrate our solid status with a party. We held it on December 6, just a few days after the builders left and the work was finished.

"Lou, you've done a wonderful job here," our friends agreed. "This is a beautiful addition."

We drank and laughed and ate long into the night, and I couldn't have been happier. I figured 1973 had just been one of those strange years every ballplayer faces. If I got a good raise despite it, I might even learn to get along with Jack McKeon. I had turned thirty that August and I had to realize my baseball years were growing fewer. It was time to make the most of them.

The party had run so late that Anita and I went to bed without cleaning up. That was the nice thing about a basement den—nobody had to see it. We woke up late the next morning, had a long breakfast, read the papers, didn't see anything in them about me from the winter baseball meetings in Houston, and went downstairs to clean up. It was December 7, 1973. I would soon know how they had felt in Hawaii thirty-two years earlier. A bomb was about to fall on me. The phone rang as I stuffed paper plates into the garbage.

"Lou, this is Cedric Tallis. I'm calling from Houston. You're a New York Yankee."

My jaw dropped. I said nothing—what was there to say? Feeling empty inside, I struggled to maintain my composure. I had friends in Kansas City like my restaurant partner Walt Coffey. Anita and the kids were happy there. We felt very settled, and now this. For a couple of hours, I moped around the house, feeling very depressed—and then I began thinking the whole thing through. I had played five years in Kansas City, and maybe that was enough. I had not gotten along with Jack McKeon, and if he was going to play Wohlford over me maybe it was time to move on. I was going to the big team in the East—they had traded a quality relief pitcher named Lindy McDaniel for me and our righthanded spot starter, Ken Wright. The more I thought about it the more I liked the idea.

The next decision was what to do about the remodeled house. We decided to sell it, along with our interest in the Honda dealership, and move back to Tampa. That wasn't so lucky. The gas crisis had exploded that year, with long lines in every station around the country. People stopped using gas foolishly. They conserved. Sales of small cars boomed. What boomed most? Sales of motorcycles, especially good ones like the Honda. Too late for me. I was out of the business.

All winter I kept thinking of what it would be like playing in New York, playing for the Yankees, this famous team that had had such players as Babe Ruth, Lou Gehrig, Joe DiMaggio, Mickey Mantle, Whitey Ford. The Yankees had been struggling in the last few years, but they had new ownership now and everybody expected the team to start coming back. There was a name I kept reading about on the sports pages and hearing players mention around the league. I didn't know much about him. I had never seen him. I just kept hearing the name: *Steinbrenner*. It always came with emotion. Nobody whispered it. They said it loud and clear. They said it forcefully. They said it with a quick laugh or a wink or a change in their expression. As the winter days passed, I was more and more curious about my new team, my new town, and my new owner, *Steinbrenner*.

Then I had another thought. I started to think clearly about with whom I would be dealing and negotiating my contract, who the man was who would hold my financial future in his hot little hands. Suddenly, I realized who had taken over the running of the New York Yankees. That man was Gabe Paul. Could Alvin Dark be far behind? Was I about to add a new name to my list of Weaver, Dark, Metro, McKeon? Who was next. The answer would be almost anybody.

Gabe called me soon after the trade, welcomed me to the Yankees and told me that the ballclub was on the rise and I could help the Yankees reach the top again.

"We are going to have a fine ballclub in New York and I know you can help us, Lou," he said. "Take care of yourself, have a good winter, report in shape, and we'll see you in the spring."

The more I thought about playing for the Yankees, the more I liked it. The team had so much tradition and pride. It had fallen on some bad years, but there seemed every indication it would be rebuilding.

Ralph Houk had resigned as the Yankee manager that fall and there was talk Dick Williams would be signed, which was fine with me. I knew Williams from playing in his Oakland ballclubs, and I thought he could certainly help the Yankees come back. As it turned out, Oakland owner Charlie Finley wouldn't let him out of his contract, so the Yankees had to forget about Williams. They signed Bill Virdon instead, a man I did not know and had never met. It really didn't matter very much to me, though, because I was certain that after a trade like mine, I would be playing every day, and I certainly had a lot of hitting room in Yankee Stadium.

As I followed the doings of the Yankees in the daily press and in *The Sporting News* that winter, I began to understand the impact of the Yankees. This was not just another big league team. I would become part of the most famous, most publicized, most admired, most successful team in all of sports history. On February 28, 1974, I reported to the Yankee spring training camp at Fort Lauderdale, Florida.

Clubhouse man Pete Sheehy, who had first started working for the Yankees in Babe Ruth's big home run season of 1927, gave me uniform number 14 and showed me where my locker was, in the near corner of the clubhouse, next to Bobby Murcer, two away from Thurman Munson, in the same row with Chris Chambliss, Roy White, Graig Nettles, and Ron Blomberg.

"Welcome, Lou, glad to have you," said Munson.

"Leave him alone," said Nettles. "He has to squeeze that bad body into a uniform."

"Ahh, shucks," said Blomberg, a good ol' boy from

Atlanta, "he doesn't have a bad body. Now, Thurman has a bad body."

Thurman hit Blomberg with a bat. The Yankees were going to be fun.

Bill Virdon called the team together, explained his spring training program, told us we had a club that was good enough to win, admitted that he was new in the league and would spend some time in the spring learning a lot himself, and asked only one thing of us.

"I just want you to hustle, every minute you are out on that field. You'll find that I'm an easy guy to get along with if you do that. If you don't do that, we'll have a lot of problems."

The players all seemed friendly, the camp was wonderfully organized, and my enthusiasm was high as I went through my first early drills as a Yankee.

I had a nice beach apartment in Fort Lauderdale that spring, and that night I sipped a Jack Daniels on the rocks and told Anita, "We are going to like it here. This is a good bunch of guys, there's a lot of talent. Honey, we're going to be in the World Series before too long."

"It will be a thrill to sit in the stands and watch you play in the World Series."

"There'll be a lot of fur coats, a lot of special things for us, in New York." I lifted my glass as Anita refilled it, and thought about what Larry Doyle had said long ago about the Giants. I looked at Anita and smiled.

"It's great to be young and a Yankee."

George

The early March Florida sun beat down heavily as I worked hard in batting practice. I rattled a few line drives to right field, moved my stance a bit, shot a couple to center and finished up with a few more against the wall in left at Fort Lauderdale's Yankee Stadium. I walked out of the batting cage and watched as Thurman took his swings. The ball just jumped off his bat. We were hitting in groups of four, Graig Nettles and Chris Chambliss behind us.

Off to the side Bobby Murcer and Gene Michael leaned on their bats, waiting to hit, casually taking the sun on their bare heads.

"Damn it," a man yelled. "Put those caps on. Look like Yankees. And you, Michael, get a haircut."

Bobby and Gene sheepishly put their caps on as the man walked away. He moved toward the dugout and bellowed something at some other players, then he marched around the field barking orders. He called Bill Virdon over to the bench with a wave. He paraded back to the batting cage as I went in for my second round. When I finished hitting, I walked out and saw him talking to Nettles and Chambliss. He was a husky man, wearing a white shirt open at the collar, long sleeves in the blistering heat—always moving, always apparently energetic.

"Who in hell is this guy?" I asked Thurman.

"That," he said, "is the new principal owner of the Yankees, George M. Steinbrenner III."

I hadn't been formally introduced, and I wasn't that

day, but I could see he was a guy who barked out orders, made sure everybody knew he was there, and became part of the workout. That was the owner, all right, and the most active owner baseball had ever seen. It wouldn't be long before we would all know George M. Steinbrenner.

His baseball history has been well documented. The son of a Great Lakes shipping family, George M. Steinbrenner III had been born into wealth on July 4, 1930. He had been an athlete as a kid, run the hurdles at Williams College, coached football at Northwestern and Purdue, entered the shipping business in 1963 in Cleveland, run a couple of basketball teams, but was always interested in baseball. He had tried to buy the Indians, but the deal had fallen through. When Gabe Paul found out the Yankees were for sale, he arranged for George to meet with Michael Burke, the Yankee chief executive who ran the club for the Columbia Broadcasting System. On January 3, 1973, in a gaudy press conference at New York's fashionable "21" restaurant, George Steinbrenner was introduced as the new principal owner of the club. It was there he uttered those famous last words, "I won't be active in the day-to-day operations of the club at all. I can't spread myself so thin. I've got enough headaches with my shipping company."

His obsession about neatness was the first thing that struck me. George always seemed concerned about cleanliness, and haircuts. He never went a week without getting one. His clothes were stylish and form-fitting, and I can't ever remember seeing him with sweat on his shirts— even on the hottest summer days—or with stubble on his face. That wasn't me. I might go two or three days without shaving—especially if I got a couple of hits. Ballplayers are that superstitious sometimes. George had a military school background, and he thought you could play better if your appearance, your uniform, your equipment were all tidy. It had something to do with discipline.

According to George's wife, Joan Steinbrenner, he was even fanatic about neatness in their home. "We might vacuum two or three times a day," she said in an interview.

His haircut fetish got me in trouble once. George has two kinds of meetings with players. One is very low-key, father–son: He speaks softly, allows you to speak, listens carefully to what you have to say, and then makes the decision he was going to make in the first place. The other is a real ball-buster: George raises his voice, prevents you from talking, gets it over with quickly, and makes the decision he was going to make in the first place. Some meetings are a combination of both.

One spring, I arrived with my hair a lot longer than usual. When I got to my locker, Pete Sheehy approached me.

"You can't dress," Pete told me.

"Why not?"

"You have long hair. George told me to send anyone with long hair directly to him."

That was so ridiculous I just walked out to the trailer that was George's spring training office with a smile on my face. He made me wait half an hour in his office while he talked on the phone. Now I was getting steamed. His secretary finally said he would see me.

"Lou," he began in the father-and-son voice, "you can't dress with hair that long."

"Why not? What has long hair to do with my ability to play?"

"It's a matter of discipline. I just won't have it."

Now his voice was getting louder. Mine was, too. I thought I would go for the big finish.

"If our Lord Jesus Christ came back down with his long hair, you wouldn't let him play on this team," I said.

George got up from his thick leather chair. "Come with me," he said.

I followed him out of his office, across the street to a motel, and through the lobby to the swimming pool.

"If you can walk across the water in that pool," he said, "you don't have to get a haircut."

The next day I reported to the park with my hair trimmed short.

In the spring of 1973, just two months after announcing he wouldn't be involved in the day-to-day operation of the club, George had gone to spring training, got on players about haircuts, became annoyed when Gene Michael ran out to shortstop one game with a hot dog in his glove, and tried to tell Ralph Houk how to manage. Soon he and Burke were disagreeing about almost everything, especially Bobby Murcer's salary after Murcer became the Yankees' hundred-thousand-a-year star. On opening day Murcer popped up with a couple of men on in the first inning. George leaped from his seat and turned to Burke. "Is that the guy we're paying one hundred thousand dollars?" Burke and Steinbrenner soon split and George became the major force on the club. By the spring of 1974 the legends about him were already growing.

Houk had quit as manager of the Yankees at the end of the 1973 season. He had been a player's manager, very well-liked, not one for petty nonsense, protective of the players with the press and a strong man himself, as evidenced by his heroic war record. Thurman had been close to Ralph.

"He just didn't like George's interference," Thurman told me one day. "George likes to call the manager in the office. Ralph didn't like that. I also hear he likes to call the manager in his hotel room and at his home. I don't think Virdon is going to like that, either."

There was something else Thurman told me that day that was far more important to me.

"George is a very generous man. He'll do anything for you if he likes you. He also pays well. I think there isn't a guy on this club who doesn't think he is getting a fair salary, maybe even better than he would be getting anyplace else."

Certainly he was always fair to me, whatever disagreements we may have had. On opening day, 1976, the *Daily News* printed a clubhouse picture showing me naked in the background. I wasn't mooning anybody, but you could clearly see it was me, and there I was, naked in a big newspaper photo. It was damn embarrassing. Catfish Hunter's attorney saw the photo.

"Lou, you ought to do something about that," he said. "If I were you, I would talk to a lawyer. That's an embarrassing photo and they have no right to print that picture."

"What can I do?"

"You can sue," he said, "and in my judgment you can collect a lot of money."

"And in my judgment," Catfish said, "you just got a legal opinion and that will cost you big money."

Catfish always had that sharp tongue, but the idea grew on me in the next few days.

I had a tough season in 1975, with only 199 at bats and a horrible .196 batting average as a result of season-long inner ear problems. When I went to sign my 1976 contract, Gabe Paul—who had promised me when I first became a Yankee that he would never cut my salary, simply didn't believe in it and would rather trade a player than do it—cut my salary a full twenty percent. I'll never forget that, even though I'm sure Gabe forgot it immediately. Then the *Daily News* photo appeared. I considered suing. Maybe I could get back some of the money from the *Daily News* that Gabe had taken from me.

"Lou, George would like to see you," Gabe told me when I arrived in the park that night.

"What's it about?"

"I think he wants to talk to you about that suit. He's in the office now. Go up and see him."

I took the elevator up to George's mezzanine-floor office in the Stadium. I told the secretary I was there, and in a few minutes she told me to go in. "Mr. Steinbrenner will see you now, Mr. Piniella." I felt a little like I had when I was in school and the Precinct of Discipline, Father Lashley, waited for me.

"Sit down, Lou. Now what's this about suing the *Daily News*?"

George had read the papers. He knew what the situation was. He didn't waste any time getting to the point. I hardly had time to catch my breath. Actually, that was the first time I had been in George's office. His desk was round and huge. He had several lush leather chairs, including the one shaped like a fielder's glove. The bar was well-stocked. He could get up, walk to his windows and see the game from high above the Stadium. It was the best seat in the house.

"I've been speaking to Catfish's attorney and he thinks I could sue the *Daily News* over that picture and collect a good amount of money."

"Lou, that wouldn't be a good idea. We don't want to get into a fight with the newspapers. If you sue the *Daily News*, the other papers will defend them. They'll start attacking us. It won't be good for the Yankees. It will all prove embarrassing for you and for the ballclub."

"Well, what do you think I should do?"

"Listen. Gabe cut your salary last year because you had the bad season with the ear infection and all. What if we give you back your money? Would that satisfy you?"

"I think that would satisfy me."

"Forget the *Daily News* photo. We'll give you your old contract for this year, what was that, sixty-six?"

"Yes."

"OK, you have it."

George had won me over. And he didn't even offer me a Jack Daniels or a game of liar's poker.

He *was* a businessman, though. In 1977 I signed a contract for eighty thousand dollars, but I had a chance at being a free agent, and sometime that summer, George called me in.

"How much would you want if I offered you a two-year contract?"

"I'd like that security. I think a hundred and ten and a hundred and twenty-five would be about right."

"Let me think about it."

We won the pennant and the World Series against the Dodgers that year, and he called me back to his office. Gabe Paul was gone to Cleveland now, and George was negotiating contracts.

"Are you ready to sign that two-year contract for a hundred ten and a hundred twenty-five?"

"George, now wait a minute. When we talked this summer, I was hitting .280. I got hot, you know, hit .330 for the season and .333 in the Championship Series and had a good World Series. I think I deserve a lot more. Don't you?"

"No, I don't."

"I don't think that's enough for the kind of year I had."

"I remember when you asked for a hundred and ten and a hundred and twenty-five and I told you I'd think about it. Are you a man of your word or what?"

I signed.

George told me once, "I can get on the back page of the *News* and *Post* anytime I want. All I have to do is holler a little bit. They love it. It sells newspapers. That's what they are interested in. I'm a businessman. If I don't raise a little hell, we don't sell tickets for us. Always remember, Lou, baseball is a business."

"A business"—those are the words to remember about George when he seems to go crazy at times. He's an ardent fan, and many of his actions grow out of the natural pleasure or disappointment of a fan—if that fan happens to own the club. But he's also a businessman. When he gets furious because the Yankees lose in "meaningless" spring training games, for example, it's because he feels it costs us ticket sales. I asked him once why it mattered so much to him.

"Lou, we've got to win in the spring," he said. "That's when we sell a good part of our season tickets. Ticket sales go way up if we have a good spring. Remember it's a business and the business is to sell tickets. And that's why we have to beat the Mets in spring training. A victory over the Mets in the spring is worth a lot of space and a lot of tickets. We can lose to Boston or Detroit, but we always have to beat the Mets."

George doesn't like it when the Mets get more attention than the Yankees, and that's just when he's most likely to pop off or say something outrageous, or do anything to get the people thinking Yankees again. "The Mets are our rivals. We can't let them ever get the jump on us. We are always fighting them for the entertainment dollar in New York, and fighting the theaters and the movies and the restaurants, and every other major attraction in New York. But mostly the Mets."

You might think baseball is the name of the game, but it's not, it's show business—and George is the consummate showman, the ringmaster directing our attention first to ring number one, where a player is in a contract dispute, then to ring number two, where a manager is in trouble, then to the center ring where—well, who else should occupy the center ring? Of course, if the team is hot and the Yankees are winning, then George doesn't need to resort to any of those tactics—the Yankees sell themselves. There's nothing like a "Pennant Fever!" headline to get the town jumping and talking. But if the spotlight's off, then watch the back pages of the papers. George'll be back—protecting his investment.

Protecting his investment, of course, means being in absolute control. He *will* listen to what you have to say, if you can make a good case. He'll take it in, roll it around, digest it, and if he agrees, then that's the decision. You feel pretty good about making a contribution. But it's *his* decision, always. No matter who the manager, or general manager, or president, or even co-owner, is—it's George who calls the shots.

An incident in 1977 illustrates both these points. We had been struggling most of the season, playing up-and-down baseball, dropping in and out of first, reading every day about Reggie and Billy and George. Now there was a marriage made in hell: three guys with massive egos, three guys who begged for attention, three guys who refused to compromise when they thought they were right. One day George was defending Billy against Reggie. The next day he was defending Reggie against Billy. The third day he was damning both of them. Each day it was big headlines in the papers and selling tickets like crazy.

It was July 12, time to start playing ball if we were going to defend our American League title. Reggie had complained to Fran Healy, Thurman's backup, that he couldn't help the club if he didn't bat fourth. That was the glamor position and that's where he belonged. Fran, who got along with everybody and had earned the nickname of Henry Kissinger for his shuttle diplomacy, told me and Thurman how unhappy Reggie was at not batting fourth. That night, after the game, Thurman joined me for a couple of drinks at the bar of the Pfister Hotel in Milwaukee.

"Why is it so damn important to him?" I asked Thurman.

"Who the hell knows? Who can figure that guy."

"But it is."

"It sure as hell is."

We had a few more drinks. We talked some more about the ballclub. We decided there was only one thing to do.

"Let's go upstairs and see George," Thurman said.

"I don't think that's our business. Let things happen the way they are going to happen."

"Lou, George likes you. If you come with me, he'll listen. I think we can help the ballclub. We're not winning, all the guys are pissed off. Why not discuss it with George? Maybe he can help."

We talked about it another few minutes. It was after midnight. We had another drink. Now we were gaining courage. "Let's do it," I said.

We took the elevator to his eighth-floor suite and knocked on his door. George answered it. He was dressed in silk pajamas. There were papers rolled up on his desk. The room had a small bar and a nice refrigerator. Our traveling secretary, Bill Kane, knew how to take care of the Boss. "C'mon in," George said. "Let me get my bathrobe."

He sat down and listened as Thurman laid out the case for Reggie batting fourth. I told him the club was better than it was playing. I told him Reggie might be more productive batting fourth. George stood up and walked over to a blackboard in the corner of the room—Kane thought of everything. George wheeled it over near the couch and began writing out names on the blackboard.

"Rivers, Randolph, Piniella, Jackson . . . Rivers, Randolph, White, Jackson . . . Rivers, White, Chambliss, Jackson . . ." Reggie had been uncomfortable not batting fourth. He was having trouble adjusting to the Yankees. He was fighting in the press with Billy almost daily. George agreed that Reggie should have the chance to bat fourth and show what he could do. He also agreed to something else. He would stop taking pot shots at Billy in the papers. He would let him manage the Yankees or he would fire him. He wouldn't torment him.

The occupant of the next-door suite was none other than manager Billy Martin. He had just arrived at his room after being out with his buddy, pitching coach Art Fowler, most of the night. It was now nearly four o'clock in the morning. Martin heard familiar voices through the walls.

He rushed over and knocked on the door.

"Go in the bathroom, you two," George said. "There might be trouble."

"Goddamn it, I know you're in there plotting against me," Billy shouted as George moved toward the door. "I'll take care of the problem," George said.

The door opened and Billy flew in. "Take your goddamn job," Billy shouted.

"Now, Billy, sit down. Just settle down."

Billy rushed past George to the bathroom. He saw us in there and shouted, "Two traitors."

"Now, c'mon, Billy," Thurman, who had been his ally, said. "We're only trying to help."

"I don't need any of your goddamn help," Billy screamed.

Billy finally calmed down. We started talking about the ballclub again. Most of it revolved around Reggie. Billy insisted he was the manager of the club, he would do it his way and he didn't need any help. At about five o'clock in the morning, Billy turned to George and said softly, "If you want it, I'll bat Reggie fourth."

We all shook hands and decided finally to call it a night or a day or whatever it was by now.

George called the press together the next day and announced he had had a meeting with Billy. He did not mention our names and he did not mention that Reggie would bat fourth. That would be Billy's decision in his own way. "Billy Martin will manage this club for the rest of the year." It was to be a familiar address by George. He would announce that Billy would manage the next year, too, and then fire him; that Bob Lemon would manage all year, and then fire him. The same would go for Gene Michael, Lemon again, Michael again, Clyde King, Billy again, and Yogi. I knew if I ever got to be the Yankee manager under George, I would get the same vote of confidence. I was also sure I'd be in big trouble if I didn't win.

Reggie was slipped into the fourth spot in the order early in August, went on to finish very strongly with fifty runs batted in for the last forty-nine games, and we won the pennant.

Out of that Milwaukee meeting a special relationship began to develop between George Steinbrenner and myself. He knew he could come to me and I knew I could go to him, as owners often do with veteran players. We trusted and respected each other, and he would start calling me into the office or calling me on the phone every once in a while to ask what I thought of this or that player in a possible trade.

I found I could kid him a bit more. One time, he came down to the clubhouse and gave us a speech. "Baseball is a game of guts. You have to be tough," he said, "you have to have discipline. You have to know how to beat other tough guys." He was rolling pretty well now, "I remember when I was in the shipping business in Cleveland and I went to the Cleveland waterfront and I had to deal with some very tough people." You could see he was trying to impress us all about the rough trade he could handle. The meeting ended, and as I was walking away to take batting practice, I turned toward him and said, "George, the only time you were on the Cleveland waterfront was when you drove your father's seventy-foot yacht to the dock and said to the guy at the gas pump, 'Fill 'er up.'" He looked at me, startled, and then started to grin. I couldn't have gotten away with that the year before.

We began to see each other a little bit outside of baseball, too. About that time, George moved from Cleveland to a new home in the Carrollwood section of Tampa. He had a big home, nothing really ostentatious, about six bedrooms, a pretty piece of property in an affluent neighborhood across town from where I was living. I had a piece of a landscaping company and we got the deal once to care for George's yard. We did the work, took care of the property, and got paid handsomely for it. There was only one problem. Like a lot of wealthy people, George was a slow payer. It took us a hell of a long time to get that check.

The both of us being in Tampa, though, we often ended up going to many of the same banquets and dinners. George also knew I liked going to the track, and since he was owner of Florida Downs, he began inviting me every year to the track opening. There'd be a grand party in his private club, with an open bar, good food, plush surroundings, comfortable chairs and tables. There were waiters to take care of your needs and runners to place your bets. It was a lot better than fighting your way to the two dollar windows downstairs. It started my interest in horses growing. In 1978, a friend of Bobby Murcer's named Carl Rosen, who owned some horses, asked me if I was interested in going over to a horse sale in Hialeah near Miami. I thought a horse or two might be a good investment and a lot of fun to own. We went over there.

The horses were paraded from their stalls and I saw some handsome animals. The bidding had not started yet, when I turned around to see George surrounded by his entourage.

"Lou, what are you doing here?"

"Oh, I thought I might get me a horse."

"You considering one of these horses?"

"Yes. A couple of them look pretty good to me."

"Forget these horses. Come with me."

He led me through a large office, through a locked

door, through another large office, past another locked door, and into a private paddock.

"This is where the good stuff is," he said.

"What about those horses I was looking at?"

"There are problems with those horses. Their ratings aren't very good. Some of them will break down. You'll spend too much money for very little horse. These horses here are where you want to put your money."

He convinced me the other horses would soon be pulling milk wagons and I started examining those special horses.

Soon the bidding began. George said that if I liked any of the horses there, I could bid on them, he would go in with me for half the cost and we would be partners. I had my eye on a particular filly. The opening bid was twenty thousand dollars and it soon escalated to forty. George nodded to me that it was well worth it, and I raised our bid to forty-three thousand dollars.

"Sold," yelled the auctioneer as he called out my number. George turned to me with a big smile on his face, like the cat who had swallowed the canary.

"We just stole one," he said. "We just stole one."

We walked over to examine our horse and take some pictures of ourselves with it. Close up, that filly looked awfully small to me, but I didn't think of saying such a thing to George. After all, I wasn't the horse expert, George was.

The horse's name was Proudly Dancing and it was an untried filly. It had never run in a race. We shipped it up north soon after we bought it and stabled it with some of the horses I had purchased through Carl Rosen at Monmouth Racetrack. One day I called the trainer.

"How's Proudly Dancing doing?"

"Well, Lou, to tell you the truth, she's awful small, but she has had some good workouts. We might see something from her soon. But there is one problem."

"What's that?"

"She's awful nervous, skitterish, can't seem to settle her down."

"Is there any way to settle her down?"

"Well, yes, we can get a goat to keep her company in the stable."

"A goat?"

"Yeah, she seems to be more nervous now. A goat would help settle her down."

George's "steal" was becoming more and more of a problem. Her workouts got a little better, though, and we were finally ready to race her. I drove down to Monmouth to see her debut there, and about a half hour before the race a violent summer thunderstorm exploded. The track was knee-deep in mud.

"Do you still think we can race her?"

"I think so," said the trainer. "She oughta be able to run in the mud."

We let her go and she was last coming out of the gate, last around the turn, last across the finish line. There were eleven horses in the race and she ran behind all of them all the way.

The poor thing was led to the area to be unsaddled and you could barely see her for the mud. I really felt sorry for the poor animal. She ran a few more times for us and that was about it. She got in foal and we sold her at a brood mare sale. We got seventy-five hundred dollars for the forty-three-thousand-dollar purchase: George's "steal."

Not all of our partnerships turned out so badly, though. We bought another horse together later on named Flip and Hold and it has run well for several years. We could make a considerable profit on it now if we sold it—but I'll still never let George forget about Proudly Dancing. If I'd checked her bloodlines before we bought her, though, I would have known. Way back in her line was a horse with a familiar-sounding name. The name was Gabe Paul.

Yankee in Exile

In 1926, a sixteen-year-old boy from Rochester, New York, hopped a freight train to New York City. He had worked as the clubhouse boy for the Rochester Red Wings and, wanting to see a World Series game, arrived at Yankee Stadium in time for the seventh game of that great 1926 Series, the Yankees against the St. Louis Cardinals. Grover Cleveland Alexander, supposedly drunk and asleep on the bullpen bench after pitching and winning the sixth game the previous day, was called into the game in the seventh inning with the bases loaded, two out, and Tony Lazzeri at bat. Alexander struck out Lazzeri and went on to hold the Yankees scoreless and save the Series.

"He wasn't drunk," Gabe Paul always insisted. "He was walking around in the bullpen. I was right there and I could lean down and see him throw a few warmup pitches. It was all a legend, a made-up newspaper story."

Paul worked for Rochester, Cincinnati, Houston, Cleveland, the Yankees, and then Cleveland again, before retiring in 1985. He was a pragmatic baseball man, a guy who enjoyed the baseball social relationships but always knew the game was a business.

"The definition of a good general manager," he once said, "is a guy who can call up another GM at three o'clock in the morning and have the guy help him out with a player, instead of screaming at him for the early wake-up call."

Paul had come to the Yankees in 1973 with George

Steinbrenner. Michael Burke had introduced him as a consultant and said it would be a nice way for Gabe to end his long, distinguished career, with the Yankees. Burke was soon ending his own short, undistinguished Yankee career and Paul was running the show. It gave him a chance to spread his aphorisms around. If it rained, Gabe was never concerned. "It will stop," he would say, "it always has." If he was arguing contract with you, he would de-emphasize the money in the deal and emphasize the joy of playing. "Don't look at the hole in the doughnut," he would say, "look at the whole doughnut."

I kept looking at the hole in the doughnut of my contract through that first winter as a Yankee. I knew I hadn't had a great year for the Royals in 1973, but I needed a cost of living increase, at least, if I was to play in the expensive Northeast. I planned to take the dispute to arbitration, if necessary. Gabe invited me to New York shortly after the first of the year to talk terms, met me and my lawyer, James Hickman, at the airport, and took us to a nice Chinese restaurant. We had a pleasant social evening. We didn't talk about the contract, we discussed what it would be like playing in New York, how much I would enjoy it and how I could make a name for myself there. I kept reminding him how he had stolen me from Kansas City for Lindy McDaniel. He kept telling me how much he had liked me as a player when I'd been with him in Cleveland, how much I had improved and how much confidence he had in my abilities. Finally the fortune cookies came, and as I broke one open, Gabe had a small smile on his face.

"Be satisfied with what you get," the fortune cookie read. Don't tell me Gabe hadn't paid off a Chinese waiter. The contract was soon settled for fifty-seven thousand five hundred dollars.

The 1974 spring training season was memorable for me, not only because I was starting my Yankee career, but also because Bill Virdon nearly ran me into exhaustion. He also made me into a damn good outfielder.

Virdon had been hired on January 3, after a fine playing career as a center fielder for the Pirates—he was the Pittsburgh player who hit that famous shot that bounced off Tony Kubek's throat in the 1960 Series—and then stints as a minor league manager in the Mets organization, a coach with the Pirates, and two seasons as Pittsburgh's manager. Virdon believed in physical fitness, hustle, and aggressive play.

He ran the most disciplined baseball camp I had ever attended. He ran us into the ground. He hit fungoes to the outfielders hour after hour after hour. I could barely limp home after workouts each night, but I felt myself becoming a better outfielder. Later that year I made a fine running catch against the Orioles. Earl Weaver came up to me at the batting cage the next day.

"When you played for me you couldn't make that catch," he said. "When in hell did you become an outfielder?"

I couldn't tell him Bill Virdon's endless fungoes had done it.

As an outfielder, Virdon had taken a lot of pride in his defensive play and he taught us defensive pride. He worked and watched us all spring. He studied out defense into the season and one day he made a most dramatic move. He shifted Elliott Maddox from right field to center field and moved Bobby Murcer from center field to right. It was the making of our ballclub, it was Bobby's undoing as a Yankee under Virdon, and it caused a press furor. Everybody on and around the Yankees was quoted about the move.

Bobby was very hurt. He had become a Yankee at the age of nineteen and had carried the team during the lean years. He felt strongly about the Yankee tradition, about being the center fielder to succeed Mickey Mantle, as Mantle had been the center fielder to succeed Joe DiMaggio. He was the highest paid player, at one hundred thousand pre–free-agent dollars, and saw the move as a slap in his face. Virdon was headstrong. He simply said, "This is the way I want it." Honestly, Maddox was a better center fielder. Bobby became a wonderful right fielder. We had a fine defensive year in the outfield with Maddox, Murcer, and me finishing one-two-three in the league in outfield assists.

Bobby never really adjusted to the loss of his status position. It hung over him all year. As hard as he tried to adjust to right field, he still felt he should be the Yankee center fielder. He believed in those pinstripes. Shortly after the season was over, Gabe Paul took care of the situation. He traded Bobby to San Francisco for right fielder Bobby Bonds.

"The trade came," Murcer later said, "just after I had told Gabe I could finally accept right field if I knew I would be a Yankee the rest of my career. He said there was no way the Yankees would trade me. Three days later, I was gone."

San Francisco was cold and Bobby hated it. He went to Chicago and hated it. He finally came back to the Yankees to stay in 1979. He had to learn to look not at the hole in the doughnut, but at the whole doughnut.

The 1974 season began with four straight wins, the best Yankee start in years, and I won a game against Detroit with a double off Mickey Lolich for my first Yankee hit. We got into first place quickly, held it through the early part of May, hit a bad streak for two months, finally started gaining momentum late in August, moved into first again early in September and stayed ahead of Baltimore throughout most of the month. We were in first place as late as September 24.

That was the season construction began on the remodeling of Yankee Stadium. We shared Shea Stadium with the Mets and Bobby kept hitting those 330-foot fly balls to right field. The wall at Shea was 338 feet. The wall at the Stadium had been 296 feet to right. We got to calling Bobby "Warning-track Murcer" for those fly balls caught just in front of the fence. I had played in Yankee Stadium as an opposing player but never as a Yankee. It was the one sour note in my rookie Yankee season. All year we felt like a team in exile.

On September 17, leading Baltimore by a game and a half, we were scheduled for a three-game series against the Orioles at Shea. Bobby and I talked before the game about ending the frustration of all those losing Yankee years since 1964.

"If we win two out of three from Earl, we win this thing," I said.

"Stay away from him," Bobby said. "Don't let him get on you."

Sure enough, Earl waddled over to me at the batting cage, pulled off his cap, scratched that gray hair of his, looked me in the eye, and said, "How the hell could you be playing the outfield so well? I keep reading the papers about your great catches and great throws. Why didn't you do that for me at Elmira?"

I just smiled. After all we were in first place. I finished my swings and walked out of the batting cage. Earl was still there.

"You know what," he suddenly said. "I'm gonna jinx you. I know damn well there's gonna be a play later on this season and you're gonna screw it up and miss a ball in the outfield, and that will give us the damn pennant."

"Earl," I said, "you're crazy."

Jim Palmer shut us out in the first game, Mike Cuellar beat us in the second game, and Dave McNally shut us out in the third game. Baltimore swept the three-game series and went into first place by a game and a half. We fought back to sweep Cleveland and regain first place, but lost a doubleheader to Boston to fall into second again.

We were still only a game out with two games to go, as we flew into Milwaukee for the last two games of the season. We had won four in a row to stay close, but the pennant pressure was intense. As always in September, Baltimore was hot. If we won, they won. If we lost, they won. They kept ahead of us that way for a week.

Our plane was delayed in Cleveland. Some of our guys drank beer. The plane ride was uncomfortable. Guys drank a little more beer. We arrived in Milwaukee, and some guys drank more beer on the bus. They had stashed a few from the plane ride. We were close to the Pfister

Hotel when the voices in the back of the bus got louder and louder. Bill Sudakis, a journeyman catcher we'd gotten from the Dodgers, was needling Rick Dempsey, who would later be the Baltimore World Series MVP in 1983, about not playing. Dempsey was behind Thurman and he wasn't about to catch very much. The needling grew more nasty as the beer flowed. Bill Virdon sat in front of the bus and heard nothing. When we arrived he immediately went to his room because his wife was meeting him in town. The rest of us were slow getting off the bus. Sudakis and Dempsey tried to go through the hotel's revolving door together. The door jammed. When it was loosened, Dempsey fired a punch at Sudakis. The big catcher grabbed Dempsey and the two of them rolled over a table, knocked over a lamp, and sprawled across a couch in the hotel lobby. It looked like one of those bad movie fights in the Westerns. Out of nowhere, Bobby Murcer jumped on the pile. He wanted to be a peacemaker. Bobby weighed all of 175 pounds, Sudakis weighed 205 pounds—Murcer wound up with a damaged hand and couldn't play the next night.

Virdon posted his lineup for that key game against the Brewers. Maddox was in center as usual, Roy White was in left field, and I was moved from left field to right. I hadn't played there once all year. The angles were different, the timing was different and the positioning was different. Earl Weaver's stupid jinx popped into my head.

We were ahead 2–0, Doc Medich was pitching a great game, and the Brewers got a couple of men on with two out in the seventh inning. Then came a slicing fly ball to right center. I started over for it. Maddox moved toward right. The ball seemed to switch directions in the wind, twist and turn and dance—damn that Earl Weaver—and nobody called it. At the last instant I lunged, but the ball bounced and fell behind me for a triple. The Brewers tied the game and went on to win in the tenth inning, 3–2. Baltimore won, of course, and it eliminated us from the pennant race. I got even with Earl by denting the watercooler.

The next day a telegram arrived in the clubhouse. It

was from Earl Weaver. It said simply, "Thanks. I knew you'd screw up someway."

The season ended the next day. George Steinbrenner and Gabe Paul entered the clubhouse together before the last game. George was in a gentle mood.

"You all played well and I'm very proud of you. Nobody expected us to go the whole way, and we almost did. I admire your guts and this is just an example of what we can do if we all play hard and pull together."

It really came from the heart. George saw what was happening and, unlike his attitude in the years to come, now he was just happy we had come as far as we had. The Yankees were coming together. Overall, it had been a happy year. Maybe if Bobby hadn't jumped into that fight, we would have won it. I should have known better. I used to drive in from Bayside every day with Sudakis. We were about fifteen minutes from the ballpark. Anita didn't particularly like the neighborhood because of the traffic congestion; after owning a beautiful home in Kansas City, we lived in a rented apartment.

"It doesn't even have a front yard," she complained.

I didn't mind. There was a coffee shop across the street and I could get a cold soda there on a hot afternoon.

Sudakis was fun to listen to, and made me laugh. Most of the time he didn't play and would say, "How can Virdon not play me? How can he not recognize my ability?"

Then he finally got a chance to start two games in a row when Thurman was hurt. The first game he took an oh-fer against Jim Palmer. The next day he took an oh-fer against Luis Tiant.

"How in hell can Virdon play me against Palmer? How in hell could he play me against Tiant?"

Sudakis was some piece of work.

The year ended with much hope for 1975. I had made a rapid adjustment to the Yankees, batted .305 with nine homers and seventy RBIs, and I liked New York—the noise, the excitement, the night life, the good restaurants, the enthusiasm of the people. Anita had a tougher time adjusting, with two small children to care for, and she was happy when the season ended and we moved back home to Tampa.

There were two dramatic changes in the Yankee cast of characters when we gathered again in Fort Lauderdale for spring training in 1975. Catfish Hunter had arrived and Bobby Murcer was gone. I really missed Bobby. He was a good friend, a good companion on the road, a good player—and he was lousy at gin rummy. I made quite a few dollars playing gin with Bobby. I would have to look for a new pigeon.

The spring of 1975 was dominated by the arrival of Catfish Hunter. He had been freed of his Oakland contract on a technicality and, unhappy that Charlie Finley hadn't come up with some big money for him, became a free agent. Every club in baseball camped at his lawyer's doorstep in Hertford, North Carolina, to bid for Cat's services. The Yankees won the auction and on New Year's Eve, 1974, in the Yankee offices at the NYC Department of Parks headquarters, where the Yankees had temporary office space, Hunter signed for something like three million.

He got off to a rough start, losing his first four games. Late in April, he walked into the clubhouse, hours before the game. Every day he was being hounded by reporters because of that big salary and the slow start, and he never seemed to have any time for himself. He started coming in earlier and earlier to beat the press. This one day, he started dressing, then walked over to me.

"I'm through trying to strike out twenty guys every game," he said.

"What do you mean, Cat?"

"I've been overthrowing. I've been trying to earn that big money on one outing. I haven't been pitching like myself. I've been throwing every pitch as hard as I could."

"You have to relax."

"That's it. The next start I'll be my old self, even if I get my ass whipped. I'll pitch the way I've always pitched."

That's exactly what he did. He settled down and pitched the way he always pitched, and finished at 23–14. He led the league in wins that year, as well as innings pitched at 328, and had a 2.58 ERA. He was a bargain at three million dollars. Of course, it wasn't my money.

We reported to spring training in 1975, worked out easily, and prepared for the exhibition season. We were scheduled for two games in Puerto Rico on March 17 and 18. They almost became the two days that ended my career.

On December 31, 1972, Roberto Clemente, the great batting star of the Pirates, had been killed in a plane crash while flying supplies to victims of an earthquake in Nicaragua. Clemente had been in an overloaded plane that took off from San Juan, circled and crashed into the water. His body was never recovered. Shortly thereafter, a sports city was created in San Juan in his honor and big league teams began to fly down from spring training to play the Pirates and raise money for Clemente's dream. That was why we were there.

The first afternoon after our arrival, several of us decided to go body surfing off one of the beautiful beaches. The waves were magnificent, the sky was blue and the temperatures balmy. It had been windy and chilly in Florida most of that spring and this was a wonderful release. Shortly after we hit the water, a small tropical disturbance kicked up, made the water rougher, and threw us around. I kept on body surfing, enjoying the challenge of the rough waters and the heat of the air. I was constantly being thrown under the water, but I thought little of it, played in the two games, and flew back to Fort Lauderdale. Then, suddenly, I began experiencing headaches and dizziness, and I had trouble maintaining my balance and coordination. It came and went throughout the spring, and I finally had to tell the ballclub about my problems. The doctors thought they could take care of it with medicine, and for a while it helped, but then the problems returned. Finally they realized that I had punctured my eardrum and would not regain my coordination and balance until the damage was repaired. I needed surgery to relieve the pressures inside my eardrum, but even that didn't help appreciably. The process of recovery was so slow that, for me, the 1975 season was a mess from start to finish. I played in only seventy-four games that year, hit only .196, and failed to hit a home run for the only time in my big league career. Every time I thought I was well enough to play every day, I went to Bill Virdon.

"I think I'm ready, Bill," I would say. "You can put me in there."

"You're not swinging that bat, Lou."

"That's because I haven't seen much pitching."

"That's because you're not healthy."

It went on like that for most of the season. I was discouraged, depressed, concerned about my health, and most certainly concerned about my career. As the year wore on, I finally accepted the situation. I would do what I could to help the ballclub, but mostly I would sit on the bench and try to regain my health.

For the Yankees, the season was over almost before it started. After his brilliant season the year before, Catfish felt enormous pressure to be perfect every time out, and when he struggled early, it seemed to have an overwhelmingly negative effect on the team. We looked to him for leadership on the staff. By the time he started winning, it was already too late. Boston was having a hot season with two rookie sluggers, Jim Rice and Fred Lynn, and we were out of the race early in July. Elliott Maddox hurt his knee. Graig Nettles suffered a leg injury. Roy White hurt his foot. It seemed as if the entire outfield was shot down and we just couldn't put our regular team out there every day. Only one player seemed to stay healthy, play every day, and have another brilliant season. He also became my best friend on the team: Thurman Munson.

Thurman had a gruff exterior. If you didn't know him, you would think he was a grumpy person, but that's what he wanted people to think. He wanted to keep people at a distance, so he pushed that image of grouchiness and aloofness, that standoffish quality. He felt more comfortable when people felt angry toward him than when they were pleasant. It was a defense mechanism, to cover up the fact that he was a little insecure, a little shy around strangers, and a little unhappy about his early life.

Thurman had been born in the working-class section of Akron, Ohio. His father had driven a cross-country truck and was away a lot. He actually became closer to the father of his childhood girlfriend and future wife, Diane Dominick. Despite some early family problems, Thurman was a fine athlete, won a scholarship to Kent State in Ohio—the same school Gene Michael attended—and signed with the Yankees in 1968. After only ninety-nine minor league games, he came to the Yankees in 1970 under Ralph Houk, batted .302, and was voted rookie of the year. He was a very strong catcher and one hell of a hitter.

He was also a very kind, very gentle person, especially around kids, his own or anybody else's. Contrary to public perception, he was funny and could take kidding—we called him Squatty Body, because he was built short and stocky, and he would needle right back. The thing was, he had to be around people he knew and with whom he felt comfortable. With his teammates, he was helpful and considerate at all times. Sure, he was self-centered. All athletes are. It is a short career with very few big earning years. He was a tough negotiator and would always say, "Get it while you can. It won't last." He invested his money wisely, got interested in real estate and was well on his way toward being independently wealthy by the time he was thirty.

Thurman was two different people, depending on whether you knew him well or not at all. To a sportswriter, the average fan coming up for an autograph, or a stranger who bothered him at a restaurant, he could be mean and abrasive. He felt he didn't have to bother with people he didn't know and didn't like. If you got close to him, however, those qualities of generosity, kindness, and caring appearing quickly and often. There is only one man I can compare him to, with those two separate personalities. George Steinbrenner is that way, different with different people. Maybe it's something in the water in Ohio.

There was another thing I liked about Thurman. He

played hurt, played every day, and played hard. I never heard him use excuses or blame anybody else for the team's misfortunes. Thurman would always say, "I have to do better." he would never say, "This guy has to do better." One time, we were in a close game, one of our young pitchers, Larry Gura, hung a curve ball, somebody hit it out and we got beaten. We talked about it later. I was mad at losing the game. Thurman didn't blame Gura.

"I should have called a fastball," said Thurman. "We had the guy set up. That was my fault. I never should have called a breaking pitch in that spot. He was looking for it."

Thurman did change drastically when Reggie Jackson joined the Yankees in 1977. He had told George he thought the Yankees should get him. He liked Reggie as an Oakland player, and George had promised Thurman, by then the Yankee captain, that no one would top Thurman's salary. When he heard how much money Reggie was making, he resented it. He felt George had been dishonest with him. He withdrew from George and from his involvement with the ballclub. He became moodier, much harder to kid. It took a lot more to make him laugh, even after a good game, even after sitting at a bar and having a couple of drinks. He would never again be the loose, comfortable guy he had been. He never could seem to shake the anger he felt with Reggie and George about the salary business. He seemed to complain more about things, about his injuries, about the lack of appreciation he felt and the lack of financial reward for what he had done.

Thurman had a marvelous season in 1975 with a .318 mark, and would repeat it in 1976 with a .302, as we won the pennant. He would be the American League MVP that year and have a fantastic World Series: .529 and nine for seventeen, with every hit a hard drive. He missed out on the World Series MVP only because Johnny Bench hit .533 as the Reds swept us in four games. As if the sweep wasn't bad enough, the Series ended on a special sour note for Thurman. Sparky Anderson, the Cincinnati manager then, was in the press interview room extolling his team. Thurman walked in to be the next interviewee, and listened as Anderson was asked, "How would you compare Munson with Bench?"

"I wouldn't embarrass him by comparing any other catcher to Bench," Anderson replied.

Thurman was very hurt. Here, he had just hit .529, and Anderson was not even generous enough to applaud both Thurman and Bench. Thurman went home from that Series feeling bad, and then Reggie came the following spring, and nothing was the same for him ever again. His knees would start bothering him severely in 1979. One thing just seemed to be piling up on another, until that fateful day, August 2, 1979.

By July 1975, it had become clear we were not the ballclub we had been in 1974. Half of our team was injured, Bobby Bonds was not hitting the way Murcer had—he would bat .270 but strike out 137 times—and on July 28, Boston led us by eleven games.

As Bob Watson would say in 1980, "When the pressure builds up, it's like being on a bus in a mudhole. The harder you press on the pedal, the further you sink in the mud." Virdon, hardly a very communicative person, seemed to withdraw more and more. He said very little, and when he did talk there was an edge of tension in his voice.

On Friday night, August 1, the story leaked in the press that Virdon was about to be fired, and that a guy named Billy Martin, fired as the skipper of the Texas Rangers just a few days earlier, would be the new manager. The press hounded Virdon.

"I don't know a thing about it," he said.

He was telling the truth. The Yankees had signed Martin before firing Virdon. They wanted to be sure before they made a public move. About an hour after the game that Friday night, Martin secretly flew into town with Gabe, and Virdon was called into Gabe's office.

"We've decided to make a change," Gabe said.

"I expected it," Virdon replied.

The next day Billy Martin was announced as the manager of the Yankees to a huge press conference at Shea Stadium. He was wearing cowboy boots, Western pants—

with those side pockets Charlie Metro loved—and a big Western hat.

"I was out hunting wild animals in Colorado when Gabe hunted me down," he explained.

George and Billy. Billy and George. It was to be the beginning of a father-son, love-hate, oil-and-water relationship that is still going strong eleven years later, a mixture of two personalities that has been alternatively bitter, happy, anguished, satisfying, disappointing, just about every emotion you can think of. George and Billy are alike in many ways, in their fierce desire to win, to lead, to possess the spotlight, to have the last word. Harry Truman, Billy Martin, and George Steinbrenner all lived by the same motto: The Buck Stops Here.

Billy Martin was born in Berkeley, California, on May 16, 1928. George Steinbrenner was born on July 4, 1930, in Cleveland, Ohio. Isn't it surprising to realize that George is younger than Billy? Billy was a tough, competitive player with the Yankees after a successful minor league career. He was close to his first big league manager, Casey Stengel, and terribly disappointed when Casey went to New York to manage the Yankees in 1949 and left young Billy back in Oakland for more seasoning. Billy joined the Yankees in 1950, however, and fit in quickly. I still remember watching television and seeing that great catch Billy made on Jackie Robinson in the 1952 World Series. The trouble that was to dog Billy's tracks, though, began in 1957 at a party with Yogi Berra, Whitey Ford, Mickey Mantle, and some other Yankees at the Copacabana night club in New York. A fight broke out, the Yankee general manager, George Weiss, blamed Billy for it, and he was gone, traded to Kansas City. He began managing in the Minnesota Twins organization in 1968, where one of his star players was Graig Nettles, and became the Twins manager in 1969. He won the division title, but was fired at the end of the season. The newspapers said he was fired because he had butted into the operations of the front office. He went to Detroit, won again there—and was fired again. The newspapers said he was fired because he had butted into the operations of the front office. He went to the Texas Rangers, made that team into a contender— and was fired in 1975. The newspapers said he was fired because he had butted into the operations of the front office.

Billy had a reputation as a fighter. He would battle for his players, battle the umpires, fight for every inch he could get on the field. He spoke out when he thought he was wronged and he was as lively a bench manager as there was in the game.

I had always enjoyed playing against Billy Martin's teams. He had a certain flair, a certain hype. He exuded confidence, and the players on his ballclubs exuded confidence about him. You could tell there was something different about him.

He was also a friendly guy on the field, very talkative, and outgoing. He would hang around the batting cage and talk to opposing players, kid them if they had big noses like he had, or had hit home runs to win games, or been involved in some controversy that had made the papers. He often asked me about my ear problem and seemed genuinely interested in my answer. I'm sure he wanted to find out if I was healthy enough to hit against him, but I also sensed that he cared.

Virdon had become tougher and more difficult as the season wore on, and when the change was made, some of the players were happy to see him go and Billy take over.

"I'm very happy to be the manager of the New York Yankees," Billy said with some emotion at that first meeting on Saturday, "and I promise you we will have a very good ballclub here very shortly."

He said little else the first few days. Mostly he watched. He had few rules—he just wanted us to play hard, have fun, and always hustle. Later on, as conflicts increased and pressure mounted, he would become withdrawn, tense, bitter—if something displeased him, he would call you out on the spot, even if it was right in the dugout—but none of that was true in 1975. Despite the

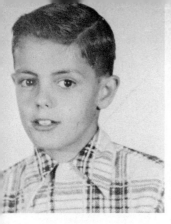

Above left: At eight, I'm already looking for a hanging curve ball. Above right: Practicing for my first love, basketball—if I can just stay out of the Precinct of Discipline. Below left: Seventeen, and just a year away from my first contract. Below right: Center fielder at Selma, my first professional baseball town—before George Wallace shut down the league rather than let in any black players.

Above left: Follow the bouncing ballplayer . . . Washington kept me just long enough to have my picture taken.

Above right: No matter what Earl Weaver said, I made it to the Orioles, where my single accomplishment was a ground out for Robin Roberts. You could look it up.

Left: The Cleveland Indians didn't think I could hit. Hah!

Right: Rookie of the year in Kansas City, where I dented a few balls—and a few water coolers.

Below: Little Lou shows he is a chip off the old block, howling at a bad call on Family Day.

Left: Playing flat-out for the Yankees: Here I'm beating a throw home with a tough slide against the Twins. (*Photo by Louis Requena*.)

Below: A textbook swing —eyes focused on the ball, weight forward, swing level, and follow-through just right. (*Photo by Louis Requena*.)

Left: And some less-than-textbook results... This one went straight up in the air like a balloon. (*Photo by Louis Requena*.)

Above left: A foul ball...hmmm, must be something wrong with the bat here. *(Photo by Louis Requena.)*

Above right: Strike three??!! You're blind! A bit of the old Tampa red-ass. *(Photo by Louis Requena.)*

Below: There's no greater thrill than making the hit that wins a World Series game—my tenth-inning single in game number four did it for us in 1978. *(Photo by Louis Requena.)*

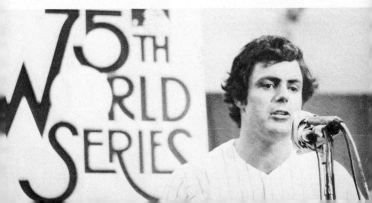

Above left: Billy Martin, that old cowhand, whispering sweet nothings in my ear. Now *there* was a soap opera. Above right: Nothing gets a pencil moving faster than a George Steinbrenner press conference. Here the Boss entertains the gentlemen of the press without a hair out of place. (*Photo by Louis Requena.*) Below: Doing what I did best in my last couple of years, relaxing with buddy Bobby Murcer. One of us is pushing a hot horse. (*Photo by Louis Requena.*)

Sharing a laugh with Yogi after my retirement was announced. He wouldn't be laughing next year when George fired him. (*Photo by Louis Requena*.)

My last at bat at Yankee Stadium. The crowd is roaring and I'm fighting back the tears. (*Photo by Louis Requena*.)

Mom, Dad, Anita, and the kids share my retirement day at the Stadium. Announcer Frank Messer tells the crowd who we all are. (*Photo by Louis Requena.*)

The whole Piniella gang in 1985 in the back of our new home in New Jersey. First we pose for pictures and then we rake those leaves.

lost year, Billy was actually enjoyable to play for, nice and loose and relaxed as that season wound down.

We finished in third place, twelve games behind Boston, and I packed my gear that final Sunday afternoon. I was preparing to head home to Tampa. Billy caught me just as I was walking out of the door of our clubhouse at Shea. It would be the last time I'd have to do that. The next year I would be a Yankee playing home games in Yankee Stadium.

"Go home, Lou, and rest. I know you couldn't play this year. Get your health back. Next year you are going to have a good year for me," Billy said, "and we are going to win the pennant."

I thought about what he had said all winter and I couldn't wait for spring training in 1976. Instead of that ringing in my ears, I kept hearing, "We're gonna win the pennant."

The Pennant
Over the Stadium

The remodeling of Yankee Stadium cost a hundred million dollars, and there were complaints in some political quarters that the whole thing was a ripoff. All I can say is that as the 1976 season drew near, we all felt a ripple of excitement. The Stadium would look a little different, a little smaller, but it was the House that Ruth Built and it was where we belonged, in the most famous baseball park in America, filled with memories of Babe Ruth, Lou Gehrig, Joe DiMaggio, Mickey Mantle, and Whitey Ford.

"It's an honor to wear these pinstripes," Billy Martin said at his opening spring meeting. "This is a team with more tradition than most. Be proud of this uniform. Don't ever embarrass it or embarrass yourself when you wear it."

More and more, I began feeling that pull to the Yankee past, I began understanding the hold this team had on the City of New York, its fans, and all baseball history. If Billy Martin taught me anything about Yankee baseball, he taught me to honor its past, its history, its traditions.

There were a couple of major changes that spring. For one thing, George was back, not that he'd ever really been away, but he'd had to push himself into the background for a while. On April 15, 1974, he'd been indicted

by the federal government for illegal contributions to
Richard Nixon's campaign through his American Ship Building Company in Cleveland. He'd pleaded guilty on August
23 and been fined fifteen thousand dollars—but that wasn't
all of it. On November 27, 1974, Commissioner Bowie
Kuhn suspended George from baseball for two years. That
just about killed him. It meant no more George on the
phone, no more George on the field for two whole years.
He had to do all his maneuvering behind the scenes
through Gabe. Can you imagine how he must have felt? I
guess he must have done a pretty good job of it, though—
Bill Virdon and Billy Martin can attest to that—because
his suspension was lifted nine months early, and on March
2, 1976, he was back in full force.

There were changes in the clubhouse, as well. Billy
always liked aggressive baseball, a stolen base, the hit and
run, the extra base when you can get it—and, if necessary,
the spitter, the hit batsman, the occasional hard takeout
slide. The sportswriters would later call it Billy Ball, and it
won games. Billy made things happen. As Frank Lane, the
general manager of the Indians, would say in 1979, "Martin's the kind of guy you'd like to kill if he's playing for the
other team, but you'd like ten of him on your side. The
little bastard."

In one quick deal pulled off by Gabe Paul on December 11, 1975, the Yankees got the guy Billy wanted for
Billy Ball. It was Mickey Rivers, Mick the Quick, the
table setter for the Yankees, the key guy in our 1976
season, the most dramatic base stealer the Yankees had in
modern times. He came to us with Ed Figueroa, a solid
starting pitcher, in a trade for Bobby Bonds. Gabe made a
great deal.

Mick the Quick. What fun it was to be his teammate.
Mickey was dumb like a fox. He had a funny way of
speaking that made it hard to understand him, especially
when he didn't want you to understand him. He had a
pathetic way of walking to the plate, ever so slowly, as if he
was in tremendous pain. He lulled a lot of pitchers to
sleep with that walk and probably got a lot of stolen bases

from unsuspecting catchers who thought his legs were too battered for him to dare run the bases. When he swung and missed a pitch at the plate, he would twirl the bat in his hands and look like a cheerleader tossing the baton around in front of the crowd at a big football game.

I once asked him, "Mickey, why do you twirl the bat like a baton?"

"Always done it."

"Yeah, I know, but why?"

"Why not?"

He had an explosive season for us in 1976 with a .312 average, forty-three stolen bases and ninety-five runs scored. Thurman, appointed the first Yankee captain since Lou Gehrig that spring, also had a brilliant year and was named the American League's Most Valuable Player. A lot of people thought Mickey deserved it.

Pretty soon Mickey became one of my best friends on the team. He liked to go to the racetrack and we spent a lot of evenings together at the track that spring. He was the worst handicapper I ever saw, absolutely the worst. He would study those charts night and day, devour the *Racing Form* and pick nothing but losers. It got to be a joke.

"Mickey, who do you like in the fifth at Aqueduct?"

"Spring Step."

"Do you like him a lot?"

"Can't lose. Just can't lose."

"There's only one horse I won't bet today."

"Who's that?"

"Spring Step."

"Spring Step?"

"Yeah, if you like him, he won't get out of the gate."

One time in Cleveland, he had an off day, and Ed Rosenthal, one of our owners, invited several of us out to Thistle Downs for a day at the track. Mickey had his usual handicapping luck through the first five races. No winners. Nothing even close. He hadn't even cashed a place or show ticket. Finally, he was all smiles as the sixth race was about to begin. The horses were at the post. They were off.

"This time I got the winner."

"I hope so, Mick."

"No, this time I got it."

"You deserve it."

"Lou, no question. This time I got it."

The horses were coming down the final straightaway. Mickey was yelling, "I got 'em, I got 'em, I got 'em."

Lo and behold, the numbers were posted, the payoffs were listed, and Mickey's winning horse had paid twelve dollars.

"I told you, Lou. I told you," he said as he walked to the window to collect his winnings.

"How many times did you have it?"

"Had one twenty-dollar ticket on him. That's enough, ain't it?"

He walked off as happy as a clam to collect his winnings. Little did I know he had a twenty-dollar ticket on *every other horse in the race*. It only cost him sixty bucks to cash that winning ticket. When we left the track that day, he had cashed a couple of other small tickets. He finally told me the story of the sixth race.

"Had to have a winner, Lou," he said. "Had to have it. Had to break my luck."

Mickey never amounted to much as a handicapper but he certainly was one whale of a ballplayer. It was Mickey who said, "Ain't no sense worrying about things you got control over, 'cause if you got control over them, ain't no sense worrying. And there ain't no sense worrying about things you got no control over, 'cause if you got no control over them, ain't no sense worrying." If we'd all listened to Mickey's advice the next few years, we'd have saved ourselves considerable wear and tear.

We lost on opening day in Milwaukee and then won five in a row. We swept two in Milwaukee and then swept two more in Baltimore. Catfish Hunter beat Ross Grimsley, and Dock Ellis, a pitcher we had obtained from Pittsburgh along with a stylish young second baseman named Willie Randolph, beat Jim Palmer. I just kept looking over into the Baltimore dugout and Earl Weaver was awful quiet that day. How sweet it was.

Ellis had supposedly been a problem pitcher in Pittsburgh, but he was seventeen and eight for us that year. Our other new acquisition, Ed Figueroa, won nineteen games and just lost his chance at twenty wins when we were rained out the final day of the season. Thurman was named the league MVP. Sparky Lyle saved twenty-three games, won another seven, had an ERA of 2.26, and sat naked on seven birthday cakes in the clubhouse. Graig Nettles had thirty-two homers and ninety-three RBIs. Catfish was 17–15, but anchored the staff with 298 innings pitched. Billy platooned me a good part of the year with Roy White, who batted .286 and led the league in runs scored with 104, and Oscar Gamble, who had seventeen homers.

I contributed a .281 season in one hundred games despite playing with a sore hand much of the season. On May 20, I had barreled into Carlton Fisk of the Red Sox at home plate while trying to score. He tagged me out with both the ball and his fist, and before we knew it, we were in the middle of a major league brawl, joined by half the players on our teams. I came out of that with some bruised tendons and ligaments on my hand. Then, just when my hand was almost better, I got so mad after making an out, I picked up a stool, tried to smash it against the wall, and got my hand caught in the middle. That's the first time the red-ass ever got me hurt.

More important than all that, though, after the inner ear problems, I regained my confidence and my batting eye that season. I also learned that a team can win without great individual stars. A ballclub wins when each player does what he can to the best of his ability. You don't *need* to have someone hitting forty home runs or knocking in 130 runs or winning twenty games. You *do* need each player contributing his own unique abilities to the entire ballclub. Earl Weaver had taught me some important lessons about winning when I played for him as a kid, and now Billy taught me about team chemistry. It's not important how the individual statistics measure up at the end of the year, but how the team standings end up—if we're number one, nothing else matters.

By the end of June we had an eight-game lead, and Billy began saying, "Nobody will catch us." By late July we had a fourteen-and-a-half game lead and we were saying, "Nobody *can* catch us." We had enormous self-confidence. Every one of us was over the moon.

We coasted home easily by ten and a half games, to the first Yankee pennant since 1964. We drew more than two million fans at home for the first time in twenty-six years, since Casey Stengel's 1950 Yankees, restored Yankee pride and tradition, brought Billy to tears with his first winning season as a Yankee manager, and got George, Gabe, and Billy hugging together for the cameras.

All I could think of that day we clinched were the long years in the minors, the doubts that I could establish myself as a big league player, the tensions, the thrown bats and battered watercoolers, the lost season of 1975—and Earl Weaver. Take that, Earl Weaver.

Now it was time for the American League Championship Series. We had won our division but we really hadn't done anything unless we could win the pennant against Kansas City. We drank a little champagne in the clubhouse the day we clinched, but we knew it would be much better-tasting when we beat the Royals. It would take some doing because manager Whitey Herzog had put together a fine club. Some of the players had come along while I was still there, but most were young newcomers, George Brett the best of them, and we had to be on our game.

The playoff began in Kansas City. We knew that if we could split the two games there we could win—after that came three in Yankee Stadium, and nobody could take two out of three from us in the Stadium. I felt pretty secure going in, and even more so coming out of the first game. Catfish Hunter, who had settled down after his shaky

Yankee start, beat Larry Gura, who had been traded away from us, with a five-hitter. Afterward Billy warned us, "We still haven't done anything yet."

He was right. In the second game, Dennis Leonard, a big righthander from Brooklyn, beat Ed Figueroa 7–3. Dock Ellis put us up 2–1 in the third game, with Chris Chambliss hitting a big homer, but Catfish didn't have it in the fourth game. Graig Nettles hit two homers, but we still got beaten, 7–4. It all came down to game five, with 56,821 people packing Yankee Stadium that Thursday night.

Leonard started again for the Royals and Billy decided to play Roy White in left. I sat. When your club is winning, nobody complains about platooning. All I could do was get nervous as the most important game of my life seesawed back and forth. We had a 6–3 lead going into the eighth, with Figueroa getting out of jams every inning. I paraded up and down on the bench, nervous as a cat. It's easier to sit down between innings of a big game when you are playing. When you're on the bench, it all rushes to your head. I didn't say anything to anybody. I just kept thinking I wanted us to win quickly. I wanted to see the game end. I was too nervous to survive it much longer.

The Royals got a couple of men on in the eighth and Brett, who had become one of the finest hitters in the game, was the next batter. Al Cowens had singled off Figueroa, who was obviously exhausted, and Billy had brought in lefthanded reliever Grant Jackson to face Jim Wohlford. Yes, that Jim Wohlford. He cracked a line drive to center for a hit, Catfish turned to me and with a little smile we both whispered, "Jim f——g Wohlford." Now the Royals had two on, with Brett facing Jackson. Boom. The ball sailed on a high line into the right-field seats for three runs and a 6–6 game. I felt ill. The Stadium was eerily silent. I never believed so many people could hold their breath at the same time.

We went out easily in the bottom of the eighth, and Dick Tidrow got the Royals out without a score in the top of the ninth. There it was, the archetypal bottom of the ninth. It was a tie game, we were coming up for our last at bats, and a run now would put the Yankees into the World Series. The crowd exploded. Paper bags, scorecards, garbage, half-eaten fruit, rubber balls, and assorted sandwiches descended from the stands. The cleanup crew took to the field as Kansas City relief pitcher Mark Littell continued throwing warmup pitches from the mound. The barrage continued and public address announcer Bob Sheppard proclaimed, "Fans who insist on throwing things on the field will be removed from the Stadium and subject to arrest." That only brought more garbage. Some fans are just flakes. It lasted for about fifteen minutes. Finally, they slowly started settling down. Chambliss was at the bat rack. He picked out his bat and walked to the plate. The roar was deafening. I wouldn't say it out loud. It would be too much of a jinx, but I kept thinking . . . he might hit it out. Chambliss had had seventeen homers with ninety-six RBIs and a .293 average for us. He had come over to the Yankees a couple of years earlier from Cleveland and had a poor season, but he'd hit .304 in 1975 and then .293 this year. The son of a Navy chaplain, he was a strong but quiet man who went out and did his job every day without much fanfare. We called him the Snatcher, because he had big hands and caught anything that came his way at first base.

"I wanted to swing at that first pitch," Chambliss said later. "I thought the fuss on the field might have cost Littell some concentration. No matter how long the delay was, I was going to jump on that first one."

At 11:13 by the huge clock in right field, Chambliss hit a high drive off Littell's first fastball into the right-field seats. Chris could see that it was gone, took a step toward first and then jumped into the air. Thurman, the on-deck hitter, still had his catching gear on for some reason and jumped even higher than Chris. The bench emptied in an instant and we all raced toward the plate. Chris was rounding second by now and a bunch of fans were in his way. He had to fight his way past them to round third. As he approached home, fans and players and cops were all around the plate. He ran past the plate and raced into the dugout. Not wanting a Fred Merkle situation—he was the

Giants first baseman who failed to touch second in a game against the Cubs in 1908, costing the Giants a win and causing a playoff won by the Cubs—Chambliss was sent back out. This time, cops and security guards accompanied him to the plate and the pennant was assured.

The clubhouse was wild. George came in and got champagne dumped on his head. Gabe hugged Billy, and they'd never been the best of friends. George's buddy, Cary Grant, was escorted around the clubhouse to congratulate some of the players and meet Billy. Cary looked and sounded just the way he had in the movies. The mayor of New York, little Abe Beame, paraded around the room as if he had lost his hat. The television lights made the place a sauna. It seemed as if thousands of people were jammed in there. Billy sat on a trunk in the middle of the clubhouse, wiped champagne from his eyes, and submitted to the press. "I wish Casey was here to see it," Billy said of his managerial hero, Casey Stengel. "This was his pennant." Stengel had died in 1975. Then Billy collected his emotions and let it all hang out. "Those guys who didn't think we could do it, who picked against us, who said I'd never win one—where are they now? Now they can kiss my dago ass. I won it. The Yankees are back where they belong, on top."

We didn't have much time to enjoy the celebration, since we left the next day for Cincinnati to open the World Series on Saturday against the Reds. It was raining and snowing when we arrived, so we never had a formal workout in Riverfront Stadium. We suited up, took a few pictures, talked to the press, played a little catch, but never had batting practice. We probably wouldn't have been too good with the bats anyway, because we were still enjoying our pennant hangovers.

The Reds had a big edge on us from the start. We had used up all our pitching in the playoffs, and Doyle Alexander, who hadn't even pitched an inning in the series against Kansas City, was our first-game starter. Billy wanted Catfish to open, of course, but Catfish had pitched in the fourth game of the playoffs on Wednesday and wasn't ready. Joe Morgan hit a homer off Alexander in the first inning to put the Reds up, 1–0. I led off the second, the first designated hitter in World Series history. I was less nervous than I thought I would be, hit Don Gullett's first pitch for a double to left, moved up on a grounder by Chambliss and scored on Graig Nettles' sacrifice fly, the first run scored by a DH in World Series history. Look, when you're not a Hall of Fame player, you have to take all the little things you can get.

It didn't help, though. We lost that game . . . and the game after that . . . and the game after that. Four straight. The Reds swept us in four straight. Oh, George was livid. This time he really felt we'd let him down—and I suppose in a way we had. There was no question we didn't perform well. The World Series got to us. These forces of emotion, excitement, and anticipation, things we hadn't experienced at that level before, simply overwhelmed us. You have to learn what the Series is all about. Nobody can tell you. You just have to live it. At the same time, the Reds were simply a better ballclub. They had the better horses, the faster horses, the stronger horses. They had been there in 1975 when they'd beaten the Red Sox in seven games and that helped them blow us away.

By the same token, our being there in 1976 was an important factor in our success against the Dodgers in 1977 and 1978. It was a great learning experience. After that defeat, we were determined to a man to see that it didn't happen again. We had caught a few fish in 1976 but let the big one get away. We weren't going to let that happen again.

Meanwhile, the baseball kettle was smoldering. Outside forces were at work that would have a distinct bearing on the ballclub, change its personality and character for years, and draw more attention to a baseball team than I could imagine was possible. It would all explode with the advent of free agency.

Baseball owners were doing their best to hold off free agency and baseball players were doing their best to see it happen. The reserve clause had bound a player to a club for life, unless traded, released, or sold, and though all players resented this arrangement, all players accepted it. Most understood that it was simply the price one paid to be a ballplayer. If you were a salesman, you could change jobs and go to a higher bidder. If you were a ballplayer, you simply went where you were told. When I was traded from Kansas City to New York I wasn't asked, I was told. I had two choices, report to the Yankees or quit baseball. There was no other choice.

Over the years, there had been discussions about changing the rules, but nothing had ever come of it—until, in 1969, Curt Flood, a St. Louis Cardinals outfielder, was traded from the Cards to the Philadelphia Phillies. He refused to report. He had business and friends in St. Louis and didn't want to give them up to live in Philadelphia. He phoned Marvin Miller, the executive director of the Major League Baseball Players Association.

"What do you think he wants?" Miller's assistant, attorney Dick Moss, asked.

"I don't know," said Miller.

"He's just been traded," said Moss. "It might have something to do with that."

It certainly did.

Flood wanted to challenge baseball's rules. He asked Miller and Moss to help him fight the reserve clause. They had been thinking about it themselves for a good long while, now they thought they might have their man.

"Will you go all the way?" Miller asked Flood.

"Yes, I'm prepared to do whatever is necessary."

Attorney Moss began preparing a legal brief on Flood's behalf. Slowly, the case moved through the legal system all the way to the United States Supreme Court, with every ballplayer watching it. The Supreme Court finally ruled that it would *not* change baseball's legal structure, but in turning the case back to the lower courts suggested that it would be advisable for players and owners to get together on the matter through negotiations.

With strike threats and work stoppages, the players continued to be militant on the issue. Catfish Hunter was declared a free agent on a contract technicality because owner Charles O. Finley hadn't paid Catfish an insurance coverage bill, but that was an isolated case. The real trigger came when Andy Messersmith and Dave McNally, playing without contracts, were declared free agents by the courts, and allowed to move to other clubs. At first, Messersmith signed with the Yankees, but the deal fell through and he landed with the Braves. McNally had already retired by the time the decision was handed down, but fought the case to help other players. The owners finally accepted the inevitable.

A new reserve clause rule was written, and players who did not sign contracts for the 1976 season were allowed to play out their option year, declare themselves free agents and put themselves up for the highest bidder.

Always an aggressive businessman, George Steinbrenner knew the new rules. He had built his father's conservative shipping companies into a two-hundred-million-dollar operation with aggressive marketing tactics. "We got out and pounded the bushes," he said. "We created business by going to the steel companies and hounding them. We simply outworked the opposition." He spent money and expected a lot in return. He demanded excellence and dedication. He wanted an operation that performed as close to perfection as he could get. He thought nothing of working a twenty-hour day, and expected his office people to perform likewise, and when they couldn't, or wouldn't, he was very displeased. He was capable of enormous kindness—helping a secretary pay for her son to go to college, donating huge sums of money to New York City police and fire aid funds—but he was also capable of exploding at the least little mistake: a wrong phone number given to him, a desk drawer left open in the office, a sandwich delivered without a pickle.

On the field, it was the same. He expected his ballplayers to perform, especially those to whom he was paying big salaries—and he was shortly to begin handing out some of the biggest. The Yankees would soon be known as The Best Team Money Could Buy. "I didn't invent the system," George said, "but I used it." Impatient for quick success, George knew the Yankees had allowed their farm system to deteriorate, and it would be years before enough players could come through the farm system to stardom. Thurman Munson, Roy White, and Ron Guidry were the only three significant Yankee-trained players in the big years of the late 1970s.

"I'm determined to build this club into a winner," George said that winter. "We'll do it any way we have to."

Winning the pennant was not enough for George and it was not enough for Billy. They wanted the whole thing—and to get it, they plunged headlong into the world of free agency.

First, George rushed after a hard-throwing twenty-six-year-old lefthanded pitcher by the name of Don Gullett. Lefthanders are vital to Yankee success because so many teams stack their lineups with lefthanded hitters to take advantage of the short right-field fences at the Stadium. Gullett had beaten us in the World Series and George had been impressed by his fastball, poise, and relative youth. He looked as if he could be a big winner for the Yankees for many years, so on November 18, 1976, Gullett became free agent number one. It was a popular signing. He was a soft-spoken young man, good-looking, a fine pitcher, an All-American type from Kentucky with a clean, wholesome, quiet, respectful image. He was a wonderful pitcher for us in 1977, with a 14–4 mark, but became bothered by arm trouble. It got worse the next season, when he would pitch in only eight games, winning four and losing two, and nurse his shoulder most of the season. He hung around for another year or so, hoping for a medical miracle, never got it, and finally was released with three years to go on his contract. George paid him something like two and a half million dollars, but he could only pitch a little more than a year of the six-year contract. He went back to his farm in Kentucky where the Yankee checks came regularly. It was a sad thing, because Donnie Gullett was a good friend and a great pitcher. He was only twenty-seven years old when he pitched his last game in the big leagues for the Yankees. What a waste of talent.

George continued to hunt for talent that winter. He was determined to get every player he could to help the Yankees win. Eleven days after the signing of Don Gullett, the Yankees called a press conference to another another free agent signing. Thurman Munson, the Yankee captain, flew in from Ohio to attend the press conference. Several other Yankees who lived in the New York area, including Roy White, Willie Randolph, and Ed Figueroa, attended the big press announcement.

Yankee president Gabe Paul stood on the rostrum in the Princess Suite of New York's Americana Hotel. He was dressed in a muted gray suit and dark tie. He put on his glasses and cleared his throat. "The New York Yankees are pleased to announce," he began, "that we have come to terms with free agent Reggie Jackson."

Jackson stood to one side and shifted from one foot to the other nervously as Paul continued. "We are very pleased that Reggie has agreed to join us and very happy to have him in a Yankee uniform."

Reggie seemed nervous as he spoke into a battery of microphones as the press listened and recorded his words. His father, brother, and girlfriend sat off to one side, listening carefully and smiling as Jackson spoke. "I am very happy to be a Yankee," Jackson said.

The chase had begun several weeks earlier, when Jackson had been drafted by thirteen big league clubs. They all pursued him vigorously. After all, he was one of baseball's premier home-run hitters, a winner with the Oakland A's, a crowd-pleaser, and a dynamic personality. He was certainly worth chasing. New York, Montreal, and San Diego were the three most intense clubs, and Reggie said he would make his final decision Thanksgiving Day in Chicago after talking one last time with all three. Reggie was in the Hyatt Regency Hotel in Chicago and George flew out there to have a breakfast meeting with him. He told Reggie and his agent, Gary Walker, that he would hang around all day and wanted to see Reggie one last time after all the other clubs had made their final offers. They agreed.

"I sat in that lobby all day, like some little kid," George said later. "I was waiting to be called at the end of their meetings. I kept thinking how I had promised my kids I would be home for Thanksgiving. This seemed more important."

Late in the afternoon, he heard a bellboy saying, "Call for Mr. Steinbrenner, call for Mr. Steinbrenner."

He picked up the phone. It was Jackson. "C'mon up, George, we're finished."

Steinbrenner took the elevator to Jackson's eleventh-floor suite, knocked on the door, and walked in. There was a smile on Reggie's face. "You're it, George," said Reggie.

Tears came to George's face. He shook hands with the big guy standing in front of him. Then he impulsively hugged him.

They shook hands all around and Jackson scribbled a note to seal the deal. "We are going on this venture together. I will not let you down." It was signed, "Reginald M. Jackson."

It was a venture that would have an overwhelming effect on the lives of many, on Thurman Munson and Graig Nettles and Fran Healy, but most especially on Billy Martin. "I hate Martin because he plays tough," Reggie had said in 1972. "But if I played for him, I'd probably love him." Well, it didn't exactly work out that way, and everybody who wore the Yankee pinstripes in those tumultuous years felt the effects.

There was no question that Reggie would create excitement and bring more attention to the Yankees. He would also bring a great deal of attention to himself. Reggie was a hot dog. Throughout his career that was the way it had always been. One of his Oakland teammates, pitcher Darold Knowles, said it concisely: "There isn't enough mustard in America to cover Reggie Jackson."

Perhaps it was his former teammate Catfish Hunter who summed up Reggie best. "Reggie's a good guy, down deep he is," Catfish said. "He'd give you the shirt off his back. Of course he'd call a press conference to announce it."

Reggie Jackson. Would he make noise in New York in the next five years!

The Summers
of Mr. October

The spring of 1977 at Fort Lauderdale's Yankee Stadium
now seems a blur of Reggie Jackson adventures. He
reported late and caused a commotion almost from the
instant he put on a Yankee uniform. Unlike Catfish Hunter, who had arrived two years earlier with almost as much
fanfare, Reggie never tried to defuse the attention. He
talked and talked and talked, always about himself, always
about what he would contribute to the Yankees, always
with the press hovering over him as if he were the only
Yankee who had ever achieved anything in the game.

"You'd think we had just won the goddamn World
Series or something," said Thurman the first day, as he
fought his way past the crowd around Reggie to his own
locker. Thurman was growing more bitter each day over
the fact that Reggie's bottom line—complete with a signing
bonus of some four hundred thousand dollars—was greater
than his. He was making more in base salary, but Reggie
was taking home a bigger paycheck. That infuriated him.

Jackson continued to hold court, as the rest of us
finished dressing and started for the field. Reggie was
holding his big black bat in his hand. "See this," he said,
as he held the bat high for all the press to see. "Nobody
will embarrass the Yankees in the World Series again as
long as I am carrying this."

Thurman and I walked out of the clubhouse together.

He turned to me with an unhappy look on his face. "Can you believe this shit?"

Fred Stanley, our fine utility infielder, once explained Thurman's early frustrations about Reggie to the press.

"See, the thing that people forgot when Reggie joined the club," Stanley said, "was that Thurman was the captain. He was Mr. Yankee. He also wanted attention. He probably wanted it as badly as Reggie did. He just didn't know how to go about it."

Stanley was talking to me in the clubhouse one day about trying to help his parents in Tempe, Arizona, get a good deal on a car. They had been quoted a price of eleven thousand dollars for the car they wanted, a steep price, and they were debating getting it. Reggie overheard the conversation. As Stanley tells it, "Reggie comes over to me and says, 'You wanna car for your folks?' I told him I did. He said he had a car dealership in Tempe and he could take care of it. He got them the same car for seven thousand dollars. I never forgot the favor. Neither did he. He made sure eleven guys heard him ask me how my folks were doing with the car he arranged for them. I didn't resent it. That's Reggie. He has to be appreciated."

Regarding Thurman, Stanley continues: "Thurman had this way of walking up and down the clubhouse when he wanted some press attention. If he didn't want it, he could hide. But when he walked, he knew one of the writers would be brave enough to stop him and ask him a question. He was waiting for them one day after hitting a game-winning home run. But they never came to him. They had all stopped at Reggie's locker, and he discussed the latest rise and fall in the stock market or something, and that just pissed Thurman off real bad."

The tension was pretty thick all spring between Thurman and Reggie. They had nothing to say to each other. Meanwhile a freelance writer named Robert Ward had followed Reggie to Florida, chased him for an interview, and finally cornered him one night after a couple of drinks in a Fort Lauderdale bar. All of us have been trapped like that. You think you are talking casually, off the record, trusting the guy's judgment not to embarrass you—then the article hits and all hell breaks loose.

Ward's article in *Sport* magazine was called "Reggie Jackson in No-Man's Land," a title I could never figure out. In it, Reggie discussed his coming role on the Yankees. He was quoted as saying, "You know, this team, it all flows from me. I've got to keep it going. I'm the straw that stirs the drink. It all comes back to me. Maybe I should say me and Munson. But really he doesn't enter into it. He's being so damn insecure about the whole thing. I've overheard him talking about me. Munson's tough, too. He's a winner, but there is nobody who can do for a club what I can do. There is nobody who can put meat in the seats [fans in the stands] the way I can. That's just the way it is. Munson thinks he can be the straw that stirs the drink, but he can only stir it bad."

Ward later asked Billy Martin if he thought there would be any leadership problems on the club with Reggie Jackson there.

"Not a chance," said Martin. "We already have a team leader. Thurman Munson."

The stage was being set.

There simply was no way to figure Reggie out. Reggie could be as charming and nice to you as you could imagine, and you would think, well, I'm getting along pretty well with Reggie; then, two days later he would walk by you in the clubhouse as if you weren't there and wouldn't talk to you for a week, and you would wonder what the hell you did to the guy. Most of the time, you never really knew how you stood with Reggie.

I felt sorry for him in the beginning. He had put this pressure on himself, he'd separated himself from the other guys with his big talk, he'd deliberately drawn the press to him, but he seemed to want to do a job. He was a professional, like everybody else in the clubhouse. Fran Healy, our backup catcher, was friendly to him, but most everybody else was aloof. Reggie wasn't dumb. He could feel it. He wasn't hated—that's too strong a word—but he certainly was disliked by everyone on the club, except maybe Healy, myself, Mike Torrez, perhaps one or two others. Thurman, Graig, Sparky, Dick Tidrow, all seemed to have little use for him. It is a very difficult situation for a ballplayer to be one of twenty-five guys, yet have nobody with whom he can share his thoughts, his emotions, his frustrations. And in Reggie's case, he couldn't even go to the manager.

Pretty soon, there was an obvious division in the clubhouse. Almost every player could be categorized as in Billy's camp or Reggie's camp or Thurman's camp. It got so if I was caught talking to Reggie, I might get a cold shoulder from Graig or Thurman. It seemed there was no way to get along with everybody, but I tried desperately to maintain some sort of neutrality. I felt terribly unhappy at what Reggie was going through. He'd brought most of it on himself, but it seemed a difficult burden for any ballplayer to carry.

Reggie had taken a luxury apartment in Manhattan across from Central Park on Fifth Avenue. I was spending that early part of the 1977 season living in a friend's apartment on East Seventy-ninth Street. The kids were in school and Anita wouldn't be coming up to New York with them until late in June. In the meantime, I stayed downtown, went to some of the city's best restaurants—I was studying the territory before I opened my own—and enjoyed some relaxing hours after the ballgame. Reggie and I had a cordial relationship and he approached me after a game.

"I'm going downtown, Lou. Want a ride?"

"Sure. Where do you go?"

"I'm right near you. Let's stop off at Oren and Aretsky's, have a piece of salmon and a couple of drinks, and I'll drive you home."

Reggie had a magnificent Rolls-Royce Corniche and it was fun to ride in it. He seemed a different person when he was out of the clubhouse, in his own car, away from the press, and on his way home.

We talked easily going back and forth to the Stadium a few times. He tried to explain the pressures he was under. He said he wished he could communicate better with Billy. He said he respected Thurman a great deal as a player and wanted to get along with him. He didn't seem as pretentious and arrogant as he did with others around the clubhouse. As I got to understand him, I really got to like the guy. He talked a lot about wanting to be liked on the team, wanting to be part of it, to get closer to the guys. He really did want to be liked. He simply did not know how to go about it.

Reggie admitted he enjoyed the spotlight. He talked of being the top dog on the team. I could see his anguish as he talked about his problems with his teammates. Inside he was terribly insecure. He desperately wanted to be one of the guys. He was just incapable of going about it the proper way.

Things didn't change very much into mid-June. Every day there seemed to be a new episode. It was the Yankee soap opera, Billy and Reggie, Reggie and Billy, Billy and George, Thurman and Reggie, and on and on and on. In the beginning it was fun. We'd buy all the papers and sit around the clubhouse table and see who said what about whom on this particular day. Most of the time, we laughed about it. Reggie was never part of it. He would walk by, see us reading the papers, make some remark under his breath and walk off. Nobody really took it very seriously. Then, as we continued to play lackluster baseball in June, it started to turn. We were not winning. We weren't playing well. We weren't doing much of anything except providing more gossip for the baseball press. Billy became more tense. This was supposed to be the year he was going to lead the Yankees to a World Series win. It wasn't working out that way. As the soap opera saga continued, it started becoming unbearable. None of the sportswriters wanted to talk about the game. All we heard, all anybody asked about, all anybody discussed, was the latest episode involving Billy and Reggie, Billy and George, Thurman and Reggie. The games hardly mattered.

"We're not in baseball anymore," I told Thurman one

day, "we're in show business. Baseball is just a sideline here."

"When I was a kid," Graig Nettles said, "I didn't know whether I wanted to be a ballplayer or run off and join the circus. Now I've been able to do both."

Reggie didn't have much of a sense of humor about himself. He was pompous and self-impressed. We would kid him on the bus about something or other, lightly, and he would ignore it or answer in a mean way. If he could only have laughed at himself a little more, the way Catfish did, he might have been accepted. Catfish made three million dollars and never talked about money. Reggie made the same and would unfurl his wallet and count off his one-hundred-dollar bills. Reggie never really tried to be part of the team. Reggie was his own team. He could go his own way, fight his own fights and get his attention from the fans and the press.

The *Sport* magazine article had come out in May and the tension between Thurman and Reggie remained heavy. They were both quality players, though. I felt that if both of them played up to their potential, we could win. Billy had won without Reggie in 1976, and thought he could win again in 1977 with little contribution from him. We were supposed to run away from the league as we had done the previous year. Billy looked for answers for why we weren't. It always came down to Reggie.

On June 18, we were playing a nationally televised game in Boston's Fenway Park against the Red Sox. It was the kind of scene Reggie loved. Those were the games he really liked to shine in. The Red Sox had beaten us Friday night and Mike Torrez was pitching against Reggie Cleveland on Saturday afternoon. Jackson was in right field, Mickey Rivers in center, and I was in left field. The Red Sox quickly pulled ahead of us again, and Jim Rice, their big righthanded slugger, was at bat. I was pulled over to left, Mickey was in left center and Reggie was shading him to right center. Torrez threw a high, outside fastball and Rice floated it toward right center field.

Reggie was brooding out there. He was batting sixth,

instead of his star spot of fourth, and that really seemed to bother him. He had batted third and fourth for those championship teams in Oakland, and batting down low for the Yankees was an insult. Billy had made remarks to the press that he had never really wanted Reggie, that he felt Reggie upset the delicate balance we'd had in 1976, that Reggie had been forced on him by George, that he wanted Reggie to understand there was only one boss on that club and that was Billy Martin. All of this had been festering for weeks as the Boston incident was about to break.

From left field I could see that Reggie hadn't gotten a a very good jump on the ball. I could also see that he was struggling to catch it. To Billy he obviously seemed content to let it bounce because it hardly mattered to him one way or another.

The ball fell for a double and Billy quickly called time. He sent Paul Blair, a superior outfielder, out to right field. Reggie hadn't seen him coming. He suddenly looked up and noticed Blair a few feet away.

"What are you doing here?"

"Billy just sent me in."

"He did what?"

By now the crowd was stirring and buzzing, the Red Sox were standing up on their bench and Reggie was jogging into the Yankee dugout. Billy yelled at him, "You show me up, I'll show you up."

"What did I do? What did I do?" yelled Reggie.

Billy was fed up. He wanted to show Reggie and show the rest of the players that nobody was bigger than the manager, that nobody was bigger than the New York Yankees, that if a player didn't hustle, he wouldn't be out there on the field.

Reggie put his glasses down on the side of the dugout steps. He moved toward Billy. The manager started over from his side of the dugout. It was certain there would be punches thrown, except that Elston Howard, one of our coaches and a Yankee teammate of Billy's, grabbed Billy around the waist and held him off. Yogi Berra, another coach then, also moved closer to the conflict. The players all stared straight ahead. It wasn't something any other player wanted to get involved in. Careers were on the line here. Mike Torrez, a Mexican-American pitcher who spoke Spanish, called to Reggie in Spanish to go inside the clubhouse. "Go inside, cool off," Torrez said. Jackson finally turned and went inside. The game continued and the inning ended. I jogged in from left field.

The clubhouse boy met me on the top step as I walked into the dugout.

"Reggie wants to see you inside," he said.

"Where is he?"

"He's by his locker."

I went inside and I could see the pain in Reggie's face. His veins stood out of his neck. He was covered in sweat. His voice seemed to crack as he talked.

"Lou, what should I do? This guy doesn't like me. He wants to embarrass me. He wants to fight me. Should I stay here after the game and fight him here in the clubhouse?"

"Reggie, look, the best thing you can do now is calm down, have a beer, take a shower, and get dressed. Then get back to the hotel room and settle down. No good will come out of anything for you, for Billy, or for the ballclub, if you two guys have a fist fight here."

"I can't stand it. He embarrassed me on national television. He humiliated me."

"When you're upset the way you are now, when you are mad, when you are visibly under this kind of strain, this is no time to discuss it or have a fight or even talk about it. Just get dressed and get out of here and deal with it tomorrow."

"How can I let him get away with it?"

"Reggie, you can't win when you fight with the manager. He has to make the decisions. That's the way it has got to be and that's the way it will always be as long as there is baseball. This is no time to get yourself into any more problems than you already have now. Now, go on back."

That's what he did. He went back to the hotel, where

he was joined by his buddy Fran Healy, and before long both Billy and George came up for a discussion. George shuffled from Billy's room to Reggie's room to go over all the aspects of the situation. It seemed George was giving serious consideration to letting Billy go, since Billy couldn't handle his three-million-dollar outfielder. According to Reggie, he told George, "I don't want to be the cause of a manager's firing. Don't fire him on my account."

Gabe Paul and George discussed the matter late into the night. They got concessions from both sides. Jackson promised he would no longer discuss the incident, and would do what Billy asked. Billy promised he would refrain from making any more antagonistic remarks in the press.

Things calmed down for a few days, but nobody really observed the code of silence. Reggie gave an interview to a reporter a couple of days later and he said, "It makes me cry, the way they treat me on this team. The Yankee pinstripes are Ruth and Gehrig and DiMaggio and Mantle. I'm not their lackey. I don't know how to be subservient."

I can't look into a man's mind. I don't know Billy's attitudes on race. I never discussed it with him, and it's not my business. I do know he seemed to treat all players alike, black and white, except for Reggie. His confrontations with Reggie had nothing to do with race, and everything to do with the personalities of two complex men. They simply could not get along. It happens sometimes. It happens on ballclubs. It happens in offices. It might even happen in your family.

After the Boston incident, tension remained high, though one thing did change. The whole affair seemed to crystallize strictly into a problem between Billy and Reggie. The rest of us pulled back. Our attitude became, "This is between Reggie and Billy. Let them settle it."

Every once in a while, maybe early in the clubhouse or driving home with Reggie after a game or even sitting together in a hotel bar someplace, we talked. Usually it was not about Billy and Reggie or Reggie and Thurman. Usually it was just about the club in general, baseball, or the pressures we all felt as professional athletes. Sometimes the conversations drifted from English into Spanish. I enjoyed talking Spanish with Reggie. His father was Spanish, so he had grown up with it and spoke it well enough to carry on a conversation. It gave me a chance to practice, too. Basically the language had left me, and it was my way of keeping my hand in.

On July 12, we remained in third place, a game and a half out of first, behind Boston and Baltimore, and were moving into Milwaukee for a three-game series. Then it was on to Kansas City and the All-Star break. Don Gullett beat Moose Haas the first night in Milwaukee, but we lost a sloppy 9–8 game the next night. Thurman and I sat at the bar after the game drowning our sorrows. George Steinbrenner had joined the club to see what he could do to get us going. We talked about that, and finally, Thurman suggested we go up to see the Boss. I loved his silk pajamas.

I've already described what happened there. There was some yelling, some reasoning, some communication, a bad CIA act when Billy saw us in the bathroom, a few more hours of arguing, and then the decision. George would leave Billy alone to manage the ballclub and Reggie would move up to fourth in the batting order. We bounced around for a couple more weeks, Billy finally made the move on his own terms in his own time, and the club got hot. Reggie started delivering big hits in big spots, he seemed more a part of the ballclub, and we moved into first place on August 23. We stayed there the rest of the way to win by two and a half games.

The clubhouse was wild again with television lights, champagne showers, and endless streams of press. It was childish, of course, for grown men to act this way, but it was also a tradition, and a pleasant one. "You have to have a lot of little boy in you to play baseball," Roy Campanella once said. A lot of that little-boy spirit comes out in the boisterous conduct of a winning clubhouse.

Reggie was part of it. He slugged champagne in

between his conversations with the press. Then he carried an opened bottle of champagne into Billy's office.

"Here, skipper," he said, "have some of this champagne."

"I will if you will," Billy said.

Reggie took a huge swallow of the bubbly stuff, then he handed the bottle to Billy. He took a huge swallow. "You had a helluva year, big guy," Billy said. "I love you." Jackson said nothing, just smiled and swallowed another mouthful.

Our American League playoff opponent was Whitey Herzog's Kansas City Royals again. We knew he would be gunning for us after the shock of the 1976 defeat, and we were right. They came roaring out of the starting gate in the opening game behind their big lefthander, Paul Splittorff. Donnie Gullet didn't have good stuff, and they won, 7–2. In the second game, Ron Guidry, who was just beginning to develop into the overpowering pitcher of the following season, allowed only two runs and three hits and we evened the count, 6–2. Now we would have to win two out of three in Kansas City to defend our title.

We went charging into Kansas City—and got stopped with a thud. Dennis Leonard beat Mike Torrez, 6–2, in the third game. Now we were down two games to one, only one game away from elimination, and in Kansas City. But we still felt we had the better ballclub. That night, a dozen of us gathered at Trader Vic's in the Crown Center Hotel, had a few drinks, talked late, and came to a consensus. Those little Kansas City Royals with tiny Fred Patek, pesky Frank White, small outfielders and designated hitters like Al Cowens and Hal McRae, were outrunning us and out-finessing us. We had to muscle them. We had to intimidate them.

"We're bigger, stronger, more powerful," I told Thurman.

"We have to show some muscle," he said.

"We have to play hard-nose baseball, kick some ass, do what has to be done to win this thing."

"Let's use our power," Nettles said. "On the bases and at bat."

"This isn't baseball tomorrow. This is survival," I said. "Whatever needs to be done on that baseball field tomorrow, let's do it. Let's not spare our bodies now."

"Let's show that we are stronger," said Thurman.

"Let's do it. We're the New York Yankees, for crissakes."

I was feeling great when I went back up to my room after that pep talk. I was ready for a good night's sleep and then I knew I would be ready to kick some ass on that ballfield. As soon as I got to the room, the phone rang. It was Bill Kane, our traveling secretary, who was in charge of the team's hotel and travel arrangements.

"Lou, this is Bill Kane."

"Yeah, Killer." We called him Killer because he walked with a limp from a bad leg and wouldn't hurt a fly. "What's up?"

"Tomorrow morning, put your bags in the lobby and check out in case we have to fly home."

"Yeah, okay."

Kane was calling every player on the team to tell them to put their bags in the lobby and check out of their rooms tomorrow morning in case we lost the fourth game and had to fly home.

After Kane hung up, though, I started thinking. Why in hell should the players be thinking about going home after the fourth game, when we couldn't go to the World Series unless we won the fourth and fifth games? That was negative thinking. It cast severe doubt on our prospects. I picked up the phone and called Killer back in his room.

"You people have done something seriously wrong here," I told the traveling secretary.

"What's that?"

"You tell us to bring our bags down and vacate our rooms in case we lose tomorrow. You're suggesting that we might not win."

Kane reported our conversation, and George exploded. "Who the hell's idea was that?"

It turned out George didn't know a thing about it. The idea had come from Gabe Paul, the old traveling secretary, who figured if we lost he could save a few bucks on a hotel room while we were busy playing the game.

A few minutes later the phone rang again. It was Killer Kane.

"Uhh, Lou," he said, "keep your bags in your room tomorrow." Then he paused. "And don't pack."

The next night we went out there for that fourth game and did just what we said we would: played real hardball. Graig Nettles drove his elbow into George Brett's face on a close play at third and set the tone for the whole game. It was tough, it was competitive, and it was fun.

We jumped ahead to a 4–0 lead, Ed Figueroa, tired from a tough season, struggled into the fourth inning, gave up a couple of runs and gave way to Dick Tidrow. Dirt—he always had a growth of beard and a uniform that never seemed to have been cleaned—came on, had nothing, and suddenly Sparky Lyle was in the game, in the fourth inning, if you can believe that. Our backs were to the wall, it was win or else, so Billy went to Sparky early. It was one of the most intense games in which I had ever played.

Sparky just kept throwing that nasty slider up there inning after inning. He had a 5–4 lead and held on to it with his fingertips. Sparky may have been a clown, with his wild, flowing mustache, outrageous sayings, and fondness for sitting naked on birthday cakes in the clubhouse—a sight everyone should have the privilege of seeing once in his life—but he was the ultimate professional, a tremendous competitor. You just loved having him in there in the kind of tight game that sent weaker men running to the bathroom. And that's what this one was.

In the nine grueling, intense, emotional, sweat-drenching innings, we beat them, 6–4. Now all we had to do was do it all over again on Sunday. It had come down to the fifth game again, just as it had in 1976. If the Yankees were to be champions, we had to beat the Royals in their own ballpark. If we wanted to keep our jobs, we had to beat the Royals in their own ballpark. A loss was certain to result in wholesale changes next year. George would accept nothing less than the championship.

We got to the ballpark early, unaware that Billy had already met with Gabe Paul and George. He had told them about a move he planned that day.

"Go ahead and do what you think is right," George had said. "You're the manager."

George and Gabe sat together in the stands several hours before the game. Reporters had heard of Billy's lineup move. They raced to George for comment. "It's Billy's decision," he said. Then he sat tight-lipped and the reporters left.

Billy Martin had posted the lineup card on the dugout wall. Reggie Jackson's name was not on it. Billy had decided to bench the lefthanded slugger against Paul Splittorff, the lefthanded pitcher, and replace him with Paul Blair, a righthanded hitter without much power but a better defensive player. Billy expected a low-scoring game and wanted defense. It was the ballsiest decision any manager ever made in a big game in my time.

The fifth game was Reggie's kind of game: big drama, big pressure, national television, Howard Cosell, all that excitement. And he was sitting. We were shocked. Billy never said anything to anybody about it. He was the manager. He didn't have to explain any decisions to his players. We knew what it meant, considering George's volatile personality.

"If we win, Billy is a genius," Sparky said. "If we lose, he's fired."

Then he laughed. Nothing was ever simple or dull around the Yankees. Billy had added incredible drama to the fifth game of the 1977 playoffs with one stroke of his pen.

The Royals jumped ahead, 2–0, against Guidry. We responded with a run in the third and when Kansas City rallied for another run and a 3–1 lead in their half of the third, Billy brought in Mike Torrez. Mike had been bombed on Friday, but he held them in a gutty performance until he could turn the ball over to Sparky, who had pitched five innings the day before. In the eighth inning, down 3–1, Willie Randolph, a quietly consistent player, singled. Thurman struck out against a tough right-handed reliever named Doug Bird. I slapped Bird's first pitch into right field and we had two runners on. The drama increased: Billy sent Reggie to the plate as a pinch hitter. This was no time for personal feuds. Whitey Herzog let Bird pitch to Reggie. After sitting all game, Reggie fouled off a couple of pitches and then pushed a ground single into center for a hit. It was 3–2.

Herzog brought in Dennis Leonard, his best pitcher, to start the ninth with a 3–2 lead. Blair singled: Billy was a genius. Roy White walked. Mickey Rivers came up and everybody expected a bunt, but using his instinct, Billy ordered Rivers to hit away, knowing his speed would make it almost impossible to double him up, even if he hit a grounder at somebody. Even an out could serve the same purpose as a bunt. Rivers cracked a single past third, and Blair scored to tie the game at 3–3. Randolph hit a sacrifice fly, George Brett made an error—and we won the game. Three runs in the ninth, 5–3.

For the second straight time, we were American League champions, and the clubhouse erupted. Reggie held his private little press conference in the corner but the rest of us shared the joy. George was walking around, shaking hands, congratulating the players, talking to the press, and beaming with satisfaction. Billy walked up behind him in the champagne-drenched clubhouse, held a bottle high above George's head and turned it over. "There," Billy said. "That's for trying to fire me." Now that is ballsy.

I had just finished my best year in the big leagues. I had been platooned the first four months of the season, but in August started playing every day, and responded with one of the best hot streaks of my career. I ended the regular season hitting .330. I had gotten seven hits in twenty-one at bats in the playoffs for a .333 average and was ready for the World Series. For the first time since Los Angeles had swept New York in 1963, the Yankees would play the Dodgers for the World Championship.

We flew into Newark Airport that night, where more than four thousand screaming baseball fans surrounded us—our flight number had been announced over the air—and we had to fight our way to the baggage counters. By the time I finally got home I was exhausted, but Anita and I stayed up a good part of the night anyway, talking and laughing about going to the World Series again.

"This time I'm after the winning share," I told her.

"This time," she kidded, "you better get it."

A lot of fans in New York still haven't forgiven the Dodgers for moving from Brooklyn and you better believe the emotions ran high that first game in the Stadium, and even higher when, in the twelfth inning of a 3–3 game, Paul Blair singled home the winning run. The next day was a letdown, as Catfish Hunter was hit hard—"The sun don't shine on the same dog's ass all the time," he said afterward—but Mike Torrez won the third game, Ron Guidry the fourth, and, after a shellacking by Don Sutton in the fifth, Torrez came on again in the sixth game and we won, 10–4. We were the world champions.

I'm reciting this because nobody remembers it. When anybody says 1977 World Series, somebody else always says, "Mr. October." Thurman Munson started calling Reggie that name after his big hit in the playoffs, and soon everybody began using it. Mr. October hit a home run in the fourth game, which we won 4–2. He hit a home run in his final time up in our losing fifth game. Then, in the sixth game, he hit three consecutive home runs off three different pitchers in three at bats, each time on the first pitch, the first off starter Burt Hooton, the second off reliever Elias Sosa, and the third, a tremendous shot to deep center off knuckleball pitcher Charlie Hough. It was the most incredible slugging performance by one hitter I had ever seen or hope to see. Steve Garvey of the Dodgers said later, "I must admit, when Reggie hit his third home run and I was sure nobody was looking, I applauded in my glove." It was as satisfying an ending to a season as anybody could have. It would carry Reggie through the winter, get a candy bar named after him, and put his name in the record books. It wouldn't end the Yankee soap opera, though. No, there was still plenty of that to come.

As for myself, it was just a thrill to walk to the plate those last few days in the Stadium that October and hear the fans screaming, "Loouu, Loouu, Loouu." It was a wonderful feeling.

"Remember to get out," Graig Nettles needled, "before it turns to boo, boo, boo."

There was still plenty of time left for that. There was still more of Sweet Lou to be heard from, more of Mr. October, more of Battling Billy. If 1977 had been dramatic and traumatic, 1978 would be even more so.

The Fun at Fenway

In the winter of 1977, George invited me to fly out in a commercial jet with him to the Jimmy Ellis–Ken Norton heavyweight championship fight in Las Vegas. It wasn't just because he was a fight fan. George wanted to see Al Rosen.

"I want to talk to him about taking over as GM of the ballclub," George said. "Gabe is leaving to go back to Cleveland and I think Al can do the job for us."

"He's a fine baseball man. I knew him well in Cleveland."

"He can take over a lot of the burden from me. I hope I can convince him to come with us. I want you to encourage him about the ballclub."

Rosen had been a star third baseman for the Cleveland Indians—and one of George's heroes—then gone into the investment business and done well. He and George had first become acquainted through an outfit called Group 66, a Cleveland civic group started by sixty-six businesses aimed at the promotion of Cleveland. Then tragedy struck: Rosen's wife become ill, suffered a mental breakdown, and eventually committed suicide. Business reversals followed shortly thereafter, and Rosen moved away from Cleveland. He went to work for Caesar's Palace, met and married a lovely lady named Rita, helped her through her own emotional crisis—the death of a teenage son—and then one day George Steinbrenner knocked on his door. Rosen leaped at the realization of a dream. He was back in baseball.

Now Gabe Paul had moved back to Cleveland and Al Rosen was named executive vice-president. He was going to be George's number-one guy in running the New York Yankees—and it was a terrific team he had taken over. We were at our peak and getting better. If the old line about the rich getting richer was ever evident, it was in 1978 when the best team in baseball added the best right-handed relief pitcher in baseball, Rich (Goose) Gossage, to the best lefthanded relief pitcher in baseball, Sparky Lyle.

George had been intent on signing Goose ever since Birdie Tebbetts, a former big league manager and catcher and one of his trusted aides, had wired the office, "Don't let any other American League East contender sign him." George knew Gossage's ninety-six-mile-an-hour fastball could turn a team around. Sparky would be hurt—there really was room for only one premier short man on a team then—but Goose had to be signed if he were available.

Spring training began as it had in 1977. Reggie was late. The press ate it up. Billy steamed. The soap opera was in high gear from opening day. Tired, tired, tired. It was becoming a depressing act.

"I wish I could afford to quit," I told one reporter. "I'm sick of coming to the park every day and hearing all this garbage about Reggie, Billy, and George. It isn't baseball anymore. I hate to walk into the clubhouse. I'm bored by it. It's disgusting."

"Lou, the kids need shoes," Anita said to me one day. "Be quiet."

It was true. I could make a few dollars in the stock market, or dabbling with the horses, or even getting into a few real estate deals—but I needed those baseball bucks. I shut up. More important, once the game started, all the nonsense was forgotten. I just loved the competition.

Besides, we would be more competitive than ever with Goose on our side. I'd known him from his days with the White Sox, where I had hit him reasonably well. He was a fastball pitcher and I was a fastball hitter. Then he'd left the league, recorded twenty-six saves for Pittsburgh in 1977, declared himself a free agent, and by the grace of George's bankroll, became a Yankee.

Goose looked like a big, fun-loving type of guy, but his personality changed on the mound. He had the heart of a lion. He loved pressure. He wanted the ball in the big spot. He could intimidate a hitter just with a stare, then throw that ball in at incredible speeds. He'd come into a game in a tight spot, take the ball from the manager without conversation, start warming up, and you knew he was telling the other team. "There is no way, no way at all, you can beat me." Few did.

As great as he was, as successful as he became, as close a friend as he developed into, there was some tinge of sadness to Goose's arrival. I was hurt watching the demise of Sparky. Everyone's success in baseball is achieved at somebody's expense. Sparky was the loser here. Sparky had been the heart and soul of the Yankees for many years. He had made them competitive out of the bullpen. He had helped the ballclub climb that mountain of success, and now he was being pushed down the other side, shunted aside, because a younger, stronger, newer arm had come by.

We tried to kid with him about it, but it was hard. He knew he was being placed in a secondary role. He knew his days as a Yankee were numbered. He showed some bitterness, but to his credit it was never addressed at Goose. He felt let down by the organization and unappreciated, but he also respected Goose as a man and as a pitcher, and knew the decisions were not his fault. He acted with much dignity at the toughest stage of his career. Still, it was painful for me to see. We would go out at night, have a drink, talk about everything but baseball, and suddenly he would look up, with that sadness in his face, his mustache drooping, his eyes a little teary, and ask, "Why me?"

As good as Goose was, we started slipping back quickly that year, and by early June had fallen eight games behind the hot Boston Red Sox. Goose had bought a home in Wyckoff, New Jersey, near my Allendale home, and I drove in with him one day. Suddenly he said, "What in hell is wrong with this team? You guys won easy last year and now I join the club and we can't win. It must be me."

There was nothing from Goose about any straws stirring the drink.

"We have a good ballclub. Don't worry. Let's all just do our jobs. The Yankees have a history of coming from behind."

It was the most prophetic thing I would say all summer.

The Yankees had an abundance of talent in 1978, and we stayed eight or ten games over .500 most of the first half of the season—but who noticed? The Red Sox were having a spectacular year, twenty games over .500 at one point, and looked like they would blow the league apart and march into the World Series. Meanwhile, at the Stadium every day brought another fuss, mostly around Reggie and Billy, sometimes around Thurman and George, once in a while involving some other disgruntled player battling over his salary or his playing time. We complained so much we were like a bunch of old ladies. We had many quality players. How could we be so far out of the race?

Of all the important players on the team, Ron Guidry alone stayed away from the controversy. The skinny left-hander from Louisiana was having a phenomenal year. Nobody ever had a better year pitching in my time. He was shy, reserved, a great athlete who could field his position, run better than anybody on the club, catch a fly ball smoothly in outfield drills, and probably even hit if he'd had the chance. And how he could pitch, with that nasty slider Sparky Lyle taught him and that ninety-five-mile-an-hour fastball coming from that skinny frame. Billy Martin and pitching coach Art Fowler both fell in love with him in 1976. I'd be having a beer with Art, and he would say in that South Carolina drawl of his, "Ahh just think that kid's gonna be a great one." Billy had wanted to keep him in 1976, but there had been roster problems and Guidry had gone back to Syracuse, worked as a relief pitcher and come to stay in 1977. Guidry spoke with a French Cajun twang, and when he joined the club he was self-conscious, shy, and withdrawn. He didn't seem to have much confidence, and struggled so badly that Gabe Paul said to him early in the year, "My eyes tell me you can throw, the reports tell me you are a great prospect, and the other clubs tell me they want you. How can so many people be wrong?" By late in 1977, however, he had gained all the confidence he needed and in 1978, when he was 25–3, he was the best I ever saw.

Just as Guidry was clearly the best pitcher in baseball in 1978, Graig Nettles was clearly the best third baseman. He was a consummate professional, a hard knocker, a guy who played the game tough and physical. When he'd first joined the club nobody had considered him that good a third baseman, but he'd just been learning his trade. He evolved into a leader of the club on the field, which is more important than being a leader in the clubhouse. He didn't give you that rah-rah bullshit. He was the kind of guy who hit a three-run homer in the eighth inning to give you the win. He had a quick wit and a mastery of one-liners, and could defuse a serious situation with one snappy remark. After Sparky Lyle was sent away to Texas, we struggled to explain it to the press. We talked of his slider, his courage, his ability to get a big hitter out in a big spot. Then Graig, who had been sitting on his soft beach chair in the corner, spoke up. "Sparky went from Cy Young to sayonara." Well, what else was there to say?

Another time, we had been ordered to attend a welcome home luncheon at the Sheraton Centre in New York after being away nearly two months in Florida spring training. George insisted we all show up. Those that didn't would be fined. Graig didn't show and he was fined. "If he wants a third baseman, he has me," Graig told the press. "If he wants an after-dinner speaker, he should get Georgie Jessel."

Though Graig tried to stay out of the controversies, he was very hard-headed, opinionated, and stubborn. If he made up his mind about something, you couldn't reason with him. He never complained about playing the game. His complaints were with George for not paying him what Graig thought he was worth, and with Reggie for bringing so much attention on Reggie. I have no deep psychological explanations for Graig's attitude toward Reggie. He just didn't like him, and Reggie didn't like Nettles. It was that simple.

All of the Yankees, it seemed, were strong personalities. Reggie, of course, was overbearing, Graig was supremely confident, Guidry quietly secure, and Willie Randolph, our second baseman, always cocky. Willie was the glue of our infield. He felt slighted because he was underpaid, compared to others, but it might have been his own fault. He wouldn't gamble on free agency and always signed long-term contracts. Two or three years into the contract, standards would change and Willie would become unhappy. He would express some of that resentment by taking an occasional day off when he was hurt. For all that, though, he was the key guy in our infield; a very tough offensive player as well as one of the best gloves around. As the years passed, he matured and became more outgoing, and is now a leader on the club. If they ever name another Yankee captain, Willie would be my candidate.

Willie's partner that year was Bucky Dent. Bucky had been the regular shortstop on the White Sox before we got him in the spring of 1977, and he was the kind of player you didn't appreciate until you saw him play every day. He was steady if not spectacular; a good hitter and a hustler. You don't need greatness at every position to win. You need steadiness and consistency, and Bucky certainly gave us that. Later on fame and fortune would come to Bucky and it would hurt him. He couldn't live up to his reputation. The pressure got to him. However, in 1977 and 1978, he was as steady a shortstop as there was in the league.

With Reggie hitting home runs, Graig slugging big hits and playing a marvelous third base, Guidry on a tear, Randolph and Dent and Munson and White and Chambliss and Rivers and, yes, Piniella, all having good years—what were we doing fourteen games back on July 17?

Billy was under enormous pressure. His job seemed to be on the line every day. As we slipped back in the race, the newspapers continued to hound George about him. One or the other of them would ask him every day what Billy's status was. George could never really say Billy was in or out, because George changed his mind about it almost every day. If we won a couple of games, he thought we were starting to move. Billy was safe. If we lost a couple of games, it appeared we had slipped out of the race for good. Billy was in danger. George simply wanted to win. Nothing else mattered. After one hard loss, reporters caught George as he left his office. "What's Billy's status?" he was asked. "Ask Al Rosen. It's his decision," George said. Nobody believed that. Only one man made the decisions on the Yankees. It wasn't Al Rosen.

Billy grew more tense as we moved into late July. "I'm sick and tired of hearing about being fired," Martin told the press. "I gave George Steinbrenner one hundred percent loyalty and I expect it in return."

I look back at those days now and realize how much Billy Martin loved the Yankees and loved wearing that pinstriped uniform. I don't think he was concerned about a baseball job. If he lost that one, he would get another—everybody knew Billy was a good baseball man. It was just that he loved the Yankees so much. I understand it now, because I feel the same way.

"When he was my manager at Texas," Jim Spencer, the lefthanded-hitting first baseman once told me, "he used to talk all the time about managing the Yankees. I always thought that was a strange thing for a Texas manager to be talking about."

There was a lot of talk about Billy's health. There were rumors of strange ailments. We heard them all, but Billy said nothing. "There's nothing wrong with my health that a few victories wouldn't cure," he said. Billy is a thin man. When things are going bad for the ballclub, he seems even thinner. In a close game, you could see the veins popping out of his neck. We always knew when George had called him on his office phone. Billy would come out of his manager's office and sit on the training table to calm down. His eyes seemed sunken and his skin seemed pulled tight on his face.

It was the only time I hated, really hated, being part of that team. We could feel an explosion coming, and it all started one Monday night at the Stadium in a game against Kansas City. The score was tied in the tenth inning and Thurman singled. Reggie, batting fourth, was ordered to bunt, which incensed him. The game was on television, remember. He wanted the opportunity to win it with a homer. The KC infield moved in. Martin, sensing that, switched signs: Reggie was to swing. Al Hrabosky, the Mad Hungarian, threw a fastball and Reggie made a half-ass attempt at a bunt, and missed it for a strike. On the bench, Billy was livid. "What the hell is he doing?" he screamed.

Dick Howser, the third-base coach, walked down the line and instructed Reggie verbally that Billy wanted him to swing. The next pitch came, Reggie tried another bunt—and missed again. This was not a case of a sign being missed. This was deliberate, a baseball mutiny. Then Reggie bunted a third time, missed, and was struck out. The Royals won, 9–7, in the eleventh inning. Billy was as angry as I had ever seen him. He stormed around the clubhouse. He threw a clock radio to the floor. He flung a drinking glass against a door. "No interviews," he screamed as reporters approached him.

Reggie Jackson was suspended for five days without pay, before rejoining us in Chicago. We had won five games in a row without him and cut the Boston lead to ten games. Jackson returned to a wild press scene, telegrams of welcome all over his locker, flowers on his footstool, press at his elbow. "I'll play as hard as I can, as I always have if the manager lets me play," Reggie told the press.

After another winning game that day, with Reggie on the bench, we prepared to fly to Kansas City. Billy waited for the team bus in the press room. He had a few pops.

Then he had a few more. While he was there, White Sox owner Bill Veeck told him that George had discussed a managerial swap earlier in the season, with Bob Lemon coming to New York and Billy going to the White Sox. That upset him. Then he read a reporter's story about what Reggie had said in the clubhouse, the sarcasm spilling all over the page. That infuriated him. Soon it all spilled over. Billy walked through the airport, talked with reporters about Reggie and George, and blurted out, "One's a born liar and the other is convicted." When we heard that, we knew he was gone. In a tearful scene before national television cameras in the lobby of the Crown Center Hotel, Billy was "resigned" by the Yankees. Bob Lemon took over on July 25.

"We'll go back to the lineup that won it last year and see what happens," Lemon said. "We'll see how far we can go."

Lemon put Thurman back behind the plate, after Billy had played him in the outfield to rest his ailing knees. Mickey Rivers would be free to run. Bucky Dent would play all nine innings without looking over his shoulder for a pinch hitter. And Reggie Jackson would play right field and bat fourth.

We still had time to regroup and win. We knew the Red Sox had a history of staggering down the stretch. We counted on it. If it had been Baltimore or Detroit in front of us, we might have been licked, but the Red Sox often folded. They were afraid of the thunder of the hoofbeats of the Yankees. It was always in their heads. History was on our side.

Bob Lemon came in and gave us a sea of calm, an air of serenity, and all of a sudden we were just baseball players. We were no longer a traveling carnival welcomed into each town with screaming headlines proclaiming Billy says this and Reggie says that and George says the other. All of a sudden, the sportswriters were writing about the games, about hits, runs, and errors, Guidry's pitching and Thurman's hitting and Graig's fielding, instead of the soap opera. Lem sat back quietly on the bench, made out the lineup card and let us play. Then, win or lose, he had a few pops at night, relaxed again, and the next day he laughed and called you "meat."

We were still nine games out on August 13. Boston started sputtering, not staggering yet, just making some strange noises. Fred Lynn was hurt. Jim Rice was hurt. Carlton Fisk was hurt. Carl Yastrzemski stopped hitting. Bill Lee, the flaky lefthander, got dropped from the Boston starting rotation, got into a shouting match with manager Don Zimmer, and called him a gerbil.

On August 15, Guidry won his seventeenth game of the season, shutting out Oakland 6–0. The Red Sox lost. We were eight games out of first place. There was more needling in the clubhouse. The guys were looser. Gossage had ended one game by getting the hitter on a long fly to centerfield where Mickey Rivers had caught it just in front of the fence. The next night, Gossage came to the park and Rivers said, "When you come in the game, man, I'm starting out with my back to the plate. I gotta chase those long ones down." Sure enough, the next time Gossage came in, Rivers did turn his back to the plate. And, sure enough, the batter hit a long fly and Rivers had to run a mile to get it. "Man, I was only kidding," he told Goose.

We lost two in a row to Seattle and fell to eight and a half games back. It was upsetting, but not depressing. We knew we were playing good baseball. "These guys are professionals," Lemon told the press. "I don't think it will bother them." Then the next night, Guidry won his eighteenth to start us on a seven-game winning streak. We knew that had to bother Boston a lot. They had to be hearing footsteps and seeing pinstripes in their sleep. We were now only six and a half games back as we entered September. The weather had cooled, the kids were getting ready to go back to school, we started watching the scoreboard and checking the schedule. We were listed for four games in Boston, starting September 7. Those were the games we watched carefully. Seattle shut us out on September 1, but the Red Sox also lost and we stayed six and a half games back. Thurman sat in front of his locker when it was over. He appeared drained. He was catching every day and his knee was giving him a lot of trouble. "I looked at the schedule. If we can pick up two and a half games this week, we can go into Boston only four down. Then we can beat them." He looked up at me with a strange expression. I drove home that night with numbers dancing in my head. We had three more with Seattle and three with Detroit before we went to Boston. I had told some sportswriters in the middle of August that we could still win the pennant. "If we get to Boston for those four games only four games out, we will win it," I said then. I don't know if I really believed it.

Ed Figueroa beat Seattle the next night, with Reggie and Chris Chambliss hitting home runs. On Labor Day, September 4, Guidry beat Detroit, 9–1, for his twentieth victory of the year. We lost a tough second game, but Tidrow beat the Tigers on September 5, and Figueroa won the next night, 8–2. We flew to Boston for the showdown series. We were exactly where we wanted to be—four games back, with four against the Red Sox at Fenway.

We could see the tension in the faces of the Red Sox players as we took batting practice. They hung around to watch us plaster that wall. They knew it was slipping away. They had had a first-place lead of eight and a half games as late as August 21, and now it was only four. We couldn't wait for the games to begin.

In my time, no team ever inflicted such a pounding on another club as we did to the Red Sox those four games. We scored forty-two runs and collected sixty-seven hits. Ken Clay beat Mike Torrez in the series opener, 15–3. Jim Beattie won the next game 13–2. We were two games out. Guidry was scheduled the next day. A reporter asked a veteran player if he thought the Red Sox were choking. "Choking? I can't say that." Then he laughed out loud. "You can say it if you want." Guidry was brilliant again, and pitched a shutout. We were one game away. The Fenway fans began filing out of the park in the seventh inning. I almost felt sorry for them. Their team had disappointed them many times before. Then it was the final game. Figueroa pitched a 7–4 victory—and we were tied for first place.

I had hit a triple, double, and a home run in the 13–2 game, and felt as confident as I had ever felt in my career. Hitting has its own momentum. When you are confident and seeing the ball well, line drives rush off your bat. When you are in a slump, the ball darts by, small, twisting, and hard to find. The next morning, after a flight to Detroit, I rushed out to get the papers and read all about it. It was the first Yankee four-game sweep in Fenway since 1943. We had picked up fourteen games in the standings in fifty-three days.

We knew we had them then. We pushed our lead to three and a half games in one week—and then suddenly cooled off. This time it was Boston's turn. With the pressure gone now and the pennant apparently lost, the Red Sox came back at us and won seven straight in the final week of the season. This was insane! One the final Saturday of the season we were one game ahead. Figueroa pitched a shutout for his twentieth win of the year, the first Puerto Rican–born pitcher ever to accomplish that feat. We had a one-game lead, one game to go, and Catfish to pitch it. I couldn't have been more confident.

Catfish had all that experience and poise. But baseball is a funny game. He was hit hard, Rick Waits had good stuff for the Indians, and Cleveland beat us, 9–2, while Boston smothered Toronto, 5–0, behind Luis Tiant. The race was tied. We had just finished playing 162 games, were 99–63, and hadn't settled a thing.

"I think it is destiny that we should settle this thing head to head," I told Thurman.

"I would rather have settled it today," he said.

"If we lose we can blame it on George," said Nettles. "He lost the coin toss."

Several weeks earlier, when it hadn't seemed important, there'd been a coin flip for the location of a one-game playoff, should one be necessary. George had lost it, and the playoff was scheduled for Boston. Now we would have fun in Fenway. That was the way the damn season should end anyway. What better way to finish? Both teams had won ninety-nine games, we had come from fourteen games back to catch them, and they had caught us on the final day of the season. We were still confident. We had Ron Guidry scheduled, the best in baseball, and they had used their best, Luis Tiant, on Sunday to tie us and so had to pitch Mike Torrez. He had been with us the year before, before Boston had obtained him as a free agent, and we knew his stuff. We had won four in a row up there less than a month ago. We were ready. As we packed our bags for the trip, George walked into the clubhouse.

He had a gloomy look on his face. He wanted that win guaranteed. I walked up to him and laughed. "George, if you hadn't lost that flip, we would at least be playing in the Stadium. You didn't do your part. Let's see if we can do our part and win."

"You guys won all four up there and only two out of three here this month," George said with bravado. "That's why I lost the flip."

"And besides," I reminded him, "you'll get another big payday at the gate."

He laughed at that one. The club seemed loose. We were looking forward to the game. We dressed easily and boarded the bus for the ride to the airport. As soon as I got onto the bus, I saw Catfish sitting in his accustomed seat. I got on him immediately.

"It's a good thing we got you out of the way," I told him. "If you pitched in Boston, with that fence, it would have been ninety runs instead of nine runs. That's what we get for trying to win a pennant with a soy bean farmer from North Carolina."

"Jim Wohlford. That's who we needed out there today. Jim f——g Wohlford."

Mickey Rivers wasn't on the bus. "Where's Mickey?" Killer Kane, the traveling secretary, yelled.

"He went to the racetrack," said Nettles. "He read the schedule and saw that today the season ended. Tomorrow's an off day."

Soon Rivers showed up. "I don't play no extra games without more money," he announced.

"Your pay gets reduced," I told him. "George has to take the expenses of this trip out of somebody's check."

The bus ride was fun, and the bantering continued on the plane, guys needling one another, everybody awake and alert, nobody depressed or worried. This was a confident bunch of professional athletes about to do a job. I walked by George and got on him a little bit.

"Remember in Milwaukee, just before the All-Star break, you told the press we were too far back to win it. You gave up on us. You have to be the luckiest guy in the world. We are going to win this thing tomorrow and you'll make all that money. Don't give up on us so soon."

The Boss laughed and said nothing. He would withhold all his comments until we finished playing the next day.

In less than an hour, we were in Boston. You could feel the drama, the excitement, the tension in the airport. This wasn't a routine game in June we were coming up for. Boston fans were waiting for planes and began yelling when they saw us, "We'll kick your ass tomorrow. The Red Sox will kill you." The shopkeepers in the airport stores poked their heads out, and a few laughingly booed us as we walked by, and even some of the airport personnel in their uniforms laughed and gave us the thumbs-down sign as we crossed their paths on the way to the team bus. We could feel the electricity in the air.

We boarded our bus for the thirty-minute ride to the Sheraton Boston and the needling was ferocious. We had all had a few pops on the plane, everybody was loose, and we ripped one another about choking the next day, about blowing our entire careers with one bad game, about embarrassing ourselves on national television before the whole country. All the time, the slow, drawling voice of

Catfish Hunter sounded in my ears. "Don't choke, Lou, don't choke."

We checked into our rooms, I turned on the television in time to see us on the news, losing to Cleveland while the Rex Sox won, and our bags were delivered. It was only about eight o'clock, and even though we had a day game tomorrow for that playoff, it was too early to settle in for the night. I decided I would follow my usual routine when I had a game the next day in Boston. I walked down the street to Daisy Buchanan's bar. I figured I could have a couple of Jack Daniels and water to relax me before I went to sleep.

I had one drink and then another, and looked around the room, and all of a sudden realized I wasn't alone. I saw Thurman and Graig and Sparky and Goose and another eight or ten guys on the team. Each of us was following his normal routine. We may have been close to playing the biggest game of our lives, but we would approach it as we approached any other game. I was happy about that. If we all had stayed in our rooms that night, the pressure may have eaten us up. We would have thought about the game, played it in our heads, and tossed all night. It's like a horse who leaves his race at the post. He is sweating while he is being saddled, he is nervous getting to the gate, and he has no energy left for the run.

Even though this was a playoff game, one other thing made it routine. No wives were with us. The Yankees had always taken the players' wives to the League Championship Series and the World Series. We'd expected to fly out to Kansas City Sunday night after winning, but instead Anita drove the car home after the Sunday loss, we flew on to Boston, and the wives watched on television. It was probably just as well. I don't think Anita and the other wives would have enjoyed sitting in the stands during that game.

I got a good night's sleep—a couple of Jack Daniels will do that for you—and woke up early. Usually I get dressed slowly, have a leisurely breakfast, and make the team bus. I dressed rapidly that sunny morning of October 2, drank a cup of coffee in my room and took a cab to the ballpark, arriving shortly before ten o'clock for the one o'clock game. I expected to be all alone—half the team was already there.

It was a spectacular day in Boston, not a cloud in the sky, hardly any wind, a perfect fall afternoon. I could imagine Harvard and Yale playing on a crisp fall Saturday afternoon like this. Six or eight guys were already dressed. A few others were in the small trainer's room getting taped. There was a pot of coffee and I took another cup. Everybody there seemed loose. It seemed routine. Most of the comments concerned the beautiful weather.

We went out for batting practice and there was very little clowning around: We were getting close to business. We took our hitting, and some of the Boston players filtered around the batting cage as the minutes ticked away. I said something to Carl Yastrzemski about the clear sky, and something to George Scott about using a heavy bat so late in the season, and something to Fred Lynn, but mostly I looked over at them and then whispered to Thurman, "They look more relaxed."

We had clobbered them four straight in early September and you could see the tenseness in their faces then. They hadn't been around to talk at the batting cage while we were out there. They'd known they were blowing a big lead. The color seemed to drain from their faces as that series went on. Not this time. They were loose, comfortable, confident. The lead had been blown, but they had come back to tie. They had won on Sunday and we had lost. I knew in my heart this would be a tough, tough baseball game. The Boston Red Sox were prepared. It was a different ballclub from the disorganized bunch we had beaten earlier, and they were in their park, in front of their fans, in their home environment.

"We'll have to beat them, they won't beat themselves," I told Reggie.

"They'll have to beat Gator."

Ron Guidry—the skinny lefthander from Louisiana's alligator country—was our confidence booster. Our regular lineup—Rivers, Munson, Piniella, Jackson, Nettles, Chambliss, White, Brian Doyle (playing for the injured Willie Randolph), and Dent—was posted on the scoreboard, and Guidry warmed up easily in the bullpen with Fran Healy. With Guidry pitching, Sparky and Goose both ready in the bullpen, our best defensive team, minus Randolph, out there and Reggie as the DH, we knew we could win if we could score a few runs.

Mike Torrez threw his first pitch for a strike to Mickey, the crowd howled, and then the ballpark grew eerily silent. The crowd seemed tense and deathly still. They wanted this game very badly, and they wanted the Red Sox to explode early so they could holler and shake off some of that tension. They knew we had beaten them four in a row in September. We went through a scoreless first inning and the silence was weird. Then Yastrzemski hit a second-inning homer, and the place erupted. The noise almost hurt my ears. Their heroes were on top. It was almost like New Year's Eve in Times Square. You could almost get caught up in the excitement. I had to fight hard to retain my concentration and not jump around with those cheers. Everybody knew this would be a fun game to remember, win or lose.

The Red Sox picked up another run on a double by Rick Burleson and a single by Jim Rice, and held that 2–0 lead into the seventh inning. The mood of our bench was still confident. This was Fenway Park, where runs are always scored in clusters, where you could easily hit one over that Green Monster and get ahead in a hurry. Going into the bottom of the sixth, I had told Guidry, "Keep them from scoring any more. We'll get those runs back somehow." This was a guy who was 24–3, and I was telling him to keep the game close. He got out of the sixth and after Nettles flied out, Chris Chambliss, who had won the pennant for us with one swing against Kansas City in 1976, started us off with a hit. Roy White, who always did his job without any fanfare, squeezed a single through the middle, and we had two runners on. Jim Spencer hit for Doyle and flied out.

"If we blow this," I told Thurman, "we're in trouble."

Bucky Dent was up. He took a pitch for a ball and fouled the next pitch off his foot. He jumped around for a while, trainer Gene Monahan sprayed his foot, and Bucky started back into the box. The next hitter was Rivers. "Here," Mickey said as he pushed a bat toward Bucky, "use this. I feel it will be lucky for you." Dent took his bat. I looked into the Boston dugout and could see manager Don Zimmer squirming. He knew Torrez had a history of getting tired late in the game. I looked out toward their bullpen and saw two pitchers throwing. I was sitting on the top step of the dugout in the corner and looked back at Bucky just as he swung. Torrez had hung a slider to Bucky and he hit it out toward left field. I watched the flight of the ball and I watched the wall and I watched Jim Rice moving back in left field all at once. I could tell from the swing and the sound that Bucky hadn't gotten it all, but it was going out there pretty well, and all of a sudden it disappeared beyond that Green Monster. All hell broke loose on our bench, with Lemon jumping out of the dugout, and the rest of us shouting and clapping and waving as Bucky made that slow journey around the bases with the three-run homer.

It was as if someone had dropped a huge tent over Fenway Park. The place was absolutely still. You could hear a fan cough and you could almost feel the air going out of their balloon. I remember the sound of a fan in a seat far behind us cracking a peanut shell open. Bucky Dent had turned Fenway Park into the world's largest morgue.

Rivers came up and walked. Zimmer emerged to a crescendo of boos and led Torrez away. Bob Stanley came in and Rivers immediately stole second. Thurman doubled him home for a 4–2 lead, and I flied out to end the inning. My heroic time was still to come.

Guidry got an out in the bottom of the seventh, walked a hitter and left for Goose. He threw hard and the Red Sox went down easily. Reggie hit a huge homer in the top of the eighth to make the score 5–2. Before the inning ended, I turned to Lemon and said, "I sure hope nobody hits a ball to me. I can't see out there."

From the sixth inning on, the sun had become a factor. In that cloudless sky it now hung over the top of the small park, just over the roof, shining directly into the eyes of the right fielder. Sunglasses were useless now—it was too bright and too direct. Just let the ball stay away from right field, I prayed. In the eighth, with Goose throwing and our confidence at a peak, the Red Sox fought back. Jerry Remy doubled and Yaz singled for a run to make it 5–3. Then Carlton Fisk singled and Fred Lynn singled. Now the game was 5–4, but Goose toughened and got Butch Hobson and George Scott to keep it at 5–4. We were three outs away from the AL East title.

Dwight Evans flied out to start the Boston ninth. Burleson walked. Remy, a line-drive lefthanded hitter, came up with that sun blinding me from above the roof. Paul Blair was in center now and he shaded a bit to right. I was hoping if Remy did hit a ball toward right center, Blair would get it. If he hit it directly at me, there would be problems. Goose threw a low inside fastball and Remy pulled it hard on a line to right. I saw the ball leave the bat and that was the last time I saw it. I knew if the ball got by me the runner would go to third or maybe score the tying run. I couldn't allow Burleson to see that I had lost it in the sun. I kept my composure and as I searched for the ball, I kept backtracking as hard as I could. I wanted to give myself more room to find it. Out of the corner of my eye, I saw that damn ball landing a few feet to my left on the grass. I had stretched out my arms to signal Blair that I couldn't see it and now it was there—I lunged and it slapped into my glove. I whirled to my right and fired a throw to third. It was the best throw I had ever made in my entire career. I would never make one like that again. Nettles later said it was knee high, right on the bag, with good stuff on it. Burleson stopped at second. I wondered later, "Was that me or God who threw that ball?"

Jim Rice was the next hitter and hit a huge fly to right

center. Blair had been pulled over to left center for the righthanded slugger, and I went over and caught the ball. That one was easy to follow, because the trajectory was so high. If he'd been on third, Burleson would have scored easily to tie the game, but from second he could only move to third.

We were down to the last out. What a way to end the game and the season, the best relief pitcher in the game against one of the greatest players of all time. Goose facing Yaz. Carl had that aura of confidence about him. The way he strode up to home plate, the way he grabbed that dirt, the way he dug in. You knew he was ready, it was something he had been waiting for all those years. With one swing, he could beat his nemesis, the Yankees, he could propel his team into the playoffs, and he could electrify that home crowd and become a lasting hero. I couldn't help but think as I stood out there in right that maybe Boston's time had come, maybe all that agony they had suffered at the hands of the Yankees was finally about to be paid back. All the frustrating days of Ted Williams would be forgotten if Yaz hit one off that screen in left. A lesser man might choke, but not Carl. Goose let go a high fastball. Yaz was a little anxious, swung at a bad pitch and hit an easy foul to third. It seemed it took an hour to come down, but it did, and Graig caught it and leaped into the air, laughing with pure exhilaration. He was never one to show emotion, but he did that time and he jumped higher than I thought was possible. We had won the AL East title.

The players leaped off the bench to hug Goose and Thurman and Nettles at third and anybody else they could catch. I had a great vantage point from right field and could see George and Al Rosen turn to each other in the box behind our dugout and hug as hard as you could imagine. Then here comes George onto the field, like a general, a conquering hero, swaggering right to one man. He reached Bob Lemon in the midst of that crowd scene and hugged him right there in front of all those fans. It was so warm and nice and wonderful—George could have blown his entire image with that one spontaneous action.

The clubhouse scene was wild. The Boston clubhouse is tiny, about the size of my living room, and it was packed. The champagne was pouring and the television lights were on and the noise was overwhelming. Mike Lupica, the *Daily News* columnist, came up to me and asked about the ninth-inning play on Remy's hit.

"Was that lucky?" he said.

"Lucky? Lucky? We're not world champions for nothing," I said, silently thanking my stars.

It was true. We had played like world champions, we knew how to win. We had become close to one another as people in the second half of that season, we had learned to depend on and have confidence in one another. We knew we would win that game. We just knew it.

When it was over, my first thought was that I was grateful to God for the opportunity to be on that field. I was excited for the moment, for myself, my family, and my teammates. Most of all, I was excited for the organization. We understood the Yankee tradition that day. Even if none of us was a Ruth or a Gehrig or a DiMaggio or a Mantle, we had each carved our own niche in Yankee history, and that was something to be very proud of.

The airplane ride to Kansas City for the start of the American League Championship Series was a lot quieter than the journey from New York to Boston. We had just finished a grueling afternoon of baseball. We had won, but the job wasn't finished. We wanted to win the World Series, and Kansas City, as always, presented a formidable task. Most of us drank a glass of wine, had a quiet dinner on the plane, and slept the rest of the way there.

Jim Beattie, a kid with a lot of promise but not many victories, was assigned the opener, because the rest of the staff had been used up. If he was going to choke, this was the time to do it. He pitched a marvelous game, lasted into the sixth, when Ken Clay took over, and, with Reggie adding a homer, we won the first game at Kansas City, 7–1. Ed Figueroa was hit hard the next day, and they evened the series, 10–4, but we had Catfish for the third game and Guidry ready for the fourth and our confidence was high. In the third game we trailed 5–4 in the eighth; Doug Bird was pitching and Thurman was at bat. He had been hurting and hitting with little power and was very concerned. He had asked me more than once, "Lou, can I still hit?" His injuries were wearing him down. He thought more and more about giving up catching and moving to the outfield or first base, but a great player rises to the occasion, and on this occasion, Thurman hit the longest home run of his career, a line shot that traveled more than 440 feet into the bullpen. It won the game for us, 6–5, and that was the turning point. Guidry was brilliant again the next day, Goose saved it, and we won 2–1 to make it to the World Series for the third straight year.

Three things stand out in my mind about that World Series. The first is how down we were after the Dodgers jumped on us for two straight in Los Angeles. It was made even worse by the fact that Dodger coach Jim Gilliam had died just before the start of the Series, and the Dodger players made a maudlin show of dedicating the Series to him. After the first two wins they kept talking about how Gilliam had been helping them win, even though he had just passed away. It was all too much. We never talked about Ruth or Gehrig helping us out.

The second thing was how Graig Nettles put on the greatest performance at third base I had ever seen, in game three. Ron Guidry, a little tired by now, had less than his best stuff, but Nettles caught every ball down his way in spectacular fashion. I know all about Brooks Robinson, but nobody ever played the position any better than Nettles did that day, as we won 5–1.

And then there was the fourth game. We went on to win the fifth and sixth games easily, so the fourth game was the turning point, and what people remember most about it was Reggie managing to get hit on the basepaths with a throw from Dodger shortstop Bill Russell after I had hit a sinking line drive to open up the play.

We were down 3–1 in the sixth, Thurman was on

second, and Reggie was on first. I hit Tommy John's fastball on a line toward short. It was a sinking liner and it handcuffed Dodger shortstop Bill Russell. The ball hit the heel of his glove and fell at his feet. Thurman, always an alert base runner, started for third. Reggie, not sure if the ball would be caught, stood in the basepath. Russell stepped on second, forcing Jackson, and threw toward first to get me, but Reggie swiveled his hip and Russell's throw hit him and flew into right field. I raced safely past first base. Thurman raced home to score. Reggie kept us alive with his hip move. I've seen him dancing, but I never saw a two-step as good as that one.

We tied the game in the eighth, and then in the tenth, Roy White walked, Reggie singled, and I came up. Bob Welch threw his fastball, I timed it perfectly and smashed a single to right center as White crossed with the winning run. Winning a World Series game with a hit in the tenth inning is about as exciting a moment as I can remember.

In the clubhouse I told Graig, "The way the Dodgers walked off the field today, it won't take us more than two games to end this thing," and after we won the next day, too, I kidded Thurman. "All that has to happen is for the plane to get us there and we're world champions." That passed for ballplayer humor. When you fly as much as we do, you have to make flying jokes. The old Yankees used to say Yogi Berra was the luckiest man in the world and no plane would go down with Yogi on it. One kidding veteran player went to a store and got a headline made up: "Yankee plane crashes, 24 killed, Yogi lone survivor."

Well, we did win that sixth game and the Series. It was finally over and a good thing, too. It had been the most dramatic season of my career, but we were all burned out from the relentless pace of that pennant race, from the endless tension involving George and Reggie and Billy and the press all over us and the tension from that tough season, from the bitching about George and the bitching about salaries and the bitching about the bitching. We had won a blistering game in Boston, beaten a good

Kansas City team in four games, and now had come back from two down to win four straight against the Dodgers. I felt simply exhausted. My mind and body were limp. We were world champions again, but it didn't have the same ring as in 1977.

I went home to Temple Terrace, just outside Tampa, spent the winter fishing, playing golf, visiting friends, visiting the horses, and attending an occasional banquet. Before you knew it, it would be Christmas, we would be out shopping for gifts for the kids, and then New Year's. With George, the off-season seemed to get shorter and shorter. It seemed that I would go from a New Year's Eve party to my New York Yankees baseball cap. Sometimes I felt as if I should take my glove and ball and bat to the New Year's Eve party and leave right from there for the Yankee spring training camp in Fort Lauderdale. As I kissed Anita, who was pregnant with our son Derek, who would be born Opening Day, a happy welcome to 1979, I could hardly imagine what lay ahead for all of us that outrageous summer.

Thurman

Interstate 10, just outside Phoenix, is a huge, four-lane superhighway, the kind that crosses America, marked by impressive red, white, and blue signs. Late in the evening of October 27, 1978, Jerry Lemon, the twenty-six-year-old youngest son of Yankee manager Bob Lemon, was driving his new jeep some thirty miles outside Phoenix. The city lights shone in the distance and Jerry, the baby behind Jeff, thirty-one, and Jim, twenty-nine, moved along the highway to visit brother Jim. He had started out earlier that day from the family's Long Beach, California, home where the excitement seemed never-ending as old friends of Bob and old teammates and neighbors called and gathered to congratulate the manager of the Yankees on an incredible season. Shortly before midnight, for no explainable reason, Jerry Lemon lost control of his jeep, flipped over twice across two lanes of traffic, was thrown loose onto the highway, and fractured his skull. Arizona state police moved him unconscious to a West Phoenix hospital. He died four days later.

Bob Lemon had never been a very talkative fellow. A kidding remark here, a little needle there, but not a very gregarious guy. He had sat quietly through the drama of the 1978 finish, showing little emotion and reacting almost the same way to wins and losses. He enjoyed the wins, of course, but it would not have changed his life if we hadn't won. Other things seemed more important to him, especially those sons and his wife, Jane, and the friends he enjoyed back home in Long Beach. Now he came to spring training with an ache in his heart.

Al Rosen tried to comfort him, spending long hours with him after workouts, trying to ease him out of his depression. Lemon had always been a heavy, convivial drinker. He enjoyed the fraternalism of a drinking bout, enjoyed telling tall tales, laughing at himself, and spreading joy among his companions. That spring he was a serious drinker, unable to see much joy in the sport; he closed the hotel bar each night, numbed more often than lightened by the alcohol. "We tried everything," Al Rosen said. "Nothing worked. The hurt was too deep."

The players took advantage of his unhappy state and sensed that Lemon had lost his heart for the job. They started cheating on him, moving lazily through a drill, skipping a few running laps, ignoring some exercises, moving slowly out of the clubhouse for practice. Lemon did nothing. Rosen protected him when George complained the club looked lethargic. "You watch," George shouted at Rosen one day, "when the season starts we won't be ready."

George had done his part to improve the club for 1979. He had signed free agent pitcher Tommy John, one of the best lefthanders in the game, and Luis Tiant, our old nemesis from Boston. After the 1978 finish, we were as confident as a ballclub would be going into spring training. There was no way we could lose. We were sleep-walking through spring training, confident we could turn it on whenever we pleased. It drove George crazy. He seemed more brusque around the clubhouse, driving us harder, even more hungry for victory. The more we won—and now we had won three pennants and two World Championships in a row—the more he wanted. The man was never satisfied with second-best. The man the press called the Boss was insatiable for victory. Why not? It was his money.

With Lemon seemingly uninterested because of his grief, we took advantage. We were mostly a veteran team, and there were days it seemed he couldn't even get enough of us on a bus to play a spring game. Every day, three or four of us came down with an ache or an ailment, especially on those days we were scheduled for the longer bus trips from Fort Lauderdale to Vero Beach, where the Dodgers played, or Winter Haven and the Red Sox, or Fort Myers and the Royals. Fort Myers? That training site could cause more injuries than World War II.

As a result, and as George had predicted, we weren't ready when the 1979 season started. We got off to a bad start, George started sniping at us in the press, and the pressure started building a mere two weeks into the season. We had won three American League pennants in a row and the Yankee-haters of the world were sick of it. We played in Cleveland, and they gave out I-hate-the-Yankee-Hankees to the fans. We played in Boston, and they booed us from the first step onto the field.

On April 19, two weeks into the season, we suffered another crushing blow. Jim Palmer of the Orioles had beaten us that day in a listless game. Cliff Johnson, our big designated hitter, had not played and was upset. He was upset any day he didn't play, because he believed he could hit any pitcher who ever lived. Johnson was undressing in the clubhouse across the room from Goose Gossage. Reggie Jackson walked by and started needling Johnson about not playing. Jackson had become more a part of the clubhouse banter as his batting skills helped us win. He began discussing Palmer's pitching and suggested he wasn't throwing as hard as he had been, certainly not with the intimidating fastball Goose had. He turned to Johnson.

"How did you hit Goose when you were in the National League, Cliff?"

"He couldn't hit what he couldn't see," Gossage answered.

Johnson fired a rolled-up tape at Gossage. Jackson laughed and walked into the trainer's room. Gossage went into the sauna to bake his big body. As he emerged, Johnson was coming from the shower.

"Did you really mean that?" Johnson asked the pitcher. "Do you think I couldn't hit you?"

Gossage laughed. The large utility catcher and designated hitter threw a punch at the huge relief pitcher. Who knows what psychological baggage Johnson was carrying when he finally exploded at Goose? All I could hear from the clubhouse was the noise of two rolling trucks. When it was over, Goose had suffered a torn right thumb and would be out of action twelve weeks. He was the one irreplaceable player on the team. Dick Tidrow tried to fill the gap, but he was no Goose. George was so angered by his failure that he ordered Tidrow traded. Al Rosen did it reluctantly, knowing that Tidrow was a valuable long relief man. George can be very impulsive when he feels a player lets him down, and we all felt it then.

On June 18, with the team's record at 34–31, eight games behind Baltimore, Lemon was fired. Rosen cried when he was forced to tell Lemon he was finished. "Sometimes," Al said later, "it is better never to hire friends in baseball. Then you don't have to fire them." A month later, ashamed at what he had been forced to do and unable to work with the new manager, Rosen resigned.

That new manager was Billy Martin. The process of his return had begun the previous year, a bare two months after Billy's tearful resignation. The move had touched off a furor among the fans—letters, phone calls, banners—and George was no fool. After he got over his anger, he saw how Billy excited the fans, brought people to the park, set those turnstiles whirling.

I was sitting in the corner of the crowded dugout in Yankee Stadium on July 29, Old-Timers' Day, watching the old-timers being introduced. The names of Johnny Mize, and my old Baltimore skipper, Hank Bauer, and Gene Woodling, guys I had always enjoyed talking hitting with, were ringing over the loudspeakers. Then Frank Messer, the Yankee announcer, suddenly said, "I'll now turn the program over to public address announcer Bob Sheppard."

Sheppard, who has been the Yankee public address announcer for more than four decades, began, "The New York Yankees are happy to announce..."

Billy Martin appeared at the corner of the dugout in

his familiar Yankee uniform with that large number 1. I could see him because I was at the opposite end. I thought it was nice that he would be introduced for a bow so soon after leaving the club. Sheppard continued. "Bob Lemon will assume the duties of general manager . . ." A murmur ran through the park. If Lemon was to be the GM, wouldn't there have to be a new manager? The dugout grew still as we listened. Sheppard stretched out the words. "Managing the Yankees in the 1980 season and hopefully for many seasons after that will be . . ." Billy was on the top step of the dugout now, moving onto the field, a huge smile on his face, his cap in his hand, his eyes staring at the line of old papers assembled on the field, the noise in the Stadium growing . . . "Number 1 . . ." There was an explosion of sound in the park. The noise grew louder and louder. Sheppard announced the name, "Billy Martin," but it was lost in the wild cheering of the fans.

I turned to Thurman. "I'll be damned," I said.

My teammates were mingled on the bench with other old-timers, press people, photographers, and Yankee officials. I could spot one player clearly. Reggie Jackson had a scowl on his face and was staring at the sky.

After the emotional ceremonies ended, the regular game against the Twins began. Whitey Ford, the Hall of Fame Yankee pitcher, tells a story about that day. "I was introduced after Billy," Ford says. "My wife was at home watching on television. They introduced Billy, they made the announcement, and they were supposed to introduce me and Mickey and DiMaggio. When I got home that night, my wife said, 'Didn't they introduce you?' She hadn't heard or seen anything after Billy came on the field."

George later told a reporter about his decision to give Billy a second chance at managing the Yankees. "I just had this uneasy feeling about the entire situation. I felt bad for Billy. I really did. I just couldn't live with myself if I didn't do something to help him. I had to give him another chance."

George had done it again.

Lemon had clearly been hurt. The official announcement was that he would be the GM, but he'd just smiled. He'd known better than that. And now he was gone.

We made a little spurt for a while under Billy, but then settled down to our level. We were not a good ballclub. We had lost some of the enthusiasm and confidence of the previous years, we had lost Goose, we were in managerial turmoil again. Our flop was the happiest news the rest of the league could get.

It seemed we had become villains across America. We were only baseball players, trying to make a living and support our families, but we were the object of everybody's hatred. The newspapers ate us up. They made fun of the managerial switch. They headlined that the circus was in town again. They called us bullies for picking on the rest of the league. They criticized George for buying pennants, said he was a sore winner and an even sorer loser. In every town the newspapers stirred up animosity. They wanted their teams to kick our asses and rub our noses in the dirt. We developed a siege mentality, us against them. George had created some of this animosity by some of the things he had said and done, but it was the players who were out there taking the abuse. The Yankees of 1979 were a very tired team. We had finally been worn down. The magic was gone. The desire seemed gone. The other teams lay for us with their best pitching. Except for the Yankees of 1936–1939 and the Casey Stengel Yankees of 1949–1953, no team had ever won four pennants in a row. We weren't about to do it, either.

There was one piece of good news shortly after Billy came back. The Yankees purchased the contract of Bobby Murcer. He had always yearned to come back, especially after we'd started winning in 1976. He had been the one bright spot in those losing Yankee years and he'd missed being part of the Yankees' comeback. He joined us in Toronto, and Graig, Thurman, and I, who had all played with him and knew he could help us on the field, rejoiced.

Thurman was especially happy to see Bobby rejoin us. They were very close friends, as were their wives and families. Thurman told Bobby how tough the 1979 season was, even more so for him, since his knees ached constantly and he was concerned that his career would be cut short. "I can't afford to quit now. I have to play another three years. Then I'll be set. Then I'll have enough money to quit." Bobby was a sympathetic listener.

In the spring of 1978, Thurman had become interested in flying airplanes. He took flying lessons in Fort Lauderdale during spring training, he read flying magazines, he visited airports all over Florida. He enjoyed the freedom it gave him, away from the pressures of the field, and, especially, he loved the total control it gave him as a pilot.

On a couple of occasions that spring of 1978, I went up with him. The pilot-instructor was at his side, Thurman was at the controls, and I was in the one passenger seat those small planes have. I would listen to the instructors talk and they all seemed impressed at how well he was doing, how fast he was learning, how rapidly he was progressing in his pilot skills. In the spring of 1979, he earned his license and bought his first prop airplane.

Thurman was very proud of that plane. He was a man who was proud of material possessions. He had come from a humble background and never had had those things as a kid. He had several cars and kept them spotlessly clean and shining. He had accumulated real estate and made some good investments. He was constantly talking about baseball being a means to the things he really wanted to do later on, which were to develop huge real estate interests, make his family comfortable and happy, and enjoy the pleasures of the material things he had worked hard to get. In the spring of 1979 he was always thinking of the transition, and talking about having enough money to be secure in the years following baseball, which he knew were soon approaching. With his knees going, he knew his career would not last much longer.

In the spring of 1979, he flew his first plane, a Beechcraft Baron, to spring training, and one afternoon we flew out together to the Bahamas. Thurman was in complete control, comfortable and secure in his skills. We flew together several more times and I became fascinated with the fun Thurman seemed to be having flying that airplane. I started thinking I might like to do the same and we talked about my taking flying lessons during the spring. I never quite got around to it, but I always enjoyed going up with him. I began to understand the emotional pull the sky and the freedom had for him.

Early that season, we played in Baltimore, and after the game, Reggie and I flew back to New York with him. He was getting along with Reggie quite well now. When we got over Pennsylvania, the weather turned bad, there were thunderstorms in the area, but Thurman calmly got a new flight plan from the control tower and we flew around the storm. We could see lightning off in the distance and Reggie and I both remarked at how professional and how calm Thurman was.

A couple of weeks later, with my family still in Florida, Thurman invited me to spend an off day with him at his home in Canton, Ohio.

"We'll go out right after the game from Teterboro Airport and have dinner when we get there. I'll call Diane and tell her you're coming," he said.

"That sounds great. I'd like that," I said.

We flew out after the Sunday game and when Thurman got close to his home, he descended and flew over his house, buzzing his family, telling Diane, his in-laws, and his kids that he was almost home. He was very proud he could do something like that, and talked about it a lot when we finally did drive up to his home.

One night we were sitting at a hotel bar after a game, Thurman, Bobby Murcer, and myself. Thurman was talking about flying and told us, "I'm buying a jet for a million and a half. A Cessna Citation. A real beauty."

Bobby made a face. "What do you need such a big plane for?"

"I think it will be great. I'll be able to get home much faster. I expect delivery in a couple of weeks."

That scared me. I know it scared Bobby, also. When

you buy a jet, you get into a different type of airplane. It takes a lot more experience to fly it. You fly at greater speeds with more power and with a lot less margin for error. It is also more expensive to fly, with greater costs for fuel, repairs, and insurance. "Now I'll have to play three or four more years to pay this thing off," Thurman said.

"You don't need it," I said quietly.

He continued talking about this new sleek jet, this powerful plane, this magnificent flying machine he would acquire for so much money. The poor kid from Canton had enough dough to buy a huge jet. He felt it was that important.

We beat the White Sox twice on July 30 and July 31. That night Bobby, Thurman, and I went back to Bobby's apartment in Chicago—he had been playing for the White Sox until joining us in June. He broke out the good Scotch and the three of us talked into the night. We talked about baseball, friendship, and how glad we were that Bobby was back with us. As the drinks were poured, we became more and more sentimental and Bobby was in tears about the joy of being back as a Yankee, a part of the only team he had ever cared about. He told us how lost he had been in Chicago and in San Francisco before that. He told us how his heart had ached when the Yankees won and he wasn't part of it. Hardly anybody ever loved being a Yankee more than Bobby Murcer.

It was almost daylight when the conversation, not surprisingly, switched to Thurman's plane.

"What the hell did you need to get that jet for?" Bobby asked. "This isn't the same as the Beechcraft. This is a horse of another color. Are you sure you know what you are doing?"

"I am comfortable. I am confident. I know I can fly this plane," Thurman said.

Thurman Munson was a very head-strong man. Once he made up his mind about something, he could not be moved. No matter what we said about his jet, he brushed it aside.

"I'll tell you what," he said. "I have it out at a local airport. I'm flying home from here after Wednesday's game. I'll take you up tomorrow before the game. I'll show you I know what I'm doing."

That seemed fair enough. We talked a little while longer, the chatter gave out, and we finally went to sleep in Bobby's apartment.

The next morning, we got up and had breakfast. Thurman insisted we see the plane, so Bobby drove us out to the airport. We talked about the plane all the way out there and Thurman insisted we would like it after we saw it. We drove to the hangar area. Thurman took us to the plane. We got into it.

The airplane looked like a rocket. It was sleek and long and forbidding. We sat in the seats and squirmed. It looked too powerful, too strong, too fast. We sat there a few minutes just talking, and finally Bobby and I looked at each other. We shook our heads. "Let's do it some other time," Bobby said. I quickly unbuckled my seat belt, Thurman let the ladder down, and we all climbed out without starting the engine up.

"Ahh, hell," Thurman said. "There's no need to worry."

We drove to the ballpark from the airport. We beat the White Sox again that night of August 1, 1979, but it hardly mattered. We were still fourteen games out of first place. Thurman started the game at first base to rest his legs, twisted his knee swinging and was removed from the game in the sixth inning. We dressed quickly for the team charter flight back to New York and Thurman left the clubhouse to get a cab to the airport. He was flying home to Canton while the rest of us went back to New York. He was carrying a suit bag over his shoulder as he walked toward the clubhouse door. He tipped the clubhouse boy and walked out the door. "Take it easy, Thurman," I said as the door half closed. I doubt that he heard me. He was on his way to the airport and then back home to Canton. That was the last time I would see my good friend Thurman Munson alive.

Thurman flew uneventfully from Chicago to Canton. He arrived home shortly after 3:00 A.M., slept a little more than four hours, and awoke to have breakfast with his wife and play with his kids. He visited his in-laws, who had always been very warm to him, and complained about some minor problems in handling the plane on the flight from Chicago. They listened without comment. They had long ago learned that Thurman did not like to be disagreed with, and any suggestion about getting rid of the plane would be met with resistance. He went downtown to Lucia's for lunch with friends. Shortly after 2:00 P.M., he drove over to the Akron-Canton airport with two friends, David Hall, thirty-two, and Jerry Anderson, thirty-one. Both were licensed pilots. He wanted to practice touch-and-go landings with the Cessna. Munson sat in the pilot's seat. Hall sat in the copilot's seat. Anderson sat in the passenger's seat.

They took off at 2:45 P.M. The men in the control tower watched the sleek silver plane with the NY 15, Thurman's Yankee uniform number, disappear to the left into a clear blue sky. The plane flew over the Ohio countryside, circled down across the terrain several times, and then Thurman called the tower for landing clearance. It was now nearly three o'clock. The plane came in slowly to the airport. Investigators would later suggest "pilot error," because the plane was moving too slowly as it neared touchdown. Thurman moved the throttle forward. Hall saw the ground coming up too rapidly. Anderson had moved out of the passenger seat and was kneeling in the open space between the two front seats.

At 3:02 P.M., a thousand feet shy of runway 19 of the Canton-Akron airport, the plane sliced into some trees, flew past Greensburg Road, and crashed into the ground below a rise that led to the runway. The plane quickly caught fire. Hall kicked out the side door and fell to the ground. Anderson, singed on the hands and neck, stumbled out after him. They turned to look for Thurman. He was still in the plane, belted into the pilot's seat. They ran around the burning plane and looked into the cockpit. Thurman's head was tilted sideways and he was motionless. From outside the burning plane, they tugged and pulled at Thurman. He was harnessed tightly into his seat.

Thirty seconds had elapsed since the crash, and as they desperately tried to pull him from the pilot's seat, the fuel ignited and the plane was covered in flames and smoke.

Detective William Evans, called to the scene by a witness from a nearby farmhouse, logged his arrival at 3:07 P.M. He found Anderson some thirty yards from the plane, on his back, gasping for breath. Hall was leaning against a tree, facing in the opposite direction, his clothes charred with flames, his eyes glassy, his mouth open as he sucked in air. Evans raced to the plane, still smoldering, and couldn't get closer than ten feet.

Thurman Lee Munson, thirty-two years old, the Yankee captain and catcher, was dead. Investigators later reporter that Thurman had died of smoke inhalation. According to the medical examiner's report, released by Anthony Gardarelli, sheriff of Summit County, Ohio, Thurman was already dead when the second fire engulfed the Cessna. He had apparently already suffered a broken neck in the crash and fatal smoke inhalation in the fire immediately after the crash landing.

At 3:34 P.M. the breathless voice of Neal Callahan of the Chicago district office of the Federal Aviation Administration, which had jurisdiction over the Canton-Akron airport, was put through to George Steinbrenner's office. Gerry Murphy, who had become George's personal aide and assistant, took the call. Callahan said he had to speak to George. "It was a matter of life and death," Murphy remembered the FAA man telling him. Murphy had been instructed to screen calls carefully. George was too busy with the details of a trade that had sent Mickey Rivers to Texas for Oscar Gamble, and with the team's overall collapse, to take unimportant phone calls. "There's a man on the phone who won't identify himself, Mr. Steinbrenner. He just says he has to speak to you. He says it's a matter of life and death."

"Sure," George said. "Put him on."

The man identified himself to George. He wanted to inform the Yankee owner that there had been an airplane crash. He told George, "Your player, Thurman Munson, he's been killed." George tensed. Shivers ran down his neck. Trickles of sweat formed on his brow. "Are you sure?" he asked.

Told by the FAA man that there was no question, George asked, "Does the family know?"

After the accident and the identification of Thurman as the victim, police had called Diane Munson's father. They asked him to accompany them to the Munson home. Soon, he, two officers, and a detective were with Diane. The children were out back playing with friends. Diane would later tell friends, "I tried to get him to stop flying. I was frightened. It just wasn't worth it." She later collected the children, Tracy, nine, Kelly, seven, and Michael, four, and told them, "Daddy has gone off to be with God."

Young Michael looked at his mother weeping and his grandfather in tears, and asked innocently, "If my Daddy's with God, why is everybody crying?"

George called Yankee general manager Cedric Tallis, who had been moved up after Al Rosen had left, and told him the sad news. George called Billy Martin, who was on a lake, fishing; a telephone message summoned him to call the office. George and Cedric began calling the players at home, not wanting them to hear the awful news on the radio. George would call Thurman's closest friends, Graig Nettles, Bobby Murcer, and myself. Cedric would call the others.

Shortly before five o'clock, the phone rang. Anita answered it. "Lou," she said, "it's for you. George." I didn't think much about the call. By now George was in the habit of calling me occasionally to talk about a player on another ballclub and ask my opinion on whether he would help the Yankees. I had no inkling of the impact of this call. I picked up the phone in my office.

George's voice was choked. He could barely talk. He was nervous and emotional. "There's been a crash in Canton, Thurman's plane, very bad . . . Thurman's passed away." Then he hung up. I ran out into the kitchen where Anita was beginning to prepare dinner for the kids. "Thurman's dead," I blurted out. "Killed in a crash."

"Oh, my God," Anita shrieked. "Diane, what about Diane?"

We stood there in the kitchen, the two of us, holding each other tightly, our bodies shaking, gasping and sobbing and with tears running down our cheeks. Anita seemed like a rag doll in my arms, about to collapse and fall.

My first reaction was anger. I was mad at Thurman. "Why in hell did he have to get into this thing? Why did he need that plane? Damn it, what did he need it for?"

Anita tried to comfort me and I tried to comfort her. It didn't work. For the first hour or so after I heard the news I couldn't shake my anger at Thurman. The poor man was gone and I was mad at him. We had talked about that plane only the day before and I'd thought maybe he was weakening a bit, maybe he was thinking more about giving it up. He had to know it was just too complicated a machine for him to handle, and too expensive. Why couldn't I have persuaded him to give it up? He had bought that big jet without selling the two small planes he owned and the financial strain of the three planes was really too much. If I couldn't convince Thurman of the logic of giving up that damn plane for safety reasons, I had thought, maybe I could convince him to give it up for financial reasons.

A reporter called shortly after six o'clock. The story had moved onto the wires now and reporters were getting reactions from Thurman's teammates. "I can't imagine the Yankees without Thurman. I can't imagine myself without Thurman. This is a death in the family," I said.

Strange things enter your mind at a time like this. I thought of a conversation I had had with Thurman a week earlier. He had been struggling with the bat and his knees were aching. "Why don't you quit," I'd said jokingly. "Why don't we both quit?" We had laughed and admitted we were too poor to just walk away when the money was still coming in from baseball. He had a lot of pride and he seemed hurt that he wasn't helping the ballclub. "They'll get another catcher. You won't have to catch so much. You'll have a better year next year," I'd said.

After a sleepless night, I arrived at the ballpark for our scheduled game against Baltimore. The press had been kept away and we dressed quietly, talking to one another in whispers about the tragedy, looking at Thurman's locker, expecting him to be there, that this entire episode had been just a nightmare. Billy Martin, a very emotional man, seemed terribly weak and small and vulnerable as he addressed us. He told us that he wanted us to go forward after this great loss, that we must continue hustling as Thurman would have wanted us to do, that we must wear the Yankee uniform with pride even in the face of such shock. As he finished, George walked into the clubhouse with Cedric at his side. He was composed, his voice nearly normal, his eyes fixed on Thurman's locker as he spoke. "To be a Yankee player, to be the owner of the Yankees has always seemed so meaningful. Now it all seems so meaningless in the light of all this," he said.

At game time, there was a moment of silence for Thurman before we ran out to our positions. We stood as a team on the top step of the dugout. Then we took the field without a catcher. As at a presidential funeral there is a riderless horse with inverted stirrups, so Thurman's loss was marked by his absence on the field. Each Yankee stood at his position as Thurman's face was flashed on the huge electronic scoreboard. The fans began applauding and would not cease their farewell to their hero until more than eight minutes had passed. Not a player moved as the entire Stadium paid unique tribute to Munson and mourned his tragic death.

We had little stomach for the game that night, and Scotty McGregor, an ex-Yankee pitching for Baltimore, shut us out, 1–0. We lost again the next day, as funeral arrangements for Thurman were announced. The press continued to elicit comment from the players. Graig Nettles probably said it best for a lot of us. "I had expected to be a friend of Thurman's for the rest of my life."

Billy Martin could not talk to the press. A statement

was issued in his name. "Thurman was a great man," Billy said. "We not only lost a great competitor, but a leader and a husband and a devoted family man. He was a close friend. I loved him."

We got beaten again the next day. The funeral was set for Monday. We had a night game scheduled against Baltimore, on national television. George had arranged for a charter flight to Canton so we could attend the funeral as a team. The players had to get up at 5:00 A.M. to drive to the Stadium and make the bus to the airport. Some of the shock had worn off by then, and they boarded the bus with the memory still fresh but the reality growing. After the funeral, life would go on for the rest of us. Thurman had been a practical man, a realist, he would have understood that. We arrived in Canton, where Thurman had missed the airport runway four days earlier, and were bused to the Civic Center. Anita was with me, as were many of the wives. Anita and I and Kay and Bobby Murcer had flown to Diane shortly after hearing of the accident. We had provided as much strength during those days as we could. Now all the wives entered a family waiting room where they hugged Diane and silently pledged their love and help. Thurman's two daughters sat quietly with their grandparents, and their young son, Michael, dressed in a cutdown Yankee uniform, number 15, scampered in and out of the room staring at his father's friends.

More than a thousand people lined up outside the Civic Center to hear the ceremony, with some five hundred sitting inside. Players and their wives sat together in the front row. Diane sat near the stage with her children and her parents. Thurman's father, Darrell, recently arrived from Phoenix where he had lived for the past four years, was also on hand. The casket was covered with an American flag. A huge portrait of a smiling Thurman, in uniform, hung on the wall. There were several dozen floral displays, one in the shape of a baseball, another with the Yankee insignia, another with his number 15 on it.

The Reverend J. Robert Coleman, pastor of St. Paul's Roman Catholic Church in Canton, who had married

Thurman and Diane eleven years earlier, moved to the rostrum. He spoke quietly and professionally of Thurman, then some of us were called on to deliver a few words. I moved slowly to the rostrum, my legs shaking, my hands sweating, my voice hollow as I spoke into the microphone. I read quietly from the Scriptures, reciting several paragraphs from Ecclesiastes, and then continued, "We don't know why God took Thurman, but as long as we wear a Yankee uniform, Thurman won't be far from us. As a baseball player he was one of the best competitors. He played rough but fair. He was also a kind, affectionate, friendly man." My voice choked and I sat down. Bobby Murcer, who had played with Thurman as far back as 1969, was next. He spoke eloquently and clearly. "He lived, he led, he loved. Whatever he was to each of us—catcher, captain, competitor, husband, father, friend—he should be remembered as a man who valued and followed the basic principles of life. . . .

"As Lou Gehrig led the Yankees as the captain of the thirties, Thurman Munson captained the Yankees of the seventies. Someone someday should earn that right to lead this team again, for that is how Thurm—Tugboat, as I called him—would want it. And that is how it will one day be—five years, ten years, whenever, if ever. . . . No greater honor could be bestowed on one man than to be the successor to this man, Thurman Munson, who wore the pinstripes with number 15. Number 15 on the field, number 15 for the records, number 15 for the halls of Cooperstown.

"But in living, loving, and legend, history will record Thurman as Number One."

That was too much for Billy Martin, uniform number one on the Yankees, who gasped, bit down hard on his lip, and seemed close to an emotional shock.

We boarded the team bus and rolled across the flat Ohio countryside to Sunset Hills Cemetery. We all stood at the gravesite as Father Coleman said the final words over the casket of Thurman Munson, "Ashes to ashes, dust to dust . . ." There was a shuffling of feet, a silence, and the final prayers. We headed back home to the Stadium, leaving Thurman behind forever.

We still had that scheduled game against Baltimore that night. We dedicated it to Thurman. We trailed 4–0, until Bobby homered, his first as a Yankee in his new tour of duty, to make it 4–3. Then, in the ninth inning, with two runners in scoring position and two out, Bobby lined a single to right to win the game. He had knocked in all five runs in the 5–4 victory, one of the most emotional games I had ever experienced.

It was near midnight when we finally left the Stadium, after starting out at 5:00 A.M. Pete Sheehy had cleaned out Thurman's locker. He left a pinstriped shirt hanging there, the NY facing out, a pair of pants on a hook, a Yankee cap, and a catcher's mask. Atop the locker was a metal plate bearing simply the number 15.

The locker stayed empty in tribute to Thurman. It was a constant reminder that, in some mystical way, he was still part of the team. There would come a time when there would no longer be any players around who knew him, and the locker could be opened up again. But for those early years after Thurman's death it seemed proper and touching that the locker remain closed, that it remain Thurman's, for the sake of the players who had known him and appreciated him and loved him.

The locker was also a constant reminder of how fickle life was. We were young athletes, healthy, strong, and vibrant, seemingly immune to disease and death, and then this tragedy hit us. It was a lesson none of us who were on that 1979 Yankee team could ever forget. You might be on top one day, and the next day gone. In a way, athletes die twice. We die the day our careers end; we are usually young men when that happens. Then we die again, finally, completely. Thurman's death left a lasting scar on all of us.

We finished the season without much heart. I had a pretty good year, batting .297 in 130 games, with eleven homers, and felt confident I would be part of our comeback in 1980 at the age of thirty-six.

On October 23, 1979, Billy Martin punched out a

marshmallow salesman in a hotel lobby after getting into an argument with the fellow in a bar. He told George a fib about what had happened, and when it was found out, he was finished. Five days later, Mickey Morabito, the publicity man of the Yankees, issued a statement to the press. "Billy Martin has been relieved of his duties as manager of the New York Yankees and Dick Howser has been named to succeed him, effective immediately."

Howser had been a Yankee coach, a good baseball man, and a good friend. It meant nothing. I would soon learn a man has to change his stripes when he changes his job, especially if it is to become a manager.

"Why Don't You
Brick It?"

This time, Billy Martin's disappearance was less surprising and less emotional for the players. Billy had been a good manager in 1976, 1977, and 1978, but the strain always wore on us. The soap opera, once funny, became heavy pressure. At my advanced baseball age, I didn't need it. I was thirty-six, and confident I could still swing the bat well, but I wanted my concentration on hitting the ball. I didn't want the press asking me if I thought Billy should go. Dick Howser seemed to be the perfect man for the job.

Just as Dick had been elevated from the coaching lines to succeed Billy, George named Gene Michael, a solid baseball man who had coached and managed at Columbus, to be the new general manager. George took pride in promoting "Stick" Michael to that spot. He had trained him and nurtured him for the job. A lot of players thought Stick was George's man, but I considered him a smart baseball man. Sure, he was George's man, but he was also a strong personality who couldn't be pushed without pushing back.

I remember him decking a Boston player named Tony Horton with a one-punch knockout. Stick Michael was no guy to fool with.

A new era was beginning for the Yankees. My buddy Catfish Hunter had retired with a bad shoulder to raise soy beans and manage his son's Little League team. He came to spring training as an instructor and, of course, the first time he saw me, he grinned and said, "Jim Wohlford." I grinned back, and said, "A Little League manager? You can't manage a grocery." Catfish and I will be needling each other as long as we are both around.

There were other dramatic changes. Thurman was gone, of course, and there was no locker left empty for him in Fort Lauderdale. The pain had worn off, and except for an occasional kidding remark about how Thurman used to hide on weigh-in day, there was little discussion of the sadness of 1979. Those of us who were there would always carry it with us, but there was a new catcher now. His name was Rick Cerone, a good, tough kid we obtained from Toronto in a deal involving Chris Chambliss, who then moved on to Atlanta. Cerone had to fight the pressure of being Thurman's successor, but he quickly won the number-one catching job. Our other big change was free agent Bob Watson, a solid, classy, long-ball-hitting, right-handed first baseman.

The spring training changes under Dick Howser were obvious. We had been close friends, kidding around a lot, sharing a few drinks, laughing on the bus, always loose and easy with one another. Now he was the boss. Camp was disciplined and organized. People paid attention to the rules. There was none of the casualness of the 1979 spring.

In 1979, as soon as we arrived at the clubhouse, we would go straight to the trainer's room, pick up an ice pack, and sit there bullshitting for half an hour before watching the bus with the young players on it leave for games at Vero Beach or Fort Myers. There were no more ice pack socials in the trainer's room in 1980. If you were hurt that badly, you could ride the bus to Vero with an ice pack on your foot and play when you got there. Dick had a rule about who made trips. "If your name is on the list," he said, "you go."

We had finished fourth in 1979 and that was embarrassing. It was our lowest finish since I had become a

Yankee and I felt as bad about that as anybody. I wanted a comeback season for the ballclub in 1980. Truthfully I had been as lazy as the rest of them in the spring of 1979, and now I played much harder. I also realized there was a new manager out there and, friend or no friend, I wanted to impress him enough to get enough playing time. I didn't mind sitting once in a while—I was thirty-six, after all—but I certainly didn't want to be a once or twice a week player.

George had always been concerned about beating the Mets in the spring and while Billy and Bob had always laughed it off, Dick took those games seriously. Before, if a guy hadn't wanted to play against the Mets, he discovered an imaginary injury and got to skip the game. Now there was no skipping any games for any reason. Pretty soon the ice packs and the excuses disappeared. George was thrilled when we beat the Mets. He came into the clubhouse smiling, congratulated the players, and announced, "The ticket windows in New York will have lines out there before they open." George always dreamed of lines forming all night outside the ticket windows. It was his dream to have a club so good, so exciting, so successful that Yankee Stadium tickets became the hottest property in town.

We opened the season in Texas, lost our first two games, and George wasn't too happy. Then it rained. It was our best day so far in the 1980 season. We regrouped and won the next two games, played .500 ball through April, showed a little spurt in May and moved into first place on May 14.

I started the season slowly. I was hitting only .185 on May 27, which concerned me. I knew I had those years advancing on me and I heard talk that I was losing a little quickness with the bat; some of the sportswriters began suggesting that I might be ready to retire. Every day I didn't hit, I would kiddingly tell somebody or other I couldn't hit anymore, I might be better off getting out of the game and that the next game might be my last. I probably felt that way when I said it, but with a few pops, a good night's sleep, and a double to left, I would change my mind.

My average stayed around the .250 mark most of the season. I played against lefthanders, but little against righthanders.

The righties saw Jim Spencer at first, and Reggie, Oscar Gamble, Bob Watson, or Bobby Murcer as the DH and in the outfield instead of me. I was getting crowded out of my playing time.

Many days, I came home and said to Anita, "This might be it."

She always encouraged me, soothed my hurt feelings, and reminded me that I had felt that way last week, last month, last year. As I played less and less, it hurt me more and more. I had been very close to Dick Howser. I felt betrayed by his moves. "Why me?" I asked Graig Nettles one day. "After all I have done for this ballclub."

"Try switch-hitting," Nettles said.

Graig was not a guy to give you much sympathy when you weren't playing. He also had his own troubles, with George—he was mad at George for not paying him what he felt he was worth—and with a bout of hepatitis, from which he suffered all year.

Instead of confronting Dick with my unhappiness, I withdrew. I grew more pensive about my career. I sat quietly in the dugout. I knew I was acting selfishly and unprofessionally, but I couldn't help it. It is easy to be a team player in the middle years of a successful career, much more difficult when you're a young player trying to establish yourself or an older player just trying to hang on for a few more years. There is a constant conflict between team and self, and if the truth be known, self always comes out on top. That is why veteran clubs usually win. More players can sacrifice individual goals for team goals. The owners force the players to think that way. They never say, "You had a good year advancing runners or hitting the cutoff man." They say you hit .300 or you didn't.

When I thought about all that, when I asked Graig or Bobby, or went home and asked Anita, "Why me?" the answer always seemed to be the same: That's what managers do. They play the players they think will help them win. They can't concern themselves with your feelings. It is easy to be a buddy when you are a coach. It is impossible to be on the same terms with your players when you are making out the lineup card. A manager can play only so many guys. All the rest want to play, too, or they wouldn't be there. And those who don't play take that anger out in a variety of ways—sometimes even at home. I was more tense around Anita and the kids that summer than I had been at any time in my baseball career.

The guys Dick played instead of me were doing a good job, and we remained in first, so I remained on the bench. If Dick had come and explained it to me, I would have dealt with it a little better, but he didn't. My contract was running out soon and I was afraid for my career.

In mid-August, we began showing some signs of wear and tear. Our lead began slipping. Baltimore, as always under Earl Weaver, began coming on. Before one Saturday night game, Dick called me into his office.

"Lou, you've been swinging the bat better. I'd like to play you every day. Can you handle it?"

"You bet I can. That's what I've been waiting for."

"OK, you're in there today against the righthander. Let's win some games."

I was happy as a clam walking out of his office. I would show Howser and everybody else that the old man of the Yankees still had some piss and vinegar left in him. I could still hit and I could still help this club. I played every day for about three weeks, we built our league lead from one game up to six games, and my average jumped more than fifty points to .310. I was feeling great. Then I took an oh-for-four in early September. Dick called me into his office again.

"Look, Lou, you look a little tired. We got a night game tonight against the lefthander and a day game tomorrow against a righthander. You play tonight and I'll rest you tomorrow," he said.

"That's fine. I can use a day off."

I had played every day for about three or four weeks in the summer heat. I was thirty-seven years old and I was tired, and I was grateful for the rest—except that the one day off turned into two weeks. I sat against the righthander the next day, and then against another righthander the next day, and the day after that. For two weeks, we didn't face a lefthander, and for two weeks I sat, and steamed, and grew angrier at my old good friend Dick Howser. I never talked to him about it and, with the division lead secure now, he didn't bother to talk to me about it.

We moved into Toronto for a three-game series. Toronto in September can be awful. That night it was rainy, cold, windy, and damn uncomfortable. I took a quick batting practice and went inside the clubhouse. We were about four games ahead, with twenty games to go, and Yankee teams just don't blow that kind of lead. I was certain we would win, but I was just as certain I wouldn't play much part in it the last three weeks.

I sat in the middle of the bench watching the game. Oscar Gamble was in left field. I was wrapped tightly in my jacket, a large towel pulled tight against my neck to break the wind. Oscar batted in the seventh and came back to the bench. Dick said something to him as the inning ended and then walked down the bench toward me.

"Grab your glove, Lou, and go out to left field."

This was a raw, cold, windy day late in September in Canada. I was not a twenty-three- or twenty-four-year-old kid trying to make a ballclub. I was a thirty-seven-year-old veteran player who had helped the Yankees make a lot of money for a lot of years. When Howser told me to get my glove, you could have fried an egg on my face, I was that hot. I mumbled some unpleasantries to myself about him, none of which would be appreciated by any sane man. He glared, but said nothing. I walked out to left field.

The game ended, and I came into the clubhouse and marched around in there for a few more minutes. I made a few more comments in the clubhouse, Nettles agitated me some more, and the matter seemed to end as Howser discussed the winning game with the press. We boarded the bus for our flight to Boston and nothing more was said. I kept thinking about the embarrassment of going in for defense in the seventh inning of that frozen game, and I continued to get hotter and hotter. We boarded the plane for the flight to Boston and I quickly had a beer. Then I had a couple more. Dick must have had a few up front in first class, where the manager and his coaches sit and discuss players who they think aren't doing the job, and I just knew I was getting cut up by the lot of them.

We started walking through the terminal in Boston toward our bus for the hotel. I was walking alone when, suddenly, Dick took a couple of quick steps and was next to me. His face was red and I knew I had been right about the few drinks.

"Why don't you brick it?" he shouted at me.

I said little, because I didn't know what he meant. "Why don't you brick it?" What was that?

Bobby Murcer had seen me talking to Howser, and walked over to me. Bobby hadn't been playing as much as he liked, either, and had spent a good part of the summer antagonizing Howser. He wanted to know what Howser had said. "Why don't you brick it?" He shook his head. He knew it wasn't a compliment, but he wasn't quite sure what the manager was telling me to do. We had to check it out with our resident language authority, Graig Nettles. If anybody on the team knew what it was supposed to mean, Nettles would. I walked over to him, and he asked me quickly what Howser had said. "Why don't you brick it?" I said.

Nettles smiled. He knew. "Why don't you brick it? Why don't you quit and get a job? Why don't you lay some bricks?" Then he laughed out loud. "You gonna brick it, Lou?"

Now I was really pissed off. Nettles managed to tell everybody else on the bus what Dick had said to me, and what it meant, and suggested that I was about to "brick it." And hot as I was leaving the plane, I was even more agitated when Nettles let everyone in on the secret. Here I am trying for a new contract and a few more years on that high salary, just trying to hang on, and Howser tells me to brick it.

We finally reached the hotel lobby and as we walked through the doors, I approached Howser again. "Brick it? Why don't you brick it? I've been playing good baseball all these years for the Yankees, and you become the manager of this ballclub and you're telling me to brick it?"

Dick seemed in better control now and he finally said, "Let's talk. C'mon up to my room."

Stan Williams, our pitching coach and a close friend of Dick's, heard the conversation. Williams, a big, tough guy we used to call the Big Hurt, because he could injure people so easily when he got mad, looked at the small manager and said, "You think you need me up there?"

Both Dick and I had calmed down enough now to anticipate a professional conversation without violence.

"Just stay in your room by your phone," said Howser. "If I need you, I'll call. Then just come through the walls."

We went up in the elevator together and got to his room. A basket of fruit, some flowers, the usual cheese and crackers, and a few bottles were on his night stand. Big league managers get certain privileges and presents from hotel managers. Dick was relaxed now. I started relaxing. We shared a couple of drinks and talked for about two hours. I told him about the anger that had been building up all year, and he told me about why he had done certain things a certain way.

If only we had had the conversation earlier in the season, it would have cleared the air. I learned then that there is no more important aspect to managing a ballclub than communicating with your players. I came out of the meeting with Dick a friend.

We finished the season with 103 wins, the most by a Yankee team since the 1963 Yankees had won 104 games. We felt confident going into the playoffs again against— yes, Kansas City, the only team we ever met in a League Championship Series. I had finished strong with a .287

mark after that slow start and felt sure we would win. I also knew I would be playing, since we were facing a lefthander, Larry Gura, in the first game, so I felt good. As we traveled to KC for the first two games, we were loose.

Well, we got shocked. Ron Guidry pitched the opener for us, and for the first time I can remember, he simply didn't have it. He gave up four quick runs; Ron Davis, who had done such a great job as Goose's setup man, came in, and we got beaten 7–2, even though I hit a home run. Now the second game was the key. It always is in the playoffs—you don't want to go home down by two games. Rudy May had one bad inning in the third and gave up three runs, but we came back with two in the fifth, trailed 3–2, but felt confident. It was false confidence. Dennis Leonard and Dan Quisenberry, with a damn sidearm fastball, kept stopping us.

Then, in the eighth inning, an incident occurred that would seal Dick's fate with George. Seventy million people saw George lose his cool on national television. It was an image of him that would remain for a long time. Besides being a businessman, George is also a fan, and he reacts the way a lot of fans do. Since he happens to own the ballclub, however, his reactions are a bit more public.

In the eighth inning, we had a chance to tie it. Willie Randolph led off with a hit, the next two batters went out, and then Bob Watson smashed a huge drive off the left-center-field wall. Willie raced around second, stumbled a bit, picked up third-base coach Mike Ferraro's waving his arms at third, and headed home. Ferraro knew their left fielder, Willie Wilson, did not have a strong and accurate arm. Wilson was a speed player, who made up for what he lacked in finesse with explosive quickness. He was the same kind of hitter, a guy without power but capable of slapping that ball on the artificial turf, driving it through the infield and beating it out.

Wilson picked the ball off the wall, threw a bad toss toward the cutoff man and got lucky when George Brett, backing up, caught the throw and fired home. Brett's throw to Darrell Porter at the plate was on the money, and Randolph was out. What one of the television cameras caught was George jumping up from behind our dugout, pulling on his sweater, and marching off with his GM, Gene Michael, trailing quickly behind him. What a sight. I saw it over and over again on television and couldn't stop laughing. Little did I know then that Stick would be my manager in a few weeks. We lost that game, 3–2.

Now we had to come home and beat the Royals three straight. It certainly seemed possible. We had a great club, and we felt the Royals were much better on their artificial turf than on our natural grass. Going into the seventh inning of the third game, we had a 2–1 lead behind Tommy John, when Wilson hit a double and with two out, Howser brought in Gossage to face light-hitting U. L. Washington. It was a perfect move, in theory. So much for theory. Washington bounced a ball over the mound, Willie Randolph fielded it cleanly, but Washington hustled down the line and beat the throw. It gave George Brett an at bat with two on and two out in a 2–1 game. He had hit .390 that year, just falling under .400 in the last couple of weeks. He was at his zenith as a player and obviously frustrated at the failure of Kansas City to get into the World Series in three previous tries against us. This time he made up for it. He caught Gossage's first fastball down the middle of the plate and clocked it. The ball rattled into the third deck for a three-run homer, and as the sportscasters say, you could have turned off your set right there. Quisenberry shut us down again, and we lost the last game, 4–2. They went to the World Series and we went home.

Was George upset? Yes, he was—upset at losing, upset at the sweep, and upset at Ferraro for sending Randolph home in that key second game. He said so publicly. Howser, a very loyal man, defended Ferraro, and when George went so far as to talk to Don Zimmer about succeeding Ferraro, Howser was quoted in the press as saying, "Managers should have the final say on who the third-base coach is." Well, George has always felt he should have the final say on anyone who works for him, and it was his ballclub. On November 21, Dick Howser attended a press conference in George's office. George told the reporters Dick was resigning to accept a wonderful real estate offer in Florida. Nobody could explain why Dick had suddenly become enchanted with the real estate business, after spending his life in baseball as a player, coach, and manager. George had summoned Dick back from college coaching in Florida to take the managerial job, and now here he was sending him back to the real estate business. Does any of this sound too fantastic for a soap opera?

Well, now Stick was the manager. I got a big chuckle out of that one when I heard about it. I had played ball with Gene Michael when I'd first come to the Yankees, and I remember clearly spending a lot of nights hearing him complain about Bill Virdon. Virdon didn't play Michael as much as Michael thought he should play, and almost every day Gene didn't make the lineup he would say to me, "Boy, that Virdon, he sure doesn't know talent."

I liked playing with Stick. He was a very competitive guy, an excellent card player, witty, and not above sticking a needle into some guys. He could also take a joke. Somebody put a cold weenie into his glove one spring training day and he jumped a foot when he slipped his fingers into that. Unfortunately, George was watching and didn't take it lightly. Oh, well.

Shortly after the managerial change was announced, I had a bad scare. It had been a rotten fall. My house was burglarized, my father was hit by a car, causing very serious injuries including several broken ribs, and I was on my way to talk with my son's soccer coach about why he wasn't playing more. On the way, though, my car got stuck in the sand, I had to call AAA to pull me out, and by that time I'd missed the coach. I came home mad, and left for a business appointment mad. Suddenly, as I was driving, I felt weak, sweaty, and sick to my stomach. Chest pains shot through me. Oh, no, I said, not that. I continued driving, straight to a Tampa hospital, where they put me through tests, kept me a couple of days, and finally decided all I needed was a good rest. I was thoroughly frightened for a while. I was only thirty-seven years old—I couldn't imagine having a heart attack. Fortunately, they diagnosed it as simple fatigue, told me to cut back on my activities, which I did, and stop smoking, which I didn't. Some things are just harder to do than other things.

On December 15, 1980, the Yankees signed Dave Winfield to a free agent contract worth something like twenty-three million dollars for ten years. Was he worth it? Is any player worth what he gets nowadays? It's supply and demand. A guy who chooses to become a free agent can command a great deal of money if he is a star player. The owners can afford it or they wouldn't pay it. I'm not privy to George's balance books, but he is a hard-headed businessman. If he wasn't making money on the New York Yankees, he would sell the club. I'm convinced that no matter how much he paid Winfield, he made money. I also knew that Reggie Jackson, whose contract with the Yankees was up after the 1981 season, would not be back after that. Reggie was getting older, George simply wasn't going to pay him the money he was paying Winfield, and Reggie probably wouldn't sign for less. Reggie would play out his final Yankee season in 1981 and moved on to California.

It was another sign that we were getting old as a ballclub. Reggie, Nettles, and I were all moving into that dangerous baseball age, closing in to our middle thirties, and the Yankees had to be rebuilt. We weren't getting enough fresh young talented players from our farm system. George went for the instant fix. He explained his reasoning to me one day.

"This is New York," he said. "We have to compete and be entertaining. Our fans won't wait for the players from the farm system to develop. We have to win now. That's why I have to sign the free agent players at their peak. We can't be like the Mets or the Tigers. We can't wait five years to put a competitive team on the field. We have to do it every year. That's why it's harder to run the Yankees."

That's one theory, anyway.

I rested a while after I got out of the hospital and then I began a workout program. It was the most work I had ever done in the winter. I was entering the final year of my contract, and I knew I had to have a good season at thirty-seven if I was going to squeeze another contract out of George.

Strike

We belong to a privileged class. We play baseball for lots of money, and there is no question we are spoiled. Just how spoiled, I found out on June 11, when the fifty-day baseball strike began. I had to take care of my own hotel bill, make my own plane reservation, get my own cab to the airport, find my own flight, pick up my own suitcase, and make my own way home. There were a lot of other things to remember about the 1981 season, but I shall always recall that that was when I made my first summer airline reservation. It shouldn't have been a big deal for a grown man to do that, but when you have a traveling secretary take care of that routine logistical chore all your life, it does become a big deal. For once, I couldn't look at a schedule or yell at Killer Kane, "What time does the flight leave?" I felt like a traveling salesman when I journeyed out to the airport in Chicago that day. There would be more shocks to come.

Gene Michael was our new manager as we began the 1981 spring training season. Some people questioned whether an ex-teammate and ex-coach could step aside and handle old friends, but he had done well as a manager in Columbus and we were willing to give him a chance. More serious were the doubts of the players that Stick would really be the manager. The real field boss was George Steinbrenner, they felt, Stick had gotten the job because he was not nearly as independent as Dick Howser and would be more likely to handle the team the way George wanted.

We got off well, were playing good ball by May and stayed close to the top into June. The strike talk had been escalating for months, and when we went into first place on June 6, the newspapers began suggesting that if there was a strike, it might mean more that we were on top. Who knew what would happen to the rest of the season?

On June 11, 1981, we beat Chicago for a two-game lead, and waited official word from our player representative, Reggie, that the strike had actually been called. Sure enough, we were suddenly out of work. Our salaries stopped. There was no bus to the airport. I shared a cab with a couple of other players and struggled to put my suitcase into the trunk.

"Damn, this thing is heavy," I said.

"That's what you get for trying to steal bats from the ballclub," Nettles said.

"I don't have any bats. It's all dirty laundry."

We struggled home and I relaxed for a couple of days around the house, following the developments in the paper. I had a lot of faith in Marvin Miller, the executive director of our association, and I knew he would do what was best for the players. I had never been very involved in the association, but I supported its goals and ideals—the players were certainly better off as a result of Miller and free agency and arbitration than they had been when I'd broken into baseball.

"How long do you think it will last?" Anita asked me after the first few days.

"I think it will be over this week," I said, all confidence.

"I just wanted to know if I should buy extra lunch meat for you," she said.

As Hazel Weiss, wife of Yankee GM George Weiss, said after his retirement in the early 1960s, "I married you for better or worse, but not for lunch." Ballplayers' wives aren't used to having their husbands around all day.

I played a little golf, watched the stock market, took care of chores around the house, and spent more time with the kids. As the strike dragged on, some younger players began to have financial problems. Some of the owners felt they would crack first and may have stretched out the strike thinking the players would crumble. I was not concerned financially—I had watched my money, and anyway, I knew it would be over in a couple of weeks, or a month, or six weeks at the most. I could deal with that. As the days went by, though, the stories in the papers were always the same—little progress. Each time the owners met, it seemed positions hardened on both sides. One day, the owners met in New York. The press had gathered in the lobby of the hotel, and Gabe Paul of Cleveland was one of the first to arrive. The press almost smothered poor old Gabe as he tried to make it up the hotel elevator. When it appeared that Gabe might faint from this pressing crowd, one reporter yelled "Steinbrenner," and pointed to the other end of the lobby. The press scattered like ants. Gabe was saved. George wasn't really there, but the press knew where the good stories would be.

Suddenly, about three weeks into the strike, life became fun. I realized that I had been a professional baseball player for nineteen years, working seven days a week all summer, with no days off except for travel days. I had never gone to the beach, or had a picnic, or watched a movie at night with my family—and now I could. I didn't have to get up in the morning swinging a bat. I didn't have to check the wind conditions or see if the sun was shining. I could sleep late, and not think about handling an inside fastball. It was the summer vacation I'd always wanted. I really got to like that strike.

For me, it was a look into the future. I was suddenly like everybody else. It had always been hard for me to go to the ballpark on a beautiful Sunday summer morning, when the sky was a perfect blue and the air was balmy and my neighbors on the other side were loading picnic baskets into their car. I always felt a little down on those days, and I could see the look in Anita's face, and the unhappiness in the faces of the kids when I took off. They understood that it was my job and that baseball paid for all the nice things they had, but it was not easy being an absentee father and husband on those summer Sundays. Maybe baseball should schedule an off day on a Sunday every couple of weeks. Some guys might even play harder from Monday to Saturday for that. It won't happen because baseball draws too well on Sundays, but it sounds like a good idea.

By late July, I figured the strike wouldn't be settled until September, if at all. I owned a forty-six-foot Hatteras with three other businessmen in New Jersey. I called the captain in Florida and told him to sail it to Bimini. The plan was for the entire family to fly to the Bahamas for about ten days, relax, fish, enjoy the sun, and forget about the game. We flew down in early August. Five days into our vacation, we got a call—the strike was over. It was Murphy's Law. My one summer vacation in nineteen years, and they had to pick then to wrap it up.

There were no winners in the strike. The owners and players suffered equally. Both lost income, and the image of the game was tarnished. I felt sorry for the fans, for all those people who lives were enriched by baseball, or who planned summer vacations around seeing their favorite teams play. The fans were cheated.

They were cheated when we came back, too. Under the strike settlement, the Yankees were automatically in the playoffs, because we had finished first in the first half, which meant that we had no incentive when play resumed. What was the use of killing yourself if it gained you nothing? Who cared how many games we won? We knew we would be in the playoff.

Gene Michael was the victim of that malaise. It wasn't Gene's fault. We had no fire after the strike, and it's hard to play winning baseball without enthusiasm. Guys were more concerned about getting hurt than playing hard. Of course, George was angered. He began warning Stick that the team wouldn't be ready for the playoffs. If Stick couldn't motivate us, he threatened, he would have to make a change again. It all came to a head when a reporter asked Stick about it, and Stick responded, "If he wants to fire me, let him get it over with." That's all George needed. George had never played professional baseball, but he thought he knew what a professional athlete needed to do to get ready for a playoff series. Stick took the bait from the press. Taunting George like that is like a boxer dropping his hands to his side and screaming for the other fighter to hit him if he can. Bang. On September 6, 1981, Gene Michael was fired and replaced by Bob Lemon again. George delivered the knockout punch. Lemon had been a starter all his life and now he was a relief pitcher.

Lemon arrived that night and held his first clubhouse meeting. His red nose shone brightly. His voice was gravelly. His speech was familiar. I thought he had brought a tape with him. It was pure corn.

"Let's just play baseball. You guys know what to do. I'm here to see if I can help win a couple of games. You guys are really the ones who have to do it. OK, let's just go out there and play baseball, meat."

Those of us who had been with Bob in 1978 tried not to laugh. It was funny to hear the same speech all over again a few years later. I wondered if he had given that speech exactly the same way to the Kansas City and Chicago ballclubs when he'd managed them.

We played a little better ball under Lemon those last couple of weeks, but not much. We still considered the regular season a tuneup for the playoffs, and now we had an extra playoff series to contend with. Milwaukee won the second half and we had to play them for the divisional title before even thinking of the pennant.

It looked like a laugher at first. We beat them two straight in Milwaukee, with the help of one of my rare home runs in the second game and, as we flew home, we were feeling pretty good. We figured the Brewers were just happy to be in it, glad for the opportunity to take their wives to New York, catch a play on Broadway, see a good movie maybe, have dinner in one of those famous restaurants, and return home proud that they had played the Yankees for the title. What arrogance! The Brewers came out playing tough, aggressive baseball, and before we knew it, we had lost two games ourselves, and the series was tied.

George hit the panic button again.

An hour before the game, George entered the clubhouse for a special meeting. He came down with a complete entourage. He had his front-office personnel with him. He had his valet with him. He had his driver. It looked like the heavyweight champion of the world walking toward the ring as the group closed in on us in the clubhouse.

"I want to tell you guys that if you lose this game today you'll be the laughingstock of New York," he began. "Your neighbors won't want to talk to you, your family won't want to talk to you, your friends won't want to talk to you. You'll be embarrassed to leave your houses. You'll be known as losers, the most famous losers in baseball history, the first team to lose a playoff for the division. That's what everybody will remember you for."

George was rolling now, like the falls at Niagara, the words pouring out rapidly, each player getting a blast before the big game, just to put them in that perfect mood. He was working his way around the clubhouse, getting on Reggie, whom he knew he would never sign again, getting on Jerry Mumphrey for not playing center field the way Joe DiMaggio had, getting on Nettles for not hitting at all, getting on me for doing nothing since my second-game homer. Then he started on Rick Cerone, our young catcher. Cerone had played wonderful baseball in 1980 under Dick Howser. He had fought off the pressure of succeeding Thurman and turned in a terrific season, batting .277 with fourteen homers, eighty-five RBIs and a great job behind the plate. In 1981, he had broken a bone in his hand in April, missed more than a month of the season, and struggled through a poor .244 year. He was a lot more sensitive about his career that year than the previous season. George moved toward him and began bellowing that he wasn't hitting, his catching stank, and he wasn't the player he had been, and . . .

"Go to hell, George."

It rang out in the clubhouse like a giant bell on a huge ship. It rocked the clubhouse. It stunned George. It froze the players. It ended the meeting. Cerone was never one of George's favorite players after that. He went to arbitration the next year and beat George, which also didn't help his Yankee career, suffered several major injuries, and finally got traded to Atlanta. I think he'll have a great career there—he's a tough kid. He just needs a chance to play. Actually, George had pretty much gotten over the incident by the time the trade was made, but it is a label Cerone will never shake. "This is the guy who told George Steinbrenner..." What a tag.

After Cerone's address ended the meeting Nettles came up to me and asked, "Does George really mean this? We won't be failures all the rest of our lives if we lose this, will we?"

"I think he went a little overboard. I really think Anita will talk to me even if we lose."

Here was a case of George clearly overreacting. He wanted to win, sure, but we wanted to win just as much. One baseball game does not change a man's life, no matter how big the game is. This wasn't a time to panic, it was a time to think about positive, winning baseball. A lot of this game is played above the shoulders. I don't like to think about defeat—that's why I reacted so strongly in Kansas City when it was suggested we might lose that fourth game and should bring our bags downstairs. I don't think about defeat until it happens.

With that meeting still on our minds, we took the field for the fifth game against the Brewers. We trailed 2–0; rallied for four runs in the fourth, I got a pinch hit for two runs; Reggie, Gamble, and Cerone, of all people, hit home runs; and with Righetti relieving Guidry in the fifth and Gossage mopping up in the eighth and ninth, we won 7–3. We were Eastern Division champions.

Nettles poked me as we got inside the clubhouse. "George's speech really did it," he said.

Maybe George's raising hell did get us into a fighting mood, in one way or another—or maybe it was Rick Cerone's reply. In an case, we were playing the Oakland

A's for the American League Championship, the A's under the leadership of—who else?—Billy Martin.

Billy had taken over the club in 1980, finished second with them, and won his division in 1981. It was a gutty performance, but we thought we could beat them easily and we were right. We were a veteran club, much deeper, and we beat them three straight.

As the champagne popped and the press moved in, I slipped out for a while and walked down the hall. I wanted to see Billy, to congratulate him for a fine season and console him for the loss of the pennant. His club was a young team with a lot of talent, and I was sure they would come on strong again in 1982. They reminded me a lot of the 1976 Yankees, Billy's first New York winner. We'd lost the World Series to Cincinnati that year, but we'd known we would be back.

His clubhouse door was open and a few writers were talking to Oakland players. His office door was also open and he sat there alone behind his desk, tears in his eyes, his green and white Oakland uniform soaked in sweat. His feet were up on his desk and he was staring straight ahead. I knew how hard this man took losing. No manager I had ever played for suffered more when he lost. He was often inconsolable after a defeat. His whole life revolved around winning. I gently called his name and he looked up.

"I just wanted to congratulate you on a great season. You got quite a team there, Skip. You're gonna win a lot of pennants, I want you to know that."

"Thanks, Lou. I appreciate that. They played hard. We were just a little short, a little short."

"Have a good winter, Skip, and good luck next year."

"Thanks, Lou. Thanks for coming in. Good luck in the Series."

His voice choked when he said that. I knew how much he wanted to be there himself, to show the world he could come back with a winner after being fired again in New York. Billy Martin had taught a lot of us how to win.

The team that was going to the World Series again had grown and matured under him. I owed him the visit.

Before we could get to the World Series, though, we had one more outing in Oakland—and it was a beauty.

All the players and their families were invited by George to celebrate the triumph in Vincent's restaurant in Oakland. George puts heat on us when we don't win, but when we do win he can be the most generous of men. It was a most enjoyable evening. There was great food, everybody was in a light mood—and then came the thunder. Reggie Jackson, who still lived in Oakland, had brought his entourage to the party, and sometimes Reggie's entourage seemed larger than George's. Reggie had friends, relatives, cousins, aides, who knew what-all there. Late in the evening, Graig Nettles' wife, Ginger, placed her purse on her chair and went off to get something to eat. When she returned, the purse was gone and somebody was sitting in her seat. It was one of Reggie's guests. Ginger searched for her purse—which later turned up on the floor—words were exchanged, and soon Reggie and Graig were at it. Bang. Graig may have been fast at third, but he was faster with two left hooks, the first knocking Reggie back and the second knocking him over. It was the culmination of five years of frustration and anger between Graig and Reggie, and needless to say, the festive atmosphere of the evening ended. People began leaving. The party was over.

It was a premonition of things to come. First of all, after winning two straight from the Dodgers in Yankee Stadium, we flew into Los Angeles and got beaten one, two, three in a row. Their screwballing phenom, Fernando Valenzuela, beat us in the third game, Reggie lost a fly ball in the sun to cost us the fourth—Billy once said, "It's not that Reggie is a bad outfielder. He just has trouble judging the ball and picking it up"—and Jerry Reuss outpitched Guidry for the fifth.

We were all in a pretty sour mood when we went back to the hotel that night before flying back to New York for the sixth game. Nobody could have been unhappier than George. The next day, he claimed two fans had accosted him in the hotel elevator, and he had hurt his hand punching them out. "I clocked them. There are two guys in this town looking for their teeth," he said, and showed up the next day wih a bandaged hand.

I turned to Bobby Murcer and said, "Did you find the teeth?" Bobby became hysterical.

To this day, I don't know the true story. George never told me and I never asked. All I know is they never found the teeth. They've been looking for the teeth all these years. If George says it's true, I've got to believe it. Two fans jostled George and he had to punch them out. Of course. For a good year afterward, Graig or Bobby and I would walk by one another and one of us would say seriously, "Have they found those teeth yet?"

When we got on the plane that day, George was sitting there, heavily bandaged, and as I passed, I said, "How are you doing, Rocky?"

He broke into a grin from ear to ear. I think he liked being thought of as a tough guy.

The flight home was comfortable and we still thought we could win, even though we were down three games to two. The Dodgers had always been intimidated by New York and we had won the first two games from them there.

Dave Winfield, playing in his first Series, had finally broken an oh-for-seventeen slump with a single and we thought maybe he would get hot and help us win. Winfield had been a major contributor to the Yankee success in 1981 after coming over from San Diego as a 23.1-million-dollar free agent. He had batted .294, hit thirteen homers, knocked in sixty-eight runs, and played great defense.

I'd been immediately impressed with Dave when he joined us that spring. He was friendly, outgoing, articulate, and a good athlete. He didn't make the mistake Reggie had. He came, not to make waves, but to be part of the ballclub. He knew enough to prove his worth to the team before popping off, and so never had to go through the purgatory Reggie did before being accepted.

He was an awesome specimen of a man. One day he

beat Oakland with a little flair hit. Billy Martin was the manager of the A's. After the game, Billy told the press, "I never saw a man so big hit a ball so soft."

We kidded him a lot about that the rest of the year. "How could a man so big hit a ball so soft?" we shouted at him any time he hit one of those flairs.

After a good season, though, he'd stopped hitting. He'd gotten only two hits in the Championship Series against Oakland. He knew he was struggling. "You guys get me through this," he told me one day, "and I'll take care of the Dodgers. I know them. I used to kill them over there. They are afraid of me."

Then he went hitless in four games against them, before finally getting a single in the fifth game. He asked the umpire to get him the ball. The game stopped. I turned to Nettles on the bench. "What the hell is this?"

"Dave got a hit," he said.

"So?"

"It's his first World Series hit ever."

After the game, we jumped on him in fun—"You got a lot of gall to do that!"—but we really hoped it had broken him out of his slump. It hadn't, and that may have cost us the Series.

We were tied at 1–1 in the sixth game when Bob Lemon made a controversial move that probably led to his early firing the next season. With two on in the fourth, Lemon sent Bobby Murcer to the plate to pinch hit for Tommy John, who was pitching well. Bobby had waited all his life to get into a World Series game. In the second game, Tommy John had had a 3–0 lead and Lemon had Goose ready. He wanted another run, wanted to remove John, and sent Murcer to the plate with instructions to bunt. He sacrificed.

In the third game, the game Valenzuela pitched, Lemon began calling "Where's my bunter, where's my bunter?" and Murcer, still angry at what he considered a demeaning insult, walked to the bat rack and said, "I've had a better career than 'Where's my bunter?'" He bunted without enthusiasm. The ball was a soft line drive and it was bunted into a double play. "Where's my bunter, my ass," said Bobby as he returned to the bench.

Now, in the sixth game, Lemon *should* have told Bobby to bunt, but he was looking for a long ball to bust the game open, a dangerous gamble. Bobby got a chance to swing, hit a long fly, but we failed to score. George Frazier gave up a couple of hits, the Dodgers pushed across three runs, and we were beaten, 9–2.

Frazier wound up losing three games in relief, the first pitcher ever to lose three Series games (which trying to win, that is—Claude Williams of the infamous Black Sox also lost three, but he was trying to lose). I ended up at .277 for the season, .600 against Oakland and .438 against the Dodgers. The Series was over. I wasn't happy losing—how can you be?—but I wasn't all that unhappy, either. I felt the Dodgers were entitled to win after the frustrations of 1977 and 1978. Baseball has its own rhythm of winning and losing.

George, needless to say, didn't want to hear anything about rhythms. He immediately reacted to our defeat, and handed out an announcement in the press box saying the Yankees had embarrassed the City of New York. Embarrassed? After making it to the World Series? It was typical. Some of us laughed about it, some didn't think it was so funny, but one thing was for sure. If George thought we had embarrassed him, there would be some changes made before the 1982 season. We held on tight.

Managerial Musical
Chairs

On a cold winter afternoon, early in January of 1982, the telephone rang in the Yankee executive offices on the mezzanine level of the stadium. Doris Walden, the head telephone operator, answered, "Yankees." Anita Piniella identified herself and asked Doris if Mr. Steinbrenner was in.

Soon George was on the other end of the phone. Anita got to the point.

"Lou just got home and told me about that wonderful contract you have given him," Anita said, "and I just wanted to thank you for it. We really appreciate it. Lou is like fine wine. He gets better with age."

I'd gone to George asking for a two-year contract. He'd given me a three-year contract for three-fifty, three seventy-five, and four hundred thousand dollars. He knew I could play two years, but he couldn't be sure about the third. He'd given it to me anyway as thanks for a lot of good years. It had been a magnificent gesture.

George told me later how touched he was by Anita's action, which she'd decided to take all on her own. He said in all the years he had owned the ballclub, Anita's call was the first of its kind he had ever received. He had signed players to millions of dollars' worth of contracts, but no player's wife had ever bothered to thank him, and it really moved him. With all his rough, tough, blustery exterior, down deep George is a softie.

Sort of. One small condition in that contract would cause me more than a little grief. George always had a thing about weight. He wanted his athletes to look like athletes. He wanted them lean and mean. I could be mean, but I couldn't be lean. When he dangled that one-million-dollar-plus contract over my head, he also forced me to sign a clause promising I would report at two hundred pounds. I would be fined a thousand dollars a day for every day I was over two hundred. When you are being offered a million dollars, you might sign with any clause.

Come weigh-in on February 22, though, and the scale said 208. George sent me a letter that said I would be fined a thousand dollars a day until I met the weight, and would be in breach of contract on March first if I did not. By March first, I weighed 199—but I had no intention of paying that fine. It was ridiculous, a grown man and veteran player like me getting harrassed like that over a few pounds.

The conflict quickly spilled out into the press, as every fight on the Yankees always seemed to do.

Me: "I'm tired of being treated like Little Orphan Annie. I'm thirty-eight years old, I'm a man, I've been a Yankee for a long time, and I deserve to be treated with respect."

George: "Lou is being fined because sometimes that is the only thing he understands. He has to be treated like a little boy, because sometimes he acts like a little boy. I've checked that out with his school coaches in Tampa, and they all told me the same thing about him."

Me: "All of a sudden, we lose a few games in the spring [we were at 2–7 at that point], and they've got to blame someone. I don't want to be a scapegoat."

George: "If I'm a man whose employer pays me three hundred fifty thousand dollars a year, which is more than the President of the United States—and there are ten million unemployed people in this country earning nothing—

I'd sure honor my contract. Some guys think contracts only go one way, but our boys will find out different."

Me: "People should be worrying about my production, not my weight."

And so forth. Finally, I called up George and said, "George, we have to get this finished. This is going too far."

"Oh, no, it isn't. You signed it. You have to live with that clause until this contract is up. It will make you mentally tough."

Well, mentally tough or not, the upshot was that I kept my weight down—and George never made me pay the fine. It was just another week in the spring follies.

The Yankees took on a different look in the spring of 1982. Reggie was gone, a free agent signed with California. George just grew tired of the squabbles, the ego problems, the press attention Reggie was taking away from George, and probably his lack of production. Reggie had hit only .237 and fifteen home runs in 1981, and they were not the kind of numbers George wanted to see for the million-or-so dollars Reggie wanted.

George also wanted to change the format of the team completely. He obtained Ken Griffey, a line drive hitter, in a trade with Cincinnati and signed Davey Collins, a switch-hitting base stealer, as a free agent. He wanted more speed. That was fine, but the problem was, Griffey and Collins were National League players, and speed is more important in the National League because that league has more parks with artificial surfaces, on which you can beat out a lot of infield grounders. We had been winning with the long ball, good defense, and tight pitching. What we needed were more lefthanded long ball hitters to take advantage of the short fence in right field in Yankee Stadium.

The arrival of Griffey, who turned out to be a marvelously productive Yankee, and Collins for big money annoyed some of the players, especially Graig Nettles, who felt he had helped carry the team to its many championships, only to find that new players who had not yet done anything for the Yankees were making more. It grated on him. I sympathized with him but I understood one thing: That was the system. There was nothing to do about the system. All you could do was get angry. Graig did, and walked out of spring training. I just moaned a little and kicked over a few watercoolers. I just have a thing about watercoolers.

We were anemic in spring training. We couldn't seem to hit the ball out of the infield and everyone was growing testy. George was on me about my weight, and Bob Lemon, carrying out his orders, was trying to get me to run more. One afternoon I was in left field during a game, and when somebody hit a foul ball down there I flipped it to a fan. Lemon started getting on me about that.

"Don't you know the rules about throwing baseballs into the stands?" he bellowed.

"I don't care about the damn rules," I shouted.

"You shouldn't be throwing balls to fans. You should be doing your laps. What was your weight today?"

Well, that did it. I exploded and marched off the field with a few obscenities for the manager occurring to me. Lemon told George and George told me I was being fined again, and we went around and around on that for a few days before calling it quits.

An early spring snowstorm cost us the first four games and we didn't start the season until April 11, against Chicago. Lefthander Kevin Hickey was pitching for the White Sox. When I looked at the lineup that day, I knew we were going to have problems that year. Dave Revering was batting fourth. When the New York Yankees had a lefthanded hitter without any real credentials batting fourth against a lefthanded pitcher in Yankee Stadium, we were in deep trouble.

Sure enough, we played badly. We didn't hit. Our two new guys, Griffey and Collins, struggled early. The team was flat. The fans and the press were all over us and George took the brunt of it. A big part of the focus was on Collins. He was a good kid, very friendly, could run well and slap a few singles, but he was not in the Yankee image of a first baseman. They had moved him there from the outfield and he hated the position. I knew after a few games that Lou Gehrig was spinning in his grave over that one.

Something had to be done, and George did it. He had told Bob Lemon he would have his job all year, but it was an awfully short year. After only fourteen games of the season, George fired him. He told the press Lemon looked tired and wanted to go back to California and get some of that sunshine. At least he didn't tell them Lemon wanted to start a career in real estate. Our new manager was Gene Michael—again. Are you beginning to notice a pattern here? Stick came down from upstairs to take over, just as he had in 1981.

When he walked into the clubhouse the next day, I cornered him before he even got to his office.

"Stick, you've just made the biggest mistake of your life."

"What do you mean?"

"You're not going to make it to the 1983 season."

"We can turn this thing around."

"Nobody will be able to turn this thing around."

"We have a good ballclub."

"No, we don't, and you know it. Your Waterloo will come in this clubhouse this summer. You should have turned George down for now, and waited until next year when we could get some new young players."

Stick didn't want to take the job with a negative attitude, but he knew I was right. The Yankees had always been good at replacing players. They had made good trades, signed the right free agents, brought up kids to help. Now, however, it was Collins instead of Reggie and Goose, Revering instead of Mickey Rivers, Rick Reuschel instead of Ed Figueroa. The Yankees seemed to have lost the art of building the club. Another case in point: On May 5, George brought over John Mayberry from the Toronto Blue Jays. Why would Toronto give up a power hitter like Mayberry if he could still hit? John had certainly been a good power hitter at one time, but truthfully that time had come and gone. Mayberry hit .209 with eight homers for us, and was gone the next season.

The organization was making errors in judgment. You could see the mistakes in every area of the operation. We were no longer doing what we needed to do to remain competitive.

In April I told Stick that he wouldn't make it to the 1983 season. He didn't even get out of the 1982 season. In August, George removed Stick and replaced him with Clyde King, who was there, more or less, just to assess the situation for George. We played a little better for him than we had for Stick, but not significantly so. We just didn't have the players.

We finished the year at 79–83, fifth in our division. At least my year was a bit better—I got into 102 games and hit a strong .307, my sixth season over .300. It lifted my career mark to .290 and my Yankee average to .295.

In addition, one day in August, George called me into his office and sat me down in the fielder's-glove chair.

"Clyde will report to me on who can play and who can't play," George said. "We will make some changes over the winter and I think we will be competitive again next year. I want to make one change now. I want you to work with the hitters, the young ones especially, as the batting coach."

"Does this mean I won't be playing anymore?"

"No, it doesn't mean that at all. It means that I want to move you more into some responsible positions. I want you to get an understanding of the workings of the club, and I think you can help now by helping these young hitters. You're still an important player, but this will start you in another direction down the road."

It was the first indication that George thought of me as someone who could contribute to the team after my playing career was over. In the midst of aging pains and a lost season, it sure made me feel good. When the sportswriters asked George if the hitting coach position meant he had long-range plans for me, maybe even as a manager someday, he said, "Certainly. Lou has been showing great maturity lately. Haven't you noticed he stopped kicking watercoolers?"

We waited all winter to get the managerial situation resolved. Clyde King was still nominally the manager, but few believed that would last, and George dragged it out until January 11 before he made the announcement. When he did, jaws dropped open. Billy Martin was back.

In came Billy Martin for the third time. He was supposed to be the quick fix, the man who would both whip us into shape and put butts in the seats, but I was surprised. If something doesn't work once, you can understand. Twice, maybe things will be different, maybe the man has learned or changed. But three times?

Contrary to my prediction, Billy's Oakland team had gone downhill in 1982, and there'd been complaints that he was listless, indifferent, that he didn't care anymore. Soon, he was out of a job, but George just couldn't leave him alone. Billy fascinated him, *he* was sure that *he* could make a winner out of Billy again, and vice versa, but I saw Billy when he came in. He was older now, and people suggested he was less enthusiastic than he had been. He seemed a little more distracted, a little more tense, a little more angry. He wanted to climb the mountain again, but he had been on top before. He didn't have the same fire, and maybe he didn't have the same burning desire to win. He let too many little things bother him. He was a tired man.

One big player change in 1983 was the addition of Don Baylor, a hard-nosed free agent slugger from California who had been the league MVP in 1979. We also landed Steve Kemp, a strong lefthanded hitter who was a more questionable acquisition, because he was not a pull hitter. For a lefthanded batter in Yankee Stadium that's a disaster. It hurts too much to see those other lefthanded hitters hit home runs while you are flying out deep to right and left center field in the power alleys. That's what almost killed Bobby Murcer when we played in Shea Studium in 1974 and 1975 while Yankee Stadium was being remodeled.

We had a terrific spring that year, with a 16–8 record, very unusual for a Yankee spring team, and I could feel a little excitement building. To everyone's delight and, I must confess, surprise, Billy had been alert and sharp in spring training, and we began to think, well, maybe we can turn this thing around this year. We opened in Seattle— and promptly lost two out of three. That was frustrating. That was the way the year went. Although we were never really out of the pennant race until nearly the very end, Baltimore was the hot team that year and raced away from us.

As the season wore on, I could see Billy changing. He had lost some of his enthusiasm quickly and his moves weren't as dramatic. He didn't seem motivated, had some trouble motivating the players. He was more and more distracted and soon the articles began appearing in the press, as they always did with Billy, reporting that George was thinking of firing him again.

Billy began snapping at the coaches, he declared war on the umpires, he yelled at a woman reporter and called another report a "scrounge." George fired Billy's buddy and pitching coach, Art Fowler, as a way of getting at Billy, and announced at one team meeting, "If you guys were working for one of my other corporations, you'd all be fired right now." Front office people called me up and tried to get me to tell them what the players thought of Billy, and I said no dice, don't get me involved. We limped into the end of the season. Just another typical Yankee year.

On December 16, 1983, the shoe dropped again. Yogi Berra was named manager of the Yankees. Billy still had a Yankee contract, so there was no need to announce that he wouldn't be back. He would be back, back in Arizona scouting, back in California watching television, back in the market as a managerial candidate if any other club wanted him.

I wasn't completely surprised by the move. George had hinted at it in our meetings. He likes to sound out his front office people and his coaches before he moves, to think aloud and look at people's faces. This time Billy hadn't punched out any marshmallow salesmen or actually hit any sportswriter or said any particularly terrible things about George. He just hadn't won and with George, winning was the bottom line. One day late in the 1983 season George told us, "I feel badly that Billy hasn't been able to turn the club around. I think it is because he has problems. Sometimes Billy is his own worst enemy."

Just before spring training, the coaches and Yogi met with George. Yogi said we had a chance to win and the decision was made to try it one more time with the veteran players. I was forty years old and I knew 1984 was my last season as a player, no matter what happened. My shoulder was getting weaker, my back ached, my legs hurt, and I was looking to retire. We decided that if a young outfielder by the name of Brian Dayett had a big spring, showed he was ready, I would quit.

"I'll be watching him all spring," said Yogi.

"I'll be working with him all spring," I said.

Unfortunately, Dayett didn't hit. Yogi kept playing me but not starting me. I didn't want to play my last spring training picking up Dave Winfield or Steve Kemp or Ken Griffey in the seventh or eighth inning of a preseason game, when the weather is hotter and the fans are restless and the games are boring, but that's the way I was being used. I would be announced and there would be a roar in the stands, the calls of, "Lou, Lou, Lou." Sure, the fans appreciated my being in there—I was the only name they recognized and they had paid good money to see the Yankees play. It was eight kids and Piniella out there. It really hurt me. It was annoying. I had had a good career, not a great one, but a consistent, solid, big league career and I was picking up other veteran outfielders. I would rather have played fifteen innings in a B game than be used like that.

I was also attending meetings every day. Since I was closer to the scene as a player, George felt I had a different perspective, and I was enthusiastic about making suggestions. I hadn't been slapped down yet by George and I made all kinds of recommendations. I saw what was wrong with the club and I thought I could remedy all of it inside a few meetings. George had debated with all the other guys and put them in place. I had never been put in place. After my fifteenth suggestion about a trade for a center fielder, George got up, looked at me and said, "Now slow this damn thing down, Piniella."

At one of those meetings, there was a discussion about a trade for a pitcher. After some lengthy discussion, George called for a vote and show of hands on the matter. About ten or twelve of the fifteen people in the room voted with George. I voted the other way. He called for another vote. There was more talk. Then another vote. Finally I agreed with him, voted as he wanted, because I didn't need any aggravation.

"The vote of the baseball committee is unanimous," said George, "and we'll go after the pitcher."

George has a strange sense of the democratic system. He doesn't cast his vote until he sees how all the votes are going. If there are twelve votes on one side and he is on the other, the final vote will be 13–12 in favor of George.

I was slowly moving into a management role from that of a player. It was touchy, being asked about players when I was still one of them. I was concerned about my integrity and honesty in everything I said. I was also learning why some hard decisions were made. I was beginning to understand the business side of baseball. As George said, "Lou doesn't kick over watercoolers anymore." That's because I found out how much a watercooler cost the ballclub.

These meetings gave me a chance not only to see George in action—certainly worth the price of admission—but also to watch how Yogi operated behind the scenes. He sometimes seemed nervous, unsure of himself, a little too anxious to please everybody in the room. He had obviously wanted the job, and maybe just seemed grateful for the opportunity. Whatever decisions were made, he went along with them. It was only later in the season, perhaps when he stopped worrying about being fired, that he became more adamant and really began to assert himself as the field leader of the ballclub. It was a lesson I took to heart. You can't manage scared. Sooner or later you'll be fired—every manager knows that—but while you have the job, you must do it your own way. In the beginning of 1984, Yogi was doing it everybody else's way. It cost him.

There were more changes around the Yankees early that year that convinced me my time had come. Bobby Murcer had been retired. Goose Gossage, with some bitterness toward George, had left the Yankees, to sign with San Diego. Graig Nettles had been traded to the Padres. Early one afternoon before a night game against Minnesota, I was playing cards with a couple of young players when the team bus arrived. I stared at those young faces—Don Mattingly, Dave Righetti, Bobby Meacham, Mike Pagliarulo—and wondered what in hell I was doing here. I was much older than everybody else in the club-house, nearly forty-one years old, and I didn't belong on the field with them anymore. My mind began to wander, and I thought back to the first time I'd been in a big league clubhouse, as a kid with the Orioles in 1964, and now twenty years later I sat there, with no old friends, feeling lonely and lost and out of place, games suddenly flashing into my mind, players I hadn't thought about for years appearing in my mind's eye, incidents and people and places all coming to me now in a rush. I could see Thurman hitting that giant home run against Kansas City, and Guidry ripping that fastball, and Graig making one of those diving stops in front of me, and Goose snarling as he walked out of the bullpen past me in left field to get to those hitters, and Murcer cracking one of those line drives into the seats.

I was too damn old to be a player. I was too damn young to be a coach. I was caught between a rock and a hard place.

In 1984, Detroit disappeared from the rest of the division early with its 35-5 start, and we bounced around the bottom of the league. I was playing once in a while, in a great deal of pain, hitting a soft .300 with some flairs, a few ground balls squeezed through the middle, and a couple of fly ball singles that dropped in front of the outfielders because they were playing too deep for me, remembering the Lou Piniella of 1978, 1979, and 1980, not seeing the Lou Piniella of this fading early spring.

Now it was only a matter of timing. It was over. Clyde King, the general manager, walked by me one day in the clubhouse. It was empty and quiet. I asked him if he had a few minutes. We walked into Yogi's office and I told Clyde I had made the decision to retire.

After it was relayed to George and announced prematurely in Boston, I looked forward to the final Stadium game on Saturday against the Orioles. There had hardly been a minute in my career I had not enjoyed. I would enjoy Saturday's game. I was at peace. That day, I went hitless, but I did knock in the game-winning run by hitting into a forceout. I was glad it happened that way. We beat the Orioles—even though it was no longer Earl Weaver's team, the victory was not without some satisfaction—and when it was over, there was a mixture of tears and smiles. Don Baylor made me cry when he told a sportswriter in front of me, "When I was an opponent of the Yankees, the one guy we hated to see up there in a tough spot was Piniella." I had to laugh when somebody asked me if I was disappointed to go out with an oh-for-five in my final game, and said, "As a batting coach, I can use those films to show young hitters just how not to hit." The fans were wonderful, chanting "Lou, Lou, Lou" each time I came to the plate; my teammates said many kind things about me; many of the Orioles came over to say goodbye. As I sat in front of my locker after my last game as a player, a reporter asked my feelings. I could smile. "I'm a fortunate man. A lot of people retire and then go home. I'm still here. I'm still in the same clubhouse. I'm still a Yankee."

The adjustment was smooth. I enjoyed coming to the park, working with the hitters and watching a brilliant young hitter like Don Mattingly develop into a batting champion. There was only one more special day for me that season. It came on August 5, Lou Piniella Day, when

George Steinbrenner arranged for the fans and my teammates to salute me.

With Anita and my kids on the field, with my parents up from Florida, with special friends and associates all emotional with me, we heard the chants for Sweet Lou, we heard the warm applause, heard the love from the stands. I walked to the microphone and my heart fluttered. As I stood at home plate to thank them, the tears rushed down my face. My knees shook and mouth was dry. I could only think of Lou Gehrig standing there on the same spot, dying but calling himself the luckiest man on the face of the earth, and here was Sweet Lou retiring with all those memories, all that joy, and in good health. How lucky could one man get? The applause ended and the Stadium grew quiet as I lifted up my head to look at that beautiful ballpark and to address the fans that one last time. "For the past ten years, every time I came up to home plate, you people supported me with chants of 'Lou, Lou, Lou,' and I can only tell you how the adrenaline flowed when I heard that, and the desire welled up in my body to do well for you. I am forever grateful for that. I thank you for all your warmth, all your kindness, all your support. I love you all. The way I feel today, this is not a farewell, this is only a hello."

The First Days
of the Rest
# of My Life

As I drove to the Stadium, there were trees along the highway I had never noticed before. There was pleasant music to listen to on the car radio. There were tall buildings and factories and schools as I drove over the George Washington Bridge and crossed into the Bronx. A new world opened for me as I gave up my playing days. My concentration could wander as I sat in the car and I could think about what restaurant I might have dinner in that night, or a gift I would buy Anita for her birthday, or what the kids would be doing over the weekend. I was still part of baseball, and proud to pull on that pinstriped uniform every day, but there were no pressures. I didn't have to think about Nolan Ryan's fastball or Dan Quisenberry's sidearm sinker or Scott McGregor's little changeup. I knew I would no longer have to fight through the pain in my shoulder or the ache in my legs. It was a little boring to be a batting coach, but it was a lot easier on my psyche after twenty-two summers of trying to hit a baseball hard to make my living. I missed the competition and the excitement, the tension and the emotional rewards. I did not miss the painful pressures, the disappointment of failing to hit in a big spot, the concern about letting down my teammates, the organization, and myself. I had done my job well for a long time. Now others would help the Yankees regain their position in the American League.

As the 1984 season wound down, I began working with undivided attention at improving our club's hitting. There are certain things about successful hitting. First of all, you have to have God-given ability: good reflexes, good eyesight, good hand-to-eye coordination. But, on the professional level, you need something else as well: desire, intensity, concentration—the willingness to work hard to the exclusion of all other concerns. I agree with Ted Williams—hitting a baseball is the single most difficult feat in sports. You have to learn to hit a baseball thrown at nearly one hundred miles an hour, to hit a curving baseball, a baseball thrown softly to throw off your timing, a baseball that sinks or spins or knuckles or even drops once in a while because one side of it is wetter than the other side. Few big league players have gone through an entire career without changing their stance to adjust to those different pitches. Most hitters adjust by changing their position in the batting box. The stance may be the same, but by moving up, moving back, moving in or out, you change the angle at which you see the ball.

I used to sit in front of the television set with my father in Tampa, and a pitch would come in and a guy would miss it, and my father would yell, "How in hell could he miss that?"

I would have to explain to him. "Dad, that guy wasn't looking for the curve. He's been throwing him fastballs all day." Those are the things amateurs miss. That's why it looks so easy to hit from the television screen, where the ball always looks straight and the speed looks the same and the trajectory always appears easy to follow. It looks easy on television, but it isn't. That's why so few guys hit .300.

Most pitchers like to pitch away. Why give them that edge? Move up in the batter's box and get closer to the ball. If the pitcher is good, he'll adjust and come inside more, but unless he has Catfish Hunter–control he'll miss, the pitch will be out over the plate, and that's where you want it, where you can get the fat part of the bat on the ball. Nettles is excellent at this. He crowds the plate, makes the pitcher come inside, the pitcher misses. Bang. Home run ball. Graig has forced the pitcher into a mistake by moving up in the batter's box.

Some pitchers have a false bravado on the mound. They play that stare game. Nolan Ryan is excellent at this. He uses intimidation. He makes sure you know he is just as wild as he wants to be. Gaylord Perry didn't have good stuff at the end of his brilliant career, but he'd beat you with tricks. He had that spitter, but he didn't use it as much as people thought; instead, he would fiddle around on the mound, throw the hitter's timing off, monkey with his cap, wipe off some sweat, grab the resin bag, and pitch when you weren't quite set. He made the hitter anxious. He drove Bobby Murcer out of his mind.

Confidence was the most important factor in my hitting success. I knew that no matter what the pitcher did, I would hit the ball hard. It was only a question of whether somebody caught it or not. I worked hard in batting practice, especially in spring training, and learned how to hit behind the runner, or hit and run, or pull a long ball when I needed it. The ability to do those things well comes from hundreds, thousands, tens of thousands of baseballs hit in batting practice. How about bunting? Why can't hitters bunt? Because they don't practice. It isn't that difficult.

Hitting a baseball hard is difficult, but it isn't impossible. You need to concentrate. You also need to relax. When I walked to the plate in a big spot, I heard the crowd—especially if it was at the Stadium and they were yelling Looooou—but I tried to relax. The more relaxed your muscles are, the more you innate ability comes forth. You do things loosely. You have better bat speed. If you don't squeeze the life out of the bat with your intensity, you have better control of your swing. You have to think about the situation. Will this pitcher give me a sinkerball because he's looking for a double play? Is there a runner on third with less than two out, so he wants the strikeout? If so, he'll give me high, hard stuff. Be ready for it. Look for keys. Is the infield pulled over? Is the outfield shading me one way or another? If they are shading me to right, look for hard stuff. If they are pulled sharply to left or start moving that way, look for the breaking ball, because they expect me to pull to left. If the shortstop is leaning to third, expect the inside pitch. Look at your runner. We have signs to help the hitter. If one hand is off the runner's body, it's a fastball. If both hands are on the knees, it is an off-speed pitch. After you see that sign, adjust and smack it. We also help each other with location. A hand off the right knee means the pitch is in. You save it for the key spot in the game. Graig and I were very good at it—he would help me when he was on base and I would help him.

Some hitters didn't want that edge. Bucky Dent didn't want it, and neither did Thurman. I couldn't believe it. A lot of people think Thurman knew what pitch was coming when he crushed that long homer off Doug Bird in the 1978 playoffs, but he had no idea. He just had a lot of confidence against Bird. He had always hit him well, he was on his pitches, he guessed right and drilled it. When you hit a guy well all your career, you almost run from the on-deck circle to the batter's box. That's what Thurman did. He didn't want Whitey Herzog to change pitchers on him. He made a quick strut, he was at the plate, and he took Bird downtown.

A good hitter has a short, quick, compact swing. There are exceptions, but most hitters who develop that type of swing will be successful. Another secret is to have your bat cocked, six inches off your shoulder, ready to drive into the ball, not way above your head or way below your shoulders. If you do that, you lose too much of your bat speed getting the bat into hitting position.

I have admired a lot of hitters in my time: George Brett, Carl Yastrzemski, Tony Oliva, Rod Carew, and, for power, Reggie Jackson. Another hitter I admire, not so much for style or mechanics or stance as for sheer durability and hitting success, is Pete Rose. I had 1,705 hits in my career and I thought I was a pretty good hitter. Here is a guy who will finish up with nearly 2,500 more hits than me and who has played the game with intensity all these years. I can't comprehend a guy getting, 4,200 hits. It could be 10,000 hits. It all seems astronomical. He has 700 more hits than Carl Yastrzemski, who was the best hitter in our league for all those years. I'm just amazed that a guy could eat, sleep, and live baseball for so long. It was his job, but he always kept it a game. I was a high school senior when he broke in with the Tampa Tarpons in 1961, and I always rooted for him. It's incredible to me that he was a professional player before I was, and he was still playing long after I was finished. He did it all with hard work.

As the 1984 season wound down, more and more people—newspaper reporters, Yankee officials, fans—began discussing my future. Would I ever manage the Yankees? Would I ever manage any other big league club? Did I want to?

A baseball career takes funny turns. There is no way to predict the future. Yes, I wanted to manage the Yankees someday. I also thought I'd be damn good at it. I knew I wouldn't have any trouble handling the offense and generating runs. Whether I could handle the pitchers and the personalities of twenty-five players were more legitimate questions.

Nobody handled pitching better than Yogi Berra did in 1984. He taught me one thing of paramount importance about managing: Pitchers have only so many throws in their arms. You have to treat them with kids gloves—they're different from the rest of the club. You can't abuse their arms. The first lesson Yogi taught me was to get the pitcher out of there at the right time, no matter whether you're way ahead or way behind. You want the pitcher to last eight or ten years, not three or four. George Steinbrenner taught me how much money it takes to develop a young pitcher. You cannot destroy all you have invested in a kid just to win this game or that one. You must understand the long-range goals of the organization. When I broke in, pitchers used to be concerned about coming out of games.

They thought more innings meant more money. Now everybody makes enough money. If you have a good young pitcher, protect him. Stretch his career out.

Yogi did a magnificent job in making Dave Righetti a fine relief pitcher. Yogi protected Righetti, brought him along slowly, and was cautious as to how he used him. When he had pitched two or three times, Yogi would sit him down for a while.

"We may lose today," Yogi once told me on the bench when he refused to warm Righetti up in a close game, "but it will win us five or six down the road." By the end of the season, Righetti was comfortable and confidence as a relief pitcher.

A manager has to look at the entire season. If you jump out fast, you have a chance to win wire to wire. If not, the idea is to keep yourself in position through the middle of the summer, so you can win it in September.

One other important aspect of successful managing is using all your personnel, not only the on-field but also the off-field people. You have to learn to depend on your specialty personnel, your pitching and hitting and fielding coaches, your front office, your scouts, all the people in the organization. Nobody is so smart that he can run a ballclub all by himself. You have to hire good people and give them authority. When I manage, my coaches will be ambitious. I don't intend to surround myself with old buddies who just want to add pension time. I want guys who want to manage, who want to better their position. They will be on top of their game. It would be a thrill to have my coaches picked as big league managers.

Just as I don't want yes men as coaches, managers shouldn't be yes men for the front office people. I will work with them, understand what they have to do, and appreciate their efforts—as a coach I've learned to understand the business aspects of the front office. It's important to work well with the front office. But I will make my own decisions.

Remember, you heard it here first!

In 1984, we salvaged some pride by finishing third.

Yogi had the club playing good ball in the second half, and could be especially proud of the second half record of 51–30. The most thrilling part of the year was the batting race between Don Mattingly and Dave Winfield, with Mattingly giving me too much credit for helping him win. That kid can flat-out hit, and will be a threat to win batting titles for years to come. In the final weeks of the season, George asked me several times what I thought of Yogi's handling of the club. I had no idea which way George was leaning—toward bringing him back or toward letting him go—but I tried to give him my honest opinion. I told him I thought Yogi had rebuilt the pitching staff. I thought he was more aggressive, in better control of the team, and had turned the place around. I didn't tell George what to do or what not to do about Yogi. Whichever way George went, I would not be surprised.

Manager-in-Waiting

He went with Yogi—or so we all thought. Early that winter, George announced to the press that he was bringing Yogi back, and I went to Fort Lauderdale confident it would be a relaxing spring as I started my first full season as a Yankee coach.

I wanted a nice, happy, winning environment where I could separate myself further from the players and move more to the side of management, where Yogi could teach me more about pitching and catching, Gene Michael could help me get a handle on infield play, Jeff Torborg and Mark Connor could give me tips on handling pitchers. Unfortunately there wasn't enough time for this ever to happen.

A couple of days before the players arrived in late February, we had our organization meetings. Yogi told each of the coaches what he expected and how spring training would be organized. We spent a couple of hours at the ballpark those early days, then went out fishing, played a little golf, had a quiet dinner, and waited for the arrival of the players. With the players came the press— and with the press came the first explosion in 1985.

Even before the pitchers and catchers had shaken the winter cobwebs from their arms I was in trouble. On February 23, George decided to tell the press, "Piniella will probably be the next Yankee manager," and soon the news swirled all around our camp. Players seemed a little more standoffish around me. The press kept badgering me about my reaction. Yogi said nothing, but it was evident he was hurt. Here he was, starting his second season as Yankee manager after a third-place finish, and before a ball had been thrown in spring training, the press was already talking about a new Yankee manager. After a sleepless night, I walked into Yogi's office early in the morning. Yogi sat in his underwear fiddling with some papers.

"Yogi, I'd like to talk to you," I said.

"Sure, Lou. What's up?"

"This manager thing that's been in the papers..."

"Aww, don't worry about that crap."

"Yogi, I'm embarrassed and I'm sorry this thing ever happened. My God, the last thing I would do would be to undermine you in any way. My loyalty is one hundred percent with you. Damn it, if you don't want me on your coaching staff, if you think it will be easier without me, I'll pack my bags now and go home and get out of your way."

"No, hell, you just stay here and do what you're doing. You're an important part of this coaching staff. You work well with the hitters. They respect you. I want you to stay. I'll teach you whatever I can. You just watch and listen and do your job."

Yogi is one of the most decent men I have ever known in baseball. I truly love the man. I felt better about things after I left his office that morning, but a little bit of tension remained, especially in those spring days when we lost a ballgame. The sportswriters continued to pick on Yogi if we lost, continued to point out that he had started the spring on a shaky spot and that George had talked about me as a manager. I was uncomfortable all spring.

It was only spring training, of course, but the Yankees aren't like other ballclubs. As I've said, George seems almost nonchalant if we win in the spring, but if we lose, everybody feels it. There is only one season that would really satisfy George: A win in every spring game, wins in all 162 games in the season, wins in all the playoff games, and a sweep of the World Series. And then, of course, he'd start fussing about doing it again next year.

We flew to Boston for three games and got our brains

beaten out. Rickey Henderson was still in Florida working his ailing ankle back into shape. Dave Winfield was weak and ill. Don Mattingly was playing on a bad knee. Ron Guidry couldn't pitch the opener. After the second loss to Boston, George announced to one and all that the third game at Boston was crucial. He told the press we had to win it or else. Everybody in baseball knows "or else" starts with the manager. We didn't win it. We didn't win the next day either, which was an *exhibition* against the *Columbus farm club*. George was upset and rightfully so. We had just started the season and we were already behind the eight ball.

Yogi called a team meeting before the opening game that Saturday in Cleveland. We were 0–3 on the season, not including the 14–5 pounding we had taken in Columbus, and things were getting tense. It doesn't take too many losing games around the Yankees for things to get tense.

"Let's just play baseball now," he said. "Let's forget all the outside stuff and concentrate on playing good ball. We got a good ballclub. Let's go out and show it."

It wasn't quite the way Knute Rockne said it, but it did the job. We beat Cleveland, 6–3, behind Ron Guidry for our first win. It is always a good idea to call a team meeting before a game Guidry is scheduled to start. I'll remember that.

We won the next day again, came home to work out and, in a great game against the White Sox, won the home opener before a full house at the Stadium. Dave Righetti got the victory in relief. We beat the White Sox again the next day, moved our record to 4–3, and started to feel much better about things. I went home and told Anita I thought we had a good ballclub now, things had settled down and we would be in the hunt all the way. Little did I know.

We won a few, lost a few over the next ten days, but help was on the way. Reports out of Florida were that Rickey Henderson was getting close to coming back from his sore ankle—and that Bobby Murcer was planning a comeback. Murcer, who was working as an assistant to GM Clyde King, was supposed to be supervising Henderson's recovery, but he had hit a couple of line drives in batting practice himself and, like any old warhorse, he had decided hitting the big league pitchers was as easy as hitting the batting practice pitcher. When we read that in the papers we had a good laugh.

"Are we that bad that we need a thirty-eight-year-old guy to bail us out?" I asked Gene Michael.

"Lou," he said, "let's you and me take BP today and scare all these guys."

"You do it. If I take BP with my weak swing now, I'll never be able to teach hitting again."

It was a big joke for most of us. Only Don Baylor acted as if he was upset. He was a full-time designated hitter, and the stories said if Murcer returned he would share the DH role with Donnie. Baylor didn't say much publicly. He just kiddingly scowled. When he scowls, the building shakes.

We lost the first two games in Chicago and our record fell to 6–9. The rumors were flying that Yogi would soon be replaced. Before the trip had started, there had been an optional workout at home and only a handful of players had attended—Yogi had decided it was more important to give the guys a day off to get settled in New York. You might say George disagreed; in fact, he was furious: Workouts were always an important point to him. Then Don Mattingly, still struggling with his knee, said *he* thought the day off was more important than the workout, and George blew up. "I'm disappointed in that young man's attitude," he said. George thought the lack of a workout and the lack of attendance showed lack of discipline. It was that old military school background. George thought discipline translated into victory.

We tried hard to comfort Yogi. He was visibly upset. He saw the job slipping away. He had originally taken it in 1984 only because he wanted to win a World Series, about the only thing he had never done in baseball. The press continued to forecast he would be gone in a few days. One reporter wrote an article with a horseracing chart describing the odds on all the potential new managers, Billy Martin, Earl Weaver, Lou Piniella, a few others. The best entry was Hank Steinbrenner, George's son, quoted at 400–1, but given a chance to get the job because he certainly had the right breeding.

Actually, if George decided to make a change, I was certain it would not be to me. One day, while the rumors had been flying in spring training, George had called me into his office. We'd discussed my future.

"Lou, I want you to take over this club at spring training. I want you to coach a full year and when you get this job to start from the beginning. I think you need the experience this year on the field. I have managerial plans for you but not this year."

I thought about that as the noose tightened around Yogi's neck. I was comfortable I would not be picked, no matter what George decided to do about Yogi. What hurt Yogi more than anything was the uncertainty. "If they want to get me, why in hell don't they get it over with?" Yogi said. "Why do they keep hunting me down?"

Saturday night in Chicago, Clyde King took Yogi and the coaches out to dinner. We were supposed to be talking about how to turn this thing around and start winning. It was more like a last supper. I'd been around long enough. I could read the message from Clyde that night, even though not a word had been said about Yogi's situation. There was another factor as well. After Chicago, we went to Texas and then to Kansas City the next week. That midwest swing had claimed more than a few Yankee managers in the past. When I'm managing the club, if we're going badly and we're about to go on that swing, I just might manage to get sick.

That Sunday afternoon, with the decision to fire Yogi already made, we lost another tough ballgame to the White Sox. As soon as the game was over, Clyde King entered a quiet clubhouse. He said nothing to anybody. He walked into Yogi's office and closed the door. They were in there alone for fifteen minutes. As he came out and left the clubhouse, a news release was already being handed out to the press. Yogi had been fired and—oh, Lord—Billy Martin would take over the club in Texas. It was the start of Billy IV.

I felt relieved for Yogi—not happy he was fired, but glad it was finished. The man had been a father figure to a lot of players and you could see that hurt, that pain, that tension in his face as the days of losing continued. Now it was finally over. He could go home and be with his family, play some golf, sit around his club playing cards, and forget the constant plone calls, the questions about losing. He was a free man.

And Billy Martin was back. What an amazing situation. At first I couldn't believe a man could be hired for the fourth time to run a ballclub, but then I thought, why the hell not? If you can bring him back a second and a third time, what was so different about a fourth? Besides, Billy was already under contract to the Yankees. He knew the talent on the team. You certainly couldn't say things would be dull with him around. It figured.

Not everybody looked at it so philosophically, however. Don Baylor kicked over a garbage can. Dale Berra was near tears. Don Mattingly looked as if he could spit bullets. Most of the players seemed angry. A lot of them had expressed negative opinions about Billy before the change had been made, and they all had liked and respected Yogi. "If they liked and respected Yogi so much," George said later, "why didn't they play harder for him?"

We flew to Texas and the coaches met with Billy. He looked wonderful: relaxed, charming, upbeat, and as healthy as I had ever seen him. He had been in Arizona and had a marvelous suntan, and as he talked about the ballclub with us in a meeting that lasted more than two hours, he sounded very enthusiastic.

"One of the first things we are going to do here is to restore discipline," he said. "The owner wants it."

The meeting ended and we all got up to leave. Billy asked me to stay a minute, and we walked into the other room in his suite and spoke for a few minutes.

"Look, Lou. I talked to George. He wants me to take this club over now. He also wants me to take you under my wing. He wants me to teach you. He wants you to manage this baseball team. You'll probably be the next one," he said.

I went back to my room and began to think about what Billy had said. I had gotten out of that situation with Yogi, that embarrassing manager-in-waiting job, and now here I was back in the same damn situation under Billy. Yogi was more predictable. His temperament was more even. Now I'd been put into a more volatile situation with Billy. I kept thinking to myself, "Why me?" Billy seemed genuine in his discussion about my managerial future. He said he wouldn't be managing this club very long, a couple more years at most, that I would be his righthand man, that I would sit with him on the bench, that he would answer my questions and help me learn. "You'll learn to manage from me the way I learned from Casey Stengel," he said.

However, I knew Billy had been fired three times and that there would always be talk in the press of his being fired again. I knew Billy had a quick temper and that things could happen. I knew Billy demanded one hundred percent loyalty from his people. My God, here I was being put into the same situation as with Yogi, only this time it was manager-in-waiting to a much more volcanic personality. The press suggested Billy was not the type of guy who would want the next manager—if that is what George had told him I was—to be sitting next to him while he ran the ballclub.

As the season moved on and we started winning under Billy, however, I became more comfortable. Billy was clearly in charge. I was doing my job well, working with the hitters and the outfielders, and learning how to run a game. Toronto had moved into first place in May, but by July 21 we had cut their lead from six and a half games to one and a half games. Don Mattingly was having an awesome year, Dave Winfield was steady, Rickey Henderson was playing well, the kids—Mike Pagliarulo, Bobby

Meacham, Dan Pasqua, Brian Fisher—were all contributing. The veterans—Dave Righetti, Ken Griffey, Don Baylor, Willie Randolph, Butch Wynegar, Phil Niekro, and free agent Ed Whitson—were all playing well. Ron Guidry, who had always enjoyed playing for Billy ever since Billy had pushed him as a kid pitcher, was pitching exceptional ball. Toronto had never been in a serious pennant race and we thought they might crack. All we had to do was stay close until September.

Then, abruptly, it all began to crumble. We suddenly lost five of six and found ourselves seven games back on July 28. And the first of a series of bizarre events hit us.

That weekend in Texas, Billy was suffering from back spasms and asked his friend, the Texas team doctor, Dr. B. J. Mycoskie, to examine him. The doctor injected Billy with a muscle relaxant—and in so doing accidentally punctured a lung. It was a one-in-a-million mishap, but it left Billy in a lot of pain.

I was in the clubhouse Sunday evening when the phone rang in the trainer's room. Gene Monahan, the trainer, came to my locker and said, "Mr. Steinbrenner wants to talk to you."

"Lou," George said, "I feel terrible about what has happened to Billy. He is going to be hospitalized. He won't be able to manage the team for a few days. I want you to assume the control of the ballclub."

"George, I'll be happy to do it—but please see that Billy is informed."

I saw the dangers immediately. If George had called Billy and Billy had come to me and said, "Lou, George and I both want you to take over the club while I'm hospitalized," it would have been easier. Instead, Billy hadn't been told, and he *wasn't* told until Bill Kane, not George, let him know. Billy never even spoke to me, he just walked out of the clubhouse. He felt it was his job to pick the manager while he was away.

What's more, the ballclub was never informed properly. Here I was the interim manager, and only George and I knew about it. I had mixed emotions. I would have preferred it if Billy had addressed the team and said, "I will be in the hospital for a few days and Lou is taking over. Treat him like you would treat the manager of this baseball team." None of that was done. I was excited about the chance to manage, and I was doing what the organization wanted me to do—but was I doing what the manager wanted me to do? I didn't even know if the manager wanted me to be the manager. I didn't know what authority I had.

We flew to Cleveland that night and I talked over the situation with other coaches, explaining what George had said. They were all very helpful and understanding. I got a good night's sleep and went to the ballpark early the next day. I didn't know if I was supposed to make out the lineup or what my duties were. In a few minutes, Doug Holmquist, one of our coaches who was close to Billy, came up to me and said, "Billy called me. He said to tell you he will call later with the lineup." So that's the way it was going to be.

About an hour later, Billy called from Arlington Memorial Hospital. He sounded awfully weak. I asked about his health. He said he was feeling better and then he said, "Here's the lineup, Henderson leading off, Mattingly batting second, Winfield batting third . . ." He gave me the entire lineup and then said, "I'll be in constant contact from here." Billy said he wanted to be in touch all game. I said that was impossible because I would be busy running the game and couldn't stop to talk on the phone. We devised a plan. Butch Wynegar, our catcher who was injured, would answer the phone and relay messages to me. Little did I know then what problems that would cause.

The first game that I was to manage was almost like my first big league game. Boy, did I have butterflies. You can always assume you can manage. You can always assume you can make decisions. The job looks easy—but when you're the guy who has to do it, the perspective changes. For instance, I had never given signs before. Stick and I devised a set that would be easy for me to give and for him to follow, and then I had to practice them. For half an hour, I stood in front of the mirror and flashed signs. It was like working on my batting stance all over again. As I walked up and down the clubhouse before the game, I stopped every time I passed the mirror and gave signs.

The club took infield practice and I called my first team meeting. "We lost a few tough games in Kansas City and Texas. Now we need to win here. Let's play good baseball. I'm the manager for these games and let's turn this club back to Billy with a winning posture. He would want that more than anything else."

About ten minutes before the game, Stick came to me and said, "Where's the lineup card?"

I had always assumed that Stick made out the lineup card that was presented to the umpires before the game. He had always posted the card for the players each day in the clubhouse.

"Don't you do that?"

"No," Stick said, "the manager does that."

I started to make out the lineup card with the names Billy had given me. I went through the order, and then on the bottom of the card, where it said manager's name, I wrote "Lou Piniella" and that certainly looked funny. Don Baylor carried out the lineup card as he had for Billy, and the game began.

Then the phone calls began.

Billy called in the first inning and in the second and in the third. He wasn't really running the game, he was checking its progress. He wanted to know who was getting up in the bullpen late in the game and whether I had made certain changes. It wasn't too bad. The problem with the calls really started after the game. The press saw Butch Wynegar on the phone and asked what it was all about, and we told them Billy had been calling from the hospital and the instructions had been relayed to me in the corner of the dugout. The headlines in the next day's paper said, "Billy manages Yankees to victory from his hospital bed."

That's all the fans had to hear. The next night the phone began ringing early in the dugout.

"Who is this?" Butch Wynegar said.

"George Steinbrenner," said a voice. "I want Mattingly out of there."

Next inning: "Who is this, who is this?" Butch yelled.

"Billy Martin," said a voice. "Bat for Meacham next inning."

Next inning: "Who is this, who is this?" Butch yelled.

"It's Billy, damn it, why is this dugout phone aways busy?" This time it really was Billy.

It had become a circus. Only with the Yankees could it happen. The fans had told the Cleveland operator that it was Billy or George calling and they had been connected to the dugout. When Billy actually called, the dugout phone was busy and his blood pressure went up. The players saw all this happening, the joking on the bench grew, and it became more difficult to run the club. A serious situation with the manager ill and the interim manager trying to do the job had turned into one big joke.

Things went downhill rapidly after that. We won the first game in Cleveland, 8–2, and the second game, 8–5. Billy got the credit for managing brilliantly from his hospital bed—I was about to get the blame for losing the next three. The second victory was the first game of a doubleheader. Between games, one player took off his uniform and showered, telling me he had some domestic problems and was going home. I told him he was getting paid to play baseball and should stick around. He could talk to Clyde King after the second game. He did, but it was only a sign of things to come.

We lost the second game of the doubleheader, and it was a strange, unpleasant feeling. Then we lost the next two games. One other player refused to go into the game as a pinch runner. Another veteran player questioned my judgment in not running him from first base with one out in the ninth inning and Mattingly at bat. Mattingly hit into a game-ending double play. The silly phone calls continued. When Billy did get through to the dugout, he sounded disjointed. The busy signals were getting to him.

I was managing, but I wasn't the manager. I was managing under complicated conditions and second-guessing myself at every move: "Would Billy make this decision if he were here?" It was too much. I felt confident in my moves, I felt secure handling the players, but without any real authority I was powerless. My job had become a mockery.

After my first victory in Cleveland, George Monahan had given me a baseball with the date, the score of the game, and the fact that it was my first managerial win inscribed on it. It was very kind of him and very touching. When I left Cleveland, I was so frustrated I heaved that baseball into the urinal in the manager's office. Earl Weaver was leading the Baltimore Orioles in there next. He would understand when he found that ball.

After the last game in Cleveland, I met with Clyde King. I had thought about what I would say to him all day. I was through. I had had enough. Billy was coming back to New York the next night, but I wasn't.

"I'm through," I told Clyde. "I've had enough. I'm resigning. I am done. I won't be a coach anymore."

"Lou, don't make any hasty decisions."

"I've thought this through. I'm finished. Tell George. You're the GM. I'll call him myself after you inform him."

He told me to think about it some more, but I told him I was going home when the plane landed and I wouldn't be back. I guess I'd made up my mind when I'd gone to the mound in one of those games and a fan yelled, "Is that your decision or is it coming from a hospital bed in Texas?" That's the problem with playing in Cleveland. There are so few fans there you can hear them when they yell at you.

As far as I was concerned, the decision was made. I had always been a guy who played the game hard and took it seriously. The time for fooling around was after the games. Now I had been made to look foolish on the field and in the dugout. My spirit was wounded.

I got home, walked in the door and Anita asked, "How did you like managing?"

"Anita, I've got to tell you something. I've made a decision that both you and I will have to live with."

"What do you mean?"

"I've resigned from the ballclub."

She looked at me, then I sat her down and explained my reasons. She was very understanding and supportive.

"You don't have to take that," Anita said. "You've been too proud of your Yankee career."

I gave her a big kiss.

The next day I relaxed at home. I felt fine. I finally understood what Yogi had gone through. I had been the manager-in-waiting under Yogi, I had been the manager-in-waiting under Billy, and when I'd finally got my chance to manage a few games, I had been made to look stupid. It had turned out to be a sham. I didn't want to be the manager-in-waiting anymore. I was tired of being the guy who had to watch everything he did, dot his *I*s and cross his *T*s, hang in limbo. I wouldn't take it anymore. I didn't want to work for Billy under those conditions.

Late that afternoon, the phone rang. It was Billy. I told him how I felt. He was sympathetic. I told him I didn't want to hear that crap about a guy managing from a hospital bed. Nobody manages from a hospital bed. He admitted he should have allowed me to do the job until he got back. Finally, he said, "Lou, come back. I need your help."

An hour later, George called. I told him I had spoken to Billy and I was coming back, but I wanted this monkey off my back. I wanted to get this thing cleared up. I was a coach now, just a coach. If he wanted to make me the manager at some future date, we'd talk about it then. For now I would be a coach and that was it. He understood and was in agreement.

The next day, back at the park, I met with Billy and cleared the air. Then I went upstairs to see George. He was very warm and friendly.

"Lou," he began, "I've been telling you if you want to

be a big league manager you must have discipline, you have to take the bull by the horns. You learned more about managing in those four days than you would have learned in four or five years as a coach."

"George, I understand things better now. I know I'm management. I'm no longer a guy who played the outfield or DHed for this club. I'm management. If a player respects you, he can be handled with respect. If he doesn't, you have to deal differently with him. I see that now."

When the press asked George later if the episode had changed my standing with him, he said, "It's made Lou stronger. Now he has learned how important discipline is." Had I ever!

Things were smooth with Billy the rest of the way. The club played good ball through August, we put together a couple of winning streaks and began feeling it could be 1978 all over again. Starting September 12, we had a four-game series with the Blue Jays at the Stadium, and we felt if we stayed no more than a couple of games behind, we could catch them. And that's exactly where we were when they came in: two and a half games behind.

The first night, Guidry beat them, 7–5, and we closed to one and a half games. You could feel the electricity in the air. Phil Niekro got beaten the next night and it was two and half again, but still, that was all right. All we had to do was split the next two games and we would be very close with more than three weeks to go, including a series in Toronto at the end. We could do it.

Or so we thought. We didn't know it then, but that victory by Guidry was to be our high point. After that, the season began to unravel in one bizarre game after another, so that even when we put together a little spurt at the end, it was too late. The Yankees were about to self-destruct—and George set off the first explosive charge.

That Saturday night, we quickly fell behind the Blue Jays, and like the ghost of Jacob Marley, George suddenly materialized in the press box. Frustrated at our failure to catch Toronto, he began to lay into everybody on the team. "We were out-ownered, out-front-officed, out-managed, and outplayed," he said. "I'll take some of the blame. We need big performances out of Winfield, Griffey, and Baylor. My big-money players aren't playing like money players . . . Where's Reggie Jackson? We need a Mr. October or a Mr. September. Dave Winfield is Mr. May."

That really stung the big fellow. The players didn't like it, because they all felt Winfield had played hard and played hurt, and, besides, it wasn't true. Dave's statistics were just as good in September as they had been in May. It was probably George's way of trying to stimulate Dave, but some guys can't take that. When George criticized me as a player, it made me concentrate on the game even more. For Dave, it was "like rattling a stick across the bars of a cage," Dave said later. "Why does he say those kinds of things?" Instead of making him go out and play harder, it just made him withdraw. George later admitted that his remark was a mistake, but by that time the damage had been done. And the slide continued.

We lost that night and again the next day and fell four and a half games out—and that's when things got really strange.

On Monday, we went into the ninth inning against the Indians leading 4–1. Brian Fisher had been pitching well in relief, but by the ninth sportswriters watching the game thought he looked tired, and he started getting hit. Run after run crossed the plate, Righetti was all loosened in the bullpen—but Billy never called on him. Instead, he left Fisher out there in the line of fire, and we ended up losing, 9–5. "I didn't want the kid to get booed," Billy yelled at reporters after the game, but Fisher was booed, plenty. Why did he leave him in? Billy told the press he thought Fisher would get out of it.

The next night against Detroit, Ron Guidry was pitching, but it was one of those nights when he just didn't have the good stuff. Even the most brilliant pitchers have those games. But Billy left him in. It wasn't until Guidry had been hammered for five home runs that Billy sent in a reliever, but by that time it was hopeless, and we lost.

9–1. Now the press and the fans were all buzzing. What had gotten into Billy?

The *next* night—even stranger. It was the sixth inning, with the score tied and the go-ahead run on third base. Billy sent Mike Pagliarulo to the plate to bat righthanded. The only problem was, Mike is a lefty. He'd never batted righthanded in the major leagues in his life. We'd fooled around in practice and intrasquad games with him switch-hitting to see if he felt comfortable with it, and I thought he had some potential there—but he needed more work on it. Pagliarulo struck out looking. We lost our sixth game in a row, 5–2. The press started criticizing Billy strongly.

Thursday was just an ordinary game. We lost, 10–3, to the Tigers, but it was one of those games that could have happened to anyone: no hitting, no pitching, a writeoff. And then we flew to Baltimore.

It was as if we were snakebitten. Friday night, we were tied, 2–2, in the seventh inning, the Orioles' Alan Wiggins was on first base and Lee Lacy had a 2–0 count. Butch Wynegar looked at the dugout and saw Billy rub his nose, the signal for a pitchout, so he figured Wiggins was going to run and he told Rich Bordi on the mount to throw a ball. Bordi did—but Wiggins didn't run. He just stood there, the next pitch was a ball, Lacy walked to first, Wiggins to second, and Cal Ripken scored him for what turned out to be the winning run. Afterward, Butch revealed that the pitchout call had been a *mistake*. Billy had rubbed his nose, all right—because it had itched. Eight losses in a row. Only with the Yankees.

That night, Billy was drinking late in the bar of the Cross Keys Inn in Baltimore. I was in another corner of the dark bar with Gene Michael and Bill Kane. None of us saw how it started, but that night Battling Billy returned. He'd been drinking with two couples, including a pair of newlyweds, then shortly after the newlyweds left, the bridegroom came back, grabbed Billy, and demanded to talk to him.

"You said my wife had a pot belly," he shouted. "I'm

not going to stand for that." Billy told him he had said nothing of the kind but had been joking about the other woman there, who confirmed it, but more words were exchanged, shoves followed, and the next thing anyone knew, Yankees and bartenders were coming from all corners of the bar to separate the two. Billy shouted that they would settle it outside, but the guy wisely beat a retreat. It's like Phil Rizzuto once said, "Billy is like a gunfighter in those Westerns. There is always some young guy who wants to take him on and prove something and Billy can't back away."

And there was more to come. The next day we beat Baltimore to finally stop our slide. Bill Kane and I went out to dinner in Baltimore's Little Italy section. We had a fine dinner, drank a little wine, and came back to the hotel in a good mood about eleven-thirty. One of our pitchers, Bob Shirley, was standing in the lobby.

"You missed the fight," he said.

I didn't pay much attention to the remark because I thought he was referring to the old news of the Friday night fight. But this is the Yankees, of course. We make news every day.

Kane pursued it a little more. "What fight?"

"Billy and Ed Whitson got into a fight here," Shirley said, "and Billy's hurt."

Friday night's game had come back to haunt Billy in another way. Ed Whitson, a free agent we had signed up over the winter, had been scheduled to pitch, but Billy had dropped him from the lineup that night without telling him, and later publicly referred to him as "Whatchamacallit." Whitson, who had little love for Billy anyway, was steamed, and it broke loose that Saturday night.

The scene was the Cross Keys bar again. Billy said he went over to break up an argument between Whitson and another guy, but it immediately became an argument between Whitson and Billy, a punching, kicking, grappling brawl first on the floor of the bar, then out in the lobby— where Whitson broke Billy's right arm with a kick—then continuing out into the parking lot of the hotel, where they were finally separated for good. Almost. They met again at the third-floor elevator and had to be dragged away screaming at each other into their rooms.

When I heard that, I immediately went up to Billy's room to see how he was. He looked terrible. The trainer was treating him for cuts and bruises and Willie Horton, one of our coaches, was trying to calm him down. Billy was furious. As soon as I saw that Billy was being cared for all right, I went to Whitson's room. By contrast, he looked fine. "Don't come to the park tomorrow," I told him. "Get packed early and go on home. The front office will talk about this in New York." Ed was already beginning to simmer down, and he agreed to go, and in fact took his regular place in the rotation that week. Billy made noises about getting him suspended, George made noises about players' being in a bar so late, but nobody ended up getting suspended, or fined, or anything.

In fact, things simmered down in general the next day as we concentrated on baseball. Astonishingly, after all we had been through, we were still capable of playing good baseball. We beat Milwaukee two out of three and flew to Canada only three games out—thanks also to a Toronto losing streak—with just three games left to play. A sweep there and it would be one-game-playoff time. Visions of 1978 danced in our heads again. Could it be possible?

On Friday night, Butch Wynegar hit a game-tying homer with two out in the ninth, Lloyd Moseby dropped Don Mattingly's routine fly to allow the winning run to cross—and we were only two games out, with two to play. All our troubles were put aside. We had the momentum. We were going to win this thing! No team could have been higher as we charged into the Saturday game—and there the momentum stopped. Doyle Alexander, a former teammate and now on the Blue Jays' staff, pitched a strong game . . . and the championship was Toronto's. We got some satisfaction Sunday when Phil Niekro won his three hundredth career game while his father lay ill in a hospital bed, but, for the Yankees, the season was over.

With the last out of the game, my year as Yankee

manager-in-waiting was over. It was a position I would never again fill and I hope no other Yankee ever has to fill. There is room for only one manager on a ballclub at one time.

I didn't know what lay ahead for me in 1986 or any other baseball season, and it still seemed unclear if Billy was coming back. There was still one act left in the continuing soap opera of Martin and Steinbrenner, however. Before heading home for Toronto Sunday, Billy told the press that since Earl Weaver and Sparky Anderson and some other managers who had not made it into the play-offs had such lucrative contracts, he ought to be paid five hundred thousand dollars next season—or he might not choose to return.

Needless to say, George was not amused. "Billy's talking a half million dollars? Well let's see. That'll be two hundred thousand dollars for managing the team and three hundred thousand dollars for being the first challenger to Michael Spinks. I think Billy shot his cannon a little too soon. If he feels he can get a better deal somewhere else, then God bless him. I don't know how many shenanigans off the field from him that I've put up with. He seems to forget that I've rescued him three times when nobody else in baseball wanted him."

Billy didn't reply. A few days later, George announced that the managerial decision would be made by Clyde King and Woody Woodward. Then things seemed to happen with incredible speed—at least for me. The press complained about the decision being dragged out and started printing those handicappers' odds again, but before I knew it, I was on the phone with Clyde King talking about managing the Yankees. On October 27, 1985, as my old team, the Kansas City Royals, was beating the Cardinals for the World Championship, I was announced as the new manager of the Yankees.

As I think about my baseball career and my life and this great challenge in the winter of 1985, I realize what a lucky guy I am. I have a beautiful family and a nice home. I have more money now than I could ever have imagined when I was a kid in Tampa. I have wonderful friends. I am a contented man, and success or failure as a Yankee manager cannot change that.

Most of all, as I approach my middle years, I have those sweet memories of playing with those great athletes, watching Ron Guidry break off a clutch slider in a big spot, Graig Nettles diving for a hard-hit ball, Thurman Munson making a courageous tag, Reggie Jackson hitting one of those monster home runs, Goose Gossage striking out a big hitter, Bobby Murcer lining one off the wall, Willie Randolph racing deep in the hole for a big fielding play, Bucky Dent lofting that ball over the wall, Chris Chambliss hitting that remarkable home run, Dave Winfield climbing the wall, Mickey Rivers chasing down a long fly—pictures in my mind that remain vivid every waking moment.

Someday when I am old, I will tell my grandchildren about the joys of being a Yankee: the excitement, the fame, the furor, the good fortune. I will remember a line drive double to left field in a tough game. As I lean back in my rocking chair, there will be a sweet smile of satisfaction on my lips.

Afterword

Well, the job of managing the New York Yankees worked out about as I expected. George made some suggestions through the year, but mostly he stayed quiet. I had no trouble with the players. Everybody played hard. We finished second to the Red Sox in our division, but we beat them four straight at the end. They'll have to think about that in 1987.

There was more pressure than I expected. The job was more demanding, more time-consuming and I was more exhausted at the end of the year than I thought I would be. There was a lot of satisfaction, too. We drew fifty thousand more in attendance than we had in 1985 and George had to like that, especially in a year when the Mets won everything. Then, on October 10, I was rehired for 1987 and 1988 at an increase in pay to two hundred fifty thousand and three hundred thousand dollars a year. Howard Cosell couldn't have liked that. He predicted I was gone and listed twelve or thirteen games I lost by poor managing. Such rubbish, Howard.

Opening day had to be my greatest thrill. I was more nervous than I had ever been as a player. The press kept asking me all during spring training if I thought I would be there on opening day. That gets pretty tiresome when you have answered the same silly question fifty times. Now I was there. So was a huge crowd of over fifty-five thousand people in the glorious setting of Yankee Stadium.

We opened against the World Champion Kansas City Royals and my good friend, Dick Howser. There was so much color and excitement at the Stadium that day, and I must have smoked two packs of cigarettes before I walked to home plate with the lineup card.

It was a terrific game, with Ron Guidry pitching strongly against Bud Black. We broke a tie when Dale Berra, Yogi's kid, put down a perfect squeeze bunt for the lead run. We won 4–2 and I was sweating and excited and still smoking furiously when the red phone in my office rang just a minute after I walked in there.

"Congratulations," George said. "That was a great game."

"Thanks, Boss. I appreciate it."

The reporters scribbled furiously as George offered a few more kind words about the game. I was really feeling high. I thought to myself how nice managing the Yankees was going to be. Then reality set in. George isn't too quick with his compliments. It was the last time he congratulated me all year.

When the squad first assembled on February 21, I felt confident in my abilities. I knew I could handle the job. I had been a player and a coach for a very long time. I also knew there was more pressure managing the Yankees than playing for the Yankees. It begins with all that talk about being fired. After all, number 14 on the Yankees, Lou Piniella, was George's fourteenth manager in fourteen seasons.

Things worked smoothly in the early spring. Guys worked hard. We used our kids early, but I knew I had to win some games. George had stressed through the years, "When you win in the spring it sells tickets." We were 17–11. We sold some tickets.

I remember the first time I exchanged lineup cards with Earl Weaver in spring training. We were playing his Orioles in Fort Lauderdale. I hadn't seen him since being named the Yankee manager. He had kidded that I was probably too hot-headed to manage. That wasn't half as bad as what Mike Ferraro said about me when he heard I would manage. Ferraro, now my third-base coach, said, "Lou will get thrown out of twenty or thirty games." He was off by seventeen. I only got thrown out of three.

Anyway, Weaver shook my hand at home plate that day and said, "Make sure you separate yourself from your players."

There were some tough decisions to make. The toughest came on March 28. I had to tell a future Hall of Famer, Phil Niekro, he no longer figured in our plans. We had to let him go. Phil and his brother Joe had signed free agent contracts with the Yankees on January 8. The Yankees had decided that at the age of forty-six, Phil could not be given a guaranteed contract. If we were to be successful and continue building, we had to go with younger people.

Phil sat in my office. He looked me in the eye. He was a man about it all. I told him how much I admired and respected him. I then said, "We are going to have to let you go."

He didn't moan. He didn't cry. He didn't make a scene. He just stood up, we shook hands and he was an ex-Yankee. I was glad that he hooked on with the Cleveland Indians a week later. He won eleven ball games for them. We replaced Phil's sixteen wins of 1985 with sixteen wins from Bob Tewksbury and Doug Drabek, two youngsters I am certain will win a lot of ball games for the Yankees.

Cutting a veteran player like Phil Niekro was about the hardest thing I had to do as a manager in the spring. It was painful. You feel for the man. But I thought it was necessary. There was also joy that came out of the same move. I was able to pitch Dennis Rasmussen more often and give him a chance to develop. He became our steadiest starter with a terrific 18–6 season. I thought he had good stuff when I played with him in 1984. I fought hard to keep him. He was in the back of my mind as a starter all spring. That was one of the most satisfying aspects of the Yankee season.

All winter long, after I had been named the Yankee manager, I considered our starting staff. I was determined to keep Dave Righetti in the bullpen despite some talk that he should be returned to the rotation. I know Dave well. I know he wants that ball with two out and two on in the ninth inning of a one-run game. Closers are special people. Not many pitchers can be closers. Righetti is the best. His record of forty-six saves proves that.

Then there was Ed Whitson. I gave him every opportunity. He had been signed as an expensive free agent in 1985. He had a miserable start and dug a hole for himself by popping off about the fans. He had a good arm and I thought if I showed confidence in him he would win. I started him in the second game of the season. He was bombed. I tried everything with him. I even attempted to protect him by starting him only on the road. That messed up our pitching rotation, but I thought it was worth a gamble. That didn't work, either. The guy just hated New York. Some players can't play here. They may not be tough enough. There is a lot of pressure playing in New York, maybe even more pressure playing in New York for a team run by George Steinbrenner. He demands excellence. All he wants to do is win. He doesn't want to listen to excuses. Whitson made excuses. We finally traded him to San Diego on July 9 for Tim Stoddard. He wasn't terribly successful there, either. He was 1–7 for the Padres. Maybe the fault wasn't New York.

We got off well and were in first place by a couple of games into the middle of May. Our starting pitching was weak. We had lost Britt Burns, the big lefthander we got from the White Sox, with a hip injury before the end of spring training. Whitson was a flop. Ronnie Guidry was having an off year. Joe Niekro was inconsistent. Rasmussen was our only consistent starter. We needed help, but couldn't get it from our Columbus club. That's one of the reasons I am optimistic about 1987. Bucky Dent—I can still see that fly ball hitting the screen in Fenway in 1978—will be the Columbus manager. We will be working closely together. He will always have two or three players ready to come up from Triple A and help the big club. We have talked about this and he understands that the idea in the organization is for the New York Yankees to win. Everything anybody in the organization does is aimed at that goal.

The Red Sox got hot. By late June they had pulled away to an eight-game lead. I still thought we could catch them if we got hot and put some pressure on them. We had done that before several times. History plays a big part in a baseball season. Teams know which teams to be concerned about. The Red Sox had to be concerned about the Yankees. Always.

One of our problems was that Dave Winfield wasn't hitting. George suggested I sit him down. George owns the ballclub and has a right to make suggestions. I manage the ballclub. I have a right to make out the lineup card. George never ordered me to play anyone. He did make a suggestion I don't play Winfield. I played him. I don't think we can win without him. I did sit Dave down for a day or two. Sometimes a guy can profit from that. One of the things I learned from Billy Martin is that a manager can profit from a day off. Go play golf on an off day. Go visit friends who won't talk baseball. Get away from it for a while. Get your head cleared. It always helped.

While I'm on the subject of help I'd like to mention Bobby Murcer. He is a Yankee broadcaster now, but he was a teammate for many years and a good friend. He helped a lot in 1986. By late May or early June I had answered the question I asked myself all spring, "Can I handle this job?" I think I ran a game well, had the respect of my players and understood pitching. After all, I was a pretty good hitter for twenty years. I did need a sounding board on some moves and that's where Bobby came in. We could talk over a lot of things. Because he was around every day but was not a coach, he could offer an opinion without it sounding as if he were protecting his own job.

The Winfield situation festered through late June and July. Everybody had an opinion. I had the ultimate responsibility. I thought all he needed was a couple of days off. Dave plays hard. He plays tough defense even when he isn't hitting. He runs hard. He hustles. I thought a few days off would help. He wound up with 104 RBIs, twenty-four homers, a .262 average and great defense. I'll take that in 1987 from Dave.

Baseball people often believe the toughest job for a young manager is handling pitching. I didn't find it so tough. I had a good feel for pitching. I know when a guy is through. I would often check with the catcher, but most of the time when I went to the mound I knew what I wanted to do. Some pitchers would be happy to see you out there, but not all of them. Drabek would growl. He's got a lot of bulldog in him. If you have to come and get him he feels as if he didn't do his job. He goes to the bench angry. I like that. The one thing fans don't understand about pitching changes is you can't always go to your bullpen. Maybe Righetti is not rested. Maybe I used him too many innings the day before. He was in seventy-four games but he only pitched 106 innings. If I was going to make a change in a batter or two anyway, I started the inning with Righetti. I always wanted to give him some margin for error. That was one of Goose Gossage's complaints about Billy Martin. Goose said Billy put him in too many games with the tying or winning run already on base.

In 1987 I'll have a new system for changing pitchers. I'll walk out to the mound with a cue card. Then I'll hold it up to the fans and they can vote yes or no on a change.

There is a great deal of responsibility in managing. It really is a lonely job. It demands enormous patience. I worked harder than I ever did in my life. I would leave home for night games about two o'clock in the afternoon. I would talk to the trainer and see what the medical reports were. I would talk to the coaching staff about that night's game. I would learn if any players were unavailable. I would make out the lineup card. I would watch batting practice. During all of this time I would be talking to the press. That was one part of the job that never stopped. There are always reporters to talk to when you manage in

New York—fewer of them when you win. If we lose, they fill my office. If we win, they talk to the players. The manager gets second-guessed on losing games. The players get the credit for winning games. I guess that's the way it has to be.

After the game I would sit in my office with the press for a while, shower and change slowly, spend some time in the press room with Billy Martin or Bobby Murcer or my coaches, and finally get home two or two and a half hours after the game. Anita knew that if I got home a half hour later than usual it was a tough game. I had stayed a little longer in the park, but I came home relaxed. I had no trouble sleeping.

We played hard all year. There was no quit in this team. We played with a lot of heart. The Red Sox had that little slump we expected, but we didn't win enough to press them. They deserved the Eastern Division title. They certainly deserved the American League pennant the way they came back against California.

We have a pretty good lineup to challenge in 1987. We start with Don Mattingly at first base, a great all-around player. Not a bad third baseman, either. Willie Randolph is our cocaptain, along with Guidry, and our infield leader. He played hurt a good part of the time, but had a fine year. He is a very solid and very smart player. Mike Pagliarulo hit twenty-eight homers, but stopped hitting them in late August after he pulled a muscle. You just couldn't get that kid out of there. I expect big things from him. Wayne Tolleson was a good pickup at shortstop for us. He was a backup player in Chicago, but I think he can do the job every day. I haven't given up on Bobby Meacham, either.

Rickey Henderson is an explosive player. He is capable of winning a game all by himself. He had twenty-eight homers and a .263 average with seventy-four RBIs in the leadoff spot. He had eighty-nine walks and stole eighty-seven bases. He had a fine year. Once in a while Rickey gets tired.

"Skip, I think I'd like to play left field," he told me

one day. "I'm awful tired. That's a lot of ground to cover out there in center field."

I told him I would think about it. I don't think Rickey will play much left field in 1987.

There was a lot of talk about how much we missed Don Baylor. We got Mike Easler for him. Mike hit .302 and he was a leader in the clubhouse. Baylor had a fine year for Boston, but he was only going to play against lefthanders for us and he wasn't happy about that. I think that trade helped both teams. That's what trades are supposed to do.

We lost Butch Wynegar in August when he left the team with psychological problems. He might just be one of those guys who shouldn't have played in New York. It might be too tough for him. I was surprised when Butch left us. He's a fine fellow. I like him a lot, but he may be happier somewhere else, or out of baseball. He just grew awfully quiet in midseason and he wasn't hitting. Guys often get quiet when their bats get quiet.

Joel Skinner is an excellent receiver. He hit .259 for us and I think he will be our regular catcher.

Everybody wants Dan Pasqua. We do too. He had a tough time in the spring of 1986 when his mother died. He struggled for a good while. We had to send him out, but when we brought him back he was ready. He hit sixteen homers and he is going to hit a lot more. I wouldn't be surprised if he became the first Yankee to hit a fair ball out of Yankee Stadium. He has that kind of power.

We won ninety ball games, finished second for the second year in a row and kept hustling all season. We are primed to win in 1987. Didn't the Mets finish second two years in a row before they won everything in 1986?

I didn't have to wait long after the season ended before I got a call from Woody Woodward, the new general manager, that George wanted to see me and talk over next season.

"You have the potential to become an excellent manager," George began. "There were some things you did well and some things you didn't do well. You showed great enthusiasm and effort. You could have handled the pitchers better. I want you back next year."

"Two years," I said.

"Two years?"

"Yes. If you think I did a good job I need two years to show the players I have that security to do some things."

"Okay, I'll give you two years at the same money."

"I have to have a raise."

We went around and around on that for a while and George finally agreed to give me a raise for each of the two seasons. When Davey Johnson of the Mets heard about that he exercised a right in his contract to get a raise so he wouldn't have "any young manager in New York" making more money than he did. I call that the Lou Piniella clause in Johnson's contract.

One more thing. I have a bonus clause in my contract. I get fifty thousand dollars if we win the division, fifty thousand if we win the pennant and fifty thousand if we win the World Series.

I intend to collect.

ABOUT THE AUTHORS

American League Rookie of the Year, All-Star, twenty-three-year veteran, Yankee manager LOU PINIELLA lives in Allendale, New Jersey, with his wife, Anita, and their three children.

MAURY ALLEN, a veteran sportswriter for the *New York Post*, is the author of twenty books, including *Mr. October, Damn Yankee,* and *You Could Look It Up*. He lives in Dobbs Ferry, New York.

Special Offer
Buy a Bantam Book
for only 50¢.

Now you can have Bantam's catalog filled with hundreds of titles plus take advantage of our unique and exciting bonus book offer. A special offer which gives you the opportunity to purchase a Bantam book for only 50¢. Here's how!

By ordering any five books at the regular price per order, you can also choose any other single book listed (up to a $4.95 value) for just 50¢. Some restrictions do apply, but for further details why not send for Bantam's catalog of titles today!

Just send us your name and address and we will send you a catalog!